THE GOSPEL HISTORY

OF OUR

LORD AND SAVIOUR JESUS CHRIST.

THE GOSPEL HISTORY

OF

OUR LORD AND SAVIOUR

JESUS CHRIST

IN A CONNECTED NARRATIVE

IN THE WORDS OF THE REVISED VERSION

ARRANGED BY

C. C. JAMES, M.A.,

RECTOR OF WORTHAM, SUFFOLK;
FORMERLY FELLOW OF KING'S COLLEGE, CAMBRIDGE,
AND ASSISTANT MASTER AT ETON COLLEGE.

LONDON:
C. J. CLAY AND SONS,
CAMBRIDGE UNIVERSITY PRESS WAREHOUSE,
AVE MARIA LANE.
1890

CAMBRIDGE UNIVERSITY PRESS
Cambridge, New York, Melbourne, Madrid, Cape Town,
Singapore, São Paulo, Delhi, Mexico City

Cambridge University Press
The Edinburgh Building, Cambridge CB2 8RU, UK

Published in the United States of America by Cambridge University Press, New York

www.cambridge.org
Information on this title: www.cambridge.org/9781107646216

First published 1890
First paperback edition 2013

A catalogue record for this publication is available from the British Library

ISBN 978-1-107-64621-6 Paperback

INDEX.

PREFACE.

I HAVE often wished when preaching or teaching to have in my hands the fullest possible History of our Lord, shewing the testimony of all the Holy Witnesses combined into one narrative; which should preserve as far as might be every minute detail and trait of the evidence, without introducing a word or thought which they had not recorded. It seemed to me that such a page would be an invaluable help to any one explaining orally, or commenting upon, such of our Saviour's actions as are recorded by more than one Evangelist; and would save him the trouble and distraction of having to keep his fingers in three or four different places in his Bible, and to refer to them perpetually; entailing close mental effort at the moment, and seriously interfering with that free use of the eye which is so important to one who would secure the attention of either a class or a congregation. For this reason also the text should be in a fairly large and clear type, so that the place is easily recovered when the eye returns to it; and for the same reason it must not be disfigured by notes, marks, etc. between the lines: at the same time it should contain such references as may best aid the teacher; and he should have at hand a table of such apparent variations between the witnesses as it would be dishonest in him to ignore.

I have not been able to find such a book in English: Stroud, Pound, White, and others have published works of the kind in Greek, and the last named I have found most useful in reading with a class of boys who knew Greek, at a Public School; but since I have become a teacher of simple English country-people I have heard of nothing in a convenient form that would supply my want. I have therefore attempted to arrange such a book for myself; and feeling certain that others must often have felt the same need, I have decided to publish it, at a price which will bring it within the reach of as many as possible.

Of course I have taken the language of the Revised Version. While I do not deny that there are therein many passages that I could wish differently expressed, and a few which even grate upon the ear, the distinct gain in accuracy and truth in the vast majority of the alterations is so overwhelming, to say nothing of the use of most probably the purest Greek text that has yet been printed, that I somewhat marvel to hear of scholars still speaking and writing against its adoption. Surely also it is unfortunate that learned bodies continue to publish, and educated men to read publicly, both such manifest interpolations as that of "the three Witnesses in Heaven," and also passages in which there occur various words, such as "hell," "damnation," "beasts," "bowels," etc. (where nothing of the sort, as the words are now generally understood by simple people, was meant by the authors) without at least suggesting an alternative rendering.

The way in which I have endeavoured to carry out my plan is this. First, I arranged the parallel passages, side by side, as denoted by the best authorities. Then taking the fullest account of each event as the groundwork, I have endeavoured to weave into that the additional facts, traits, or illustrations which are found in the other narratives; assuming first of all that S. Luke did what he tells us he intended to do, viz. to write his history 'in order'—καθεξῆς γράψαι. In the narrative itself I have treated the plural as including the singular, the stronger expression as including the weaker, and the more definite as including the less distinct. Whatever I have not been able thus to weave in, I have placed in the "table of Variations" at the end of the volume.

The Italics of the Revised Version are printed in the *History* in Roman type. Where Italics do occur they denote words which it has been necessary to insert for the connection of sentences, etc. These are very few.

The order of the references at the bottom of each page is that of the greater or less fulness of the narrative of each event, and not that of any supposed order of their composition. The parallel passages themselves I propose to print in full, side by side, in a second part[1], in a form which I hope will be found very convenient for comparison. Tables, etc. are added, and such a selection of marginal references as may make the book more generally useful.

I do not in the least pretend to have solved any of those dozen or so problems as to the order of events, which will probably for ever remain matters of opinion; nor do I think that we have, or were intended to have, the materials for forming a complete itinerary of our Saviour's movements : my object has been to obtain the most complete picture possible of each event; which appears to me far more important than the chronological order. We have, if I may so speak, what an artist might call a study by S. Mark; two profiles, the one looking towards the Jewish, the other towards the Gentile world, by S. Matthew and S. Luke respectively; and a full-face portrait by S. John. From all of them, from whatever point they are viewed, the same divine Eye, so full of awful majesty, yet so tender in its infinite love, looks straight into the soul of the beholder. It is my earnest hope that in this attempt to combine the four portraits into one no single feature will be found to have suffered.

My best thanks are due to the Universities of Oxford and

---

[1] This is not yet ready. Till it is, I cannot do better than recommend the use of Mr S. D. Waddy's *Harmony of the Four Gospels in the Revised Version*. His sections do not exactly correspond with mine, but very nearly so : a table on the last page of this volume will facilitate ready reference. His preface and introduction are well worth careful reading.

Cambridge for their kind permission to print from the Revised Version; to Professors Westcott and Hort for permission to make use of their table of quotations from the Old Testament; to the Rev. T. Kenworthy Brown and the Rev. E. Ll. Savory for most careful help in correcting proofs, and for several valuable suggestions; and to Mr S. D. Waddy, M.P., for permission to make use of and to refer to his *Harmony of the Four Gospels in the Revised Version.*

I have made every effort that occurred to me as practicable to ensure accuracy. As however it is certain that there will be some errors in every human work, and probable that there will be many in this, I shall be grateful to any person who will kindly point any of them out to me by letter or post-card.

C. C. JAMES.

WORTHAM RECTORY, DISS,
    March 25, 1890.

NOTE ON THE SERMON ON THE MOUNT.

Whether the discourse in S. Luke vi. 20—49 is another report of the same as that in S. Matthew v. vi. vii. or not is one of those questions which must continue to be matters of opinion. I have printed them independently, as it is perfectly impossible to blend them into one, from their being reported from different points of view. S. Luke cannot have been acquainted with S. Matthew's report before his own was written, as the latter is so perfect a composition that had he known it he could not have varied so greatly from it ; on the other hand, S. Matthew perhaps did know S. Luke's report, and explain some phrases in it.

Many of the passages which at first sight appear peculiar to S. Matthew are found in other parts of S. Luke, mostly in chapters xi. and xii. In the "Harmony" these will be printed in brackets. References to them are given in the margin of section 43*, but none are given from 43* to 43, or vice versa, as the two stand close together in the volume.

An able writer has recently called the Sermon on the Mount "a collection of loosely connected and aphoristic utterances." I do not know of any more perfect composition in the world, or any hortatory moral treatise in which the train of thought is more connected and logically evolved. It begins by declaring who are good citizens of the new kingdom (v. 3—12); sets forth the duties of such citizens, both in the way of example and precept ; (13—17) enlarges on the principles on which the laws of that kingdom, the ancient commandments of God, are to be interpreted and kept; (17—48) treats of the great religious duties of the citizens, Almsgiving, Prayer and Fasting (vi. 1—18), and warns us against the chief hinderances to our spiritual life: worldliness (19—34); self-righteousness (vii. 1—5); irreverence (6); want of confidence (7—12), or earnestness (13—14) ; and hypocrisy, whether in teachers (15—23), or hearers (24—27). The more it is studied as a whole the more does its wonderful beauty shine forth, and the attainment of its glorious standard of perfection commend itself as the worthiest object of human ambition. He might as well have called the human skeleton a string of disconnected ossifications.

NOTE ON THE MARGINAL REFERENCES.

I have endeavoured in these to suggest every passage to which I should wish to be able to refer a class that I was teaching. I have therefore given not only the places quoted from the Old Testament, but many others also that occurred to me or were suggested by others as illustrating the text, whether by throwing light upon obscure or unusual phrases or words, or the general thought; and in many cases also passages in the Acts and Epistles, as shewing the evolution as it were of our Lord's teaching in the minds of those who first heard Him, and the application of His principles to their own circumstances and times. I know of few things more interesting than thus to trace the history of a thought, dug up from the rich mine of the Old Testament, stamped as current coin by our Saviour, and applied by His Apostles to the various uses of Christian life. The two millennia which have nearly passed since the words were spoken have added infinite variety to such application, but have in no way altered the principles themselves.

Where H. or Gr. is printed, attention is called to the Hebrew or the Greek. When more than one or two verses should be read for the reference, two or three dots are in most cases added; but the exigences of the margin have prevented this being always done, as for the sake of clearness each reference is contained for the most part in one line. For the same reason the names of the books have been abbreviated as much as possible, but not, I hope, so as to be in any case unintelligible. Other abbreviations will explain themselves: such as cp, compare; ph, perhaps; pr, probably, etc.

Cross references to other sections are added where the illustration applies to the general thought of a passage, and not merely to a particular word or phrase. These are not repeated on the same page.

TABLE OF CONTENTS.

TABLE FOR FINDING ANY PASSAGE.

S. MATTHEW.

S. MARK.

S. LUKE.

S. JOHN.

S. PAUL. I CORINTHIANS.

MIRACLES OF OUR LORD, OR ACTS SHOWING HIS SUPREMACY OVER

    α. Inanimate Nature, and the lower animals.
    β. Human diseases and infirmities.
    γ. Evil Spirits.
    δ. Death and Hades.

Besides these, several instances are recorded of the general healing of all who came or were brought to Him. Sections 31, 41, 46, 67, 117, 127.

PARABLES OF OUR LORD.

PRINCIPAL DISCOURSES OF OUR LORD.

THE GOSPEL HISTORY

OF OUR LORD AND SAVIOUR

JESUS CHRIST.

JESUS THE WORD OF GOD.

1. *The divinity, humanity, and office of Jesus Christ, the
Word of God, and himself God.*

In the beginning was the Word, and the Word was Rev. 19. 13.
with God, and the Word was God. The same was in Pro. 8. 22..
the beginning with God. All things were made by
him; and without him was not anything made that Col. 1. 16.
5 hath been made. In him was life; and the life was Heb. 1. 2.
the light of men. And the light shineth in the darkness; and the darkness apprehended it not. There Jn. 3. 19.
came a man, sent from God, whose name was John.
The same came for witness, that he might bear witness
10 of the light, that all might believe through him. He
was not the light, but came that he might bear witness
of the light. There was the true light, even the light Lk. 11. 35..
which lighteth every man, coming into the world. He
was in the world, and the world was made by him, Heb. 11. 3.
15 and the world knew him not. He came unto his own,
and they that were his own received him not. But as
many as received him, to them gave he the right to
become children of God, even to them that believe on Rom. 8. 15.
his name: which were born, not of blood, nor of the 1 Pet. 1. 23.
20 will of the flesh, nor of the will of man, but of God. Jn. 3. 5.
And the Word became flesh, and dwelt among us (and
we beheld his glory, glory as of the only begotten from Col. 2. 9.
the Father), full of grace and truth.

---

1. S. John i. 1—14.

2. *The genealogy of Jesus Christ from Abraham to Joseph.*

1 Chron.
17. 12... THE book of the generation of Jesus Christ, the son of David, the son of Abraham.

Ps.89.27...
Gen.22.18.
Abraham begat Isaac;
and Isaac begat Jacob;
and Jacob begat Judah and his brethren;
5 and Judah begat Perez and Zerah of Tamar;
and Perez begat Hezron;
and Hezron begat Ram;
and Ram begat Amminadab;
and Amminadab begat Nahshon;
10 and Nahshon begat Salmon;
and Salmon begat Boaz of Rahab;
and Boaz begat Obed of Ruth;
and Obed begat Jesse;
and Jesse begat David the king.
15 And David begat Solomon of her that had been the wife of Uriah;
and Solomon begat Rehoboam;
and Rehoboam begat Abijah;
and Abijah begat Asa;
and Asa begat Jehoshaphat;
20 and Jehoshaphat begat Joram;

1 Ch. 22. 1; and Joram begat Uzziah;

and Uzziah begat Jotham;
and Jotham begat Ahaz;
and Ahaz begat Hezekiah;
and Hezekiah begat Ma- 25 nasseh;
and Manasseh begat Amon;
and Amon begat Josiah;
and Josiah begat Jechoniah and his brethren, at the time of the carrying away to Babylon.
And after the carrying away to Babylon,
Jechoniah begat Shealtiel; 30
and Shealtiel begat Zerubbabel;
and Zerubbabel begat Abiud;
and Abiud begat Eliakim;
and Eliakim begat Azor;
and Azor begat Sadoc; 35
and Sadoc begat Achim;
and Achim begat Eliud;
and Eliud begat Eleazar;
and Eleazar begat Matthan;
and Matthan begat Jacob; 40
and Jacob begat Joseph the husband of Mary, of whom was born Jesus, who is called Christ.

— 22. 11;
— 24. 27;
— 26. 1. So all the generations from Abraham unto David are fourteen generations; and from David unto the carrying 45 away to Babylon fourteen generations; and from the carrying away to Babylon unto the Christ fourteen generations.

3. *The age and genealogy of Christ from Joseph upwards.*

AND Jesus himself, when he began to teach, was about thirty years of age, being the son (as was supposed) of Joseph,

Num. 4. 3.

the son of Heli,
the son of Matthat,
the son of Levi,
5 the son of Melchi,
the son of Jannai,
the son of Joseph,
the son of Mattathias,
the son of Amos,
10 the son of Nahum,
the son of Esli,
the son of Naggai,
the son of Maath,
the son of Mattathias,
15 the son of Semein,
the son of Josech,
the son of Joda,
the son of Joanan,
the son of Rhesa.
20 the son of Zerubbabel,
the son of Shealtiel,
the son of Neri,
the son of Melchi,
the son of Addi,
25 the son of Cosam,
the son of Elmadam,
the son of Er,
the son of Jesus,
the son of Eliezer,
30 the son of Jorim,
the son of Matthat,
the son of Levi,
the son of Symeon,
the son of Judas,
35 the son of Joseph,
the son of Jonam,
the son of Eliakim,
the son of Melea,
the son of Menna,

40 the son of Mattatha,
the son of Nathan,
the son of David,
the son of Jesse,
the son of Obed,
45 the son of Boaz,
the son of Salmon,
the son of Nahshon,
the son of Amminadab,
the son of Arni,
50 the son of Hezron,
the son of Perez,
the son of Judah,
the son of Jacob,
the son of Isaac,
55 the son of Abraham,
the son of Terah,
the son of Nahor,
the son of Serug,
the son of Reu,
60 the son of Peleg,
the son of Eber,
the son of Shelah,
the son of Cainan,
the son of Arphaxad,
65 the son of Shem,
the son of Noah,
the son of Lamech,
the son of Methuselah,
the son of Enoch,
70 the son of Jared,
the son of Mahalaleel,
the son of Cainan,
the son of Enos,
the son of Seth,
75 the son of Adam,
the son of God.

1 Chron. 17. 12...
Ps. 89. 27...

Gen. 22. 18.

Gen. 3. 15.

3. S. Luke iii. 23—38.

4. *The plan and purpose of S. Luke's Gospel.*

FORASMUCH as many have taken in hand to draw up
a narrative concerning those matters which have been
fulfilled among us, even as they delivered them unto us,
Acts 10. 41. which from the beginning were eyewitnesses and ministers
of the word, it seemed good to me also, having traced 5
the course of all things accurately from the first, to write
Acts 1. 1. unto thee in order, most excellent Theophilus; that thou
mightest know the certainty concerning the things wherein
Gal. 6. 6 thou wast instructed.
Gr.

5. *Birth of John Baptist promised.*

THERE was in the days of Herod, king of Judæa, a
1 Ch. 24. 10. certain priest named Zacharias, of the course of Abijah:
and he had a wife of the daughters of Aaron, and her
Gen. 7. 1. name was Elisabeth. And they were both righteous
before God, walking in all the commandments and 5
Phil. 3. 6. ordinances of the Lord blameless. And they had no
child, because that Elisabeth was barren, and they both
were *now* well stricken in years.
Now it came to pass, while he executed the priest's
2 Ch. 8. 14. office before God in the order of his course, according 10
to the custom of the priest's office, his lot was to enter
Ex. 30. 7.. into the temple of the Lord and burn incense. And
the whole multitude of the people were praying without at the hour of incense. And there appeared unto
him an angel of the Lord standing on the right side 15
Ex. 30. 1. of the altar of incense. And Zacharias was troubled
Jud. 13. 22. when he saw him, and fear fell upon him. But the
angel said unto him, Fear not, Zacharias: because thy
supplication is heard, and thy wife Elisabeth shall bear
thee a son, and thou shalt call his name John. And 20
thou shalt have joy and gladness; and many shall
Num. 6. 3. rejoice at his birth. For he shall be great in the sight
Jud. 13. 7. of the Lord, and he shall drink no wine nor strong
drink; and he shall be filled with the Holy Ghost,
even from his mother's womb. And many of the children 25
of Israel shall he turn unto the Lord their God. And he
Mal. 4. 5. shall go before his face in the spirit and power of Elijah,
to turn the hearts of the fathers to the children, and the
disobedient to walk in the wisdom of the just; to make

4. S. Luke 1. 1—4.   5. S. Luke 1. 5—25.

30 ready for the Lord a people prepared for him. And
Zacharias said unto the angel, Whereby shall I know
this? for I am an old man, and my wife well stricken in *Gen.17.17.*
years.   And the angel answering said unto him, I am *— 18.12.*
Gabriel, that stand in the presence of God; and I was *Dan.8.16.*
35 sent to speak unto thee, and to bring thee these good
tidings.   And behold, thou shalt be silent and not able to *Eze.3.26..*
speak, until the day that these things shall come to pass, *— 24.27.*
because thou believedst not my words, which shall be
fulfilled in their season.   And the people were waiting
40 for Zacharias, and they marvelled while he tarried in
the temple.   And when he came out, he could not
speak unto them: and they perceived that he had seen a
vision in the temple: and he continued making signs
unto them, and remained dumb.   And it came to pass,
45 when the days of his ministration were fulfilled, he *1 Ch.9.25.*
departed unto his house.

And after these days Elisabeth his wife conceived;
and she hid herself five months, saying, Thus hath the
Lord done unto me in the days wherein he looked upon
50 me, to take away my reproach among men.   *Gen.30.23.*

6. *The Annunciation.   Visit to Elisabeth.   Magnificat.*

Now in the sixth month the angel Gabriel was sent
from God unto a city of Galilee, named Nazareth, to a
virgin betrothed to a man whose name was Joseph, of
the house of David; and the virgin's name was Mary.
5 And he came in unto her, and said, Hail, thou that art
highly favoured, the Lord is with thee.   But she was *Jud. 6. 12.*
greatly troubled at the saying, and cast in her mind
what manner of salutation this might be.   And the angel
said unto her, Fear not, Mary: for thou hast found favour
10 with God.   And behold, thou shalt conceive in thy womb, *Is. 7. 14.*
and bring forth a son, and shalt call his name JESUS.
He shall be great, and shall be called the Son of the
Most High: and the Lord God shall give unto him the *Ps. 72. 8...*
throne of his father David: and he shall reign over the *Is. 9. 7.*
15 house of Jacob for ever; and of his kingdom there shall *Dan. 7. 14.*
be no end.   And Mary said unto the angel, How shall *Mic. 4. 7.*
this be, seeing I know not a man ?   And the angel
answered and said unto her, The Holy Ghost shall come

upon thee, and the power of the Most High shall over-
shadow thee : wherefore also that which is to be born 20
Jn. 20. 31. shall be called holy, the Son of God.   And behold,
Elisabeth thy kinswoman, she also hath conceived a son
in her old age : and this is the sixth month with her that
Is. 55. 11. was called barren.   For no word from God shall be
Rom. 4. 21. void of power.   And Mary said, Behold, the handmaid 25
of the Lord ; be it unto me according to thy word.   And
the angel departed from her.

And Mary arose in these days and went into the hill
Jos. 21. 9.. country with haste, into a city of Judah ; and entered
into the house of Zacharias and saluted Elisabeth.   And 30
it came to pass, when Elisabeth heard the salutation of
Mary, the babe leaped in her womb ; and Elisabeth was
filled with the Holy Ghost ; and she lifted up her voice
with a loud cry, and said, Blessed art thou among
women, and blessed is the fruit of thy womb.   And 35
whence is this to me, that the mother of my Lord should
come unto me ?   For behold, when the voice of thy
salutation came into mine ears, the babe leaped in my
womb for joy.   And blessed is she that believed ; for
there shall be a fulfilment of the things which have been 40
spoken to her from the Lord.   And Mary said,

1 Sa. 2. 1...   My soul doth magnify the Lord,
And my spirit hath rejoiced in God my Saviour.
1 Sa. 1. 11.   For he hath looked upon the low estate of his
handmaiden :
For behold, from henceforth all generations shall 45
call me blessed.
Ps. 126. 2..   For he that is mighty hath done to me great
things ;
Ps. 111. 9.   And holy is his name.
Ps. 103. 17.   And his mercy is unto generations and generations
On them that fear him.
Is. 52. 10.   He hath shewed strength with his arm ;   50
Ps. 33. 10 ;   He hath scattered the proud in the imagination
— 89. 10.   of their heart.
Job 12. 19 ;   He hath put down princes from their thrones,
— 5. 11.   And hath exalted them of low degree.
Ps. 107. 9 ;   The hungry he hath filled with good things ;
— 34. 10.   And the rich he hath sent empty away.   55
Is. 41. 8.   He hath holpen Israel his servant,
Mic. 7. 20.   That he might remember mercy

(As he spake unto our fathers)
Toward Abraham and his seed for ever.   Gen.17.19.
60   And Mary abode with her about three months, and
returned unto her house.

7. *The conception immaculate.*

Now the birth of Jesus Christ was on this wise :
When his mother Mary had been betrothed to Joseph,
before they came together she was found with child of
the Holy Ghost. And Joseph her husband, being a
5 righteous man, and not willing to make her a public
example, was minded to put her away privily. But Deut.24.1.
when he thought on these things, behold, an angel of the
Lord appeared unto him in a dream, saying, Joseph,
thou son of David, fear not to take unto thee Mary thy
10 wife : for that which is conceived in her is of the Holy
Ghost. And she shall bring forth a son ; and thou shalt
call his name JESUS ; for it is he that shall save his Nu.13.16.
people from their sins. Now all this is come to pass, Acts 4. 12.
that it might be fulfilled which was spoken by the Lord
15 through the prophet, saying,

> Behold, the virgin shall be with child, and shall Is. 7. 14.
>   bring forth a son,
> And they shall call his name Immanuel ;

which is, being interpreted, God with us. And Joseph
arose from his sleep, and did as the angel of the Lord
20 commanded him, and took unto him his wife ; and knew
her not till she had brought forth a son : and he called
his name JESUS.

8. *Birth of John Baptist. Benedictus.*

Now Elisabeth's time was fulfilled that she should be
delivered ; and she brought forth a son. And her neighbours and her kinsfolk heard that the Lord had magni-
fied his mercy towards her ; and they rejoiced with her.
5 And it came to pass on the eighth day, that they came Gen.17.12.
to circumcise the child ; and they would have called him Lev. 12. 3.
Zacharias, after the name of his father. And his mother
answered and said, Not so ; but he shall be called John.
And they said unto her, There is none of thy kindred

---

7. **S. Matt. i. 18—25.**   8. **S. Luke i. 57—80.**

that is called by this name. And they made signs to 10
his father, what he would have him called. And he
2 Cor. 3. 3. asked for a writing tablet, and wrote, saying, His name
is John. And they marvelled all. And his mouth was
Eze. 3. 27. opened immediately, and his tongue loosed, and he spake,
— 24. 27. blessing God. And fear came on all that dwelt round 15
about them: and all these sayings were noised abroad
throughout all the hill country of Judæa. And all that
heard them laid them up in their heart, saying, What
Neh. 2. 8. then shall this child be? For the hand of the Lord was
Acts 11. 21. with him.   20
And his father Zacharias was filled with the Holy
Ghost, and prophesied, saying,
1 Ki. 1. 48.   Blessed be the Lord, the God of Israel;
Ex. 3. 16..   For he hath visited and wrought redemption for his
— 4. 31.   people,
Ps. 132. 17.   And hath raised up a horn of salvation for us
Jer. 23. 5;   In the house of his servant David   25
— 30. 9.   (As he spake by the mouth of his holy prophets
Acts 3. 24.   which have been since the world began),
Ps. 106. 10.   Salvation from our enemies, and from the hand of
all that hate us;
Ps. 105. 8.   To shew mercy towards our fathers,
— 106. 45.   And to remember his holy covenant;
Ge. 22. 16..   The oath which he sware unto Abraham our father, 30
Mic. 7. 20.   To grant unto us that we being delivered out of the
hand of our enemies
1 Jn. 4. 18.   Should serve him without fear,
Eph. 4. 24.   In holiness and righteousness before him all our
1 Pet. 1. 15.   days.
Yea and thou, child, shalt be called the prophet of
the Most High:
Is. 40. 3.   For thou shalt go before the face of the Lord to 35
Mal. 3. 1.   make ready his ways;
To give knowledge of salvation unto his people
In the remission of their sins,
Because of the tender mercy of our God,
Nu. 24. 17.   Whereby the dayspring from on high shall visit us,
Mal. 4. 2.   To shine upon them that sit in darkness and the 40
Is. 9. 2.   shadow of death;
To guide our feet into the way of peace.
1 Sa. 3. 19.   And the child grew, and waxed strong in spirit, and
was in the deserts till the day of his shewing unto Israel.

9. *Birth of Jesus.*

Now it came to pass in those days, there went out a
decree from Cæsar Augustus, that all the world should
be enrolled. This was the first enrolment made when Acts 5. 37.
Quirinius was governor of Syria. And all went to enrol
5 themselves, every one to his own city. And Joseph also
went up from Galilee, out of the city of Nazareth, into
Judæa, to the city of David, which is called Bethlehem, 1 Sa. 16. 1.
because he was of the house and family of David ; to Jn. 7. 42.
enrol himself with Mary, who was betrothed to him,
10 being great with child. And it came to pass, while they
were there, the days were fulfilled that she should be
delivered. And she brought forth her firstborn son ;
and she wrapped him in swaddling clothes, and laid him Ezek. 16. 4.
in a manger, because there was no room for them in the
15 inn.

10. *Shepherds at Bethlehem.*

AND there were shepherds in the same country abiding in the field, and keeping watch by night over their
flock. And an angel of the Lord stood by them, and
the glory of the Lord shone round about them : and
5 they were sore afraid. And the angel said unto them,
Be not afraid ; for behold, I bring you good tidings of
great joy which shall be to all the people : for there is Gen. 12. 3.
born to you this day in the city of David a Saviour, Is. 9. 6.
which is Christ the Lord. And this is the sign unto
10 you ; Ye shall find a babe wrapped in swaddling clothes,
and lying in a manger. And suddenly there was with
the angel a multitude of the heavenly host praising God, Rev. 5. 11..
and saying,

Glory to God in the highest,
15   And on earth peace among men in whom he is well Is. 26. 3.
    pleased.   — 57. 19.

And it came to pass, when the angels went away
from them into heaven, the shepherds said one to another, Let us now go even unto Bethlehem, and see this
thing that is come to pass, which the Lord hath made
20 known unto us. And they came with haste, and found
both Mary and Joseph, and the babe lying in the manger.
And when they saw it, they made known concerning the

---

9. S. Luke ii. 1—7.　　　　**10. S. Luke ii. 8—20.**

saying which was spoken to them about this child.   And
all that heard it wondered at the things which were
spoken unto them by the shepherds.   But Mary kept 25
Gen.37.11. all these sayings, pondering them in her heart.   And
the shepherds returned, glorifying and praising God for
all the things that they had heard and seen, even as it
was spoken unto them.

11.   *Circumcision.   Presentation.   Nunc Dimittis. Anna.*

Gen.17.12.   AND when eight days were fulfilled for circumcising
him, his name was called JESUS, which was so called by
the angel before he was conceived in the womb.

Lev. 12. 2.   And when the days of their purification according to
the law of Moses were fulfilled, they brought him up to 5
Jerusalem, to present him to the Lord (as it is written in

Ex. 13. 2.   the law of the Lord, Every male that openeth the womb
shall be called holy to the Lord), and to offer a sacrifice
according to that which is said in the law of the Lord,

Lev. 12. 8. A pair of turtle-doves, or two young pigeons.   And be- 10
hold, there was a man in Jerusalem, whose name was
Simeon ; and this man was righteous and devout, look-

Is. 40. 1.   ing for the consolation of Israel : and the Holy Spirit
was upon him.   And it had been revealed unto him by
the Holy Spirit, that he should not see death, before he 15
had seen the Lord's Christ.   And he came in the Spirit
into the temple : and when the parents brought in the
child Jesus, that they might do concerning him after the
custom of the law, then he received him into his arms,
and blessed God, and said,   20

Gen.46.30.   Now lettest thou thy servant depart, O Lord,
According to thy word, in peace ;

Is. 40. 5.   For mine eyes have seen thy salvation,
— 52. 10.   Which thou hast prepared before the face of all
peoples ;

Is. 9. 2 ;   A light for revelation to the Gentiles,   25
— 35. 7 ;   And the glory of thy people Israel.
— 49. 6.   And his father and his mother were marvelling at the
things which were spoken concerning him ; and Simeon
blessed them, and said unto Mary his mother, Behold,

Is. 8. 14.   this child is set for the falling and rising up of many in 30
Rom.9.32. Israel ; and for a sign which is spoken against ; yea

and a sword shall pierce through thine own soul; that Jn. 19. 25.
thoughts out of many hearts may be revealed. And
there was one Anna, a prophetess, the daughter of
35 Phanuel, of the tribe of Asher (she was of a great age,
having lived with a husband seven years from her vir-
ginity, and she had been a widow even for fourscore and
four years), wh¹ch departed not from the temple, worshipping with fastings and supplications night and day. 1 Tim. 5.5.
40 And coming up at that very hour she gave thanks unto
God, and spake of him to all them that were looking for
the redemption of Jerusalem. And when they had accomplished all things that were according to the law of
the Lord, they returned into Galilee, to their own city
45 Nazareth.

And the child grew and waxed strong, filled with 1 Sa. 3. 19.
wisdom : and the grace of God was upon him.

12. *Epiphany.*

Now when Jesus was born in Bethlehem of Judæa in
the days of Herod the king, behold, wise men from the 1 Ki. 4. 30.
east came to Jerusalem, saying, Where is he that is born
King of the Jews? for we saw his star in the east, and Nu. 24. 17.
5 are come to worship him. And when Herod the king Is. 60. 3.
heard it, he was troubled, and all Jerusalem with him.
And gathering together all the chief priests and scribes 2Ch.34.13.
of the people, he inquired of them where the Christ
should be born. And they said unto him, In Bẹthlehem
10 of Judæa: for thus it is written by the prophet,
    And thou Bethlehem, land of Judah,   Mic. 5. 2.
    Art in no wise least among the princes of Judah :   Jn. 7. 42.
    For out of thee shall come forth a governor,
    Which shall be shepherd of my people Israel.   Jn. 10. 11.
15 Then Herod privily called the wise men, and learned of
them carefully what time the star appeared. And he
sent them to Bethlehem, and said, Go and search out
carefully concerning the young child ; and when ye have
found *him*, bring me word, that I also may come and
20 worship him. And they, having heard the king, went
their way ; and lo, the star, which they saw in the east,
went before them, till it came and stood over where the
young child was. And when they saw the star, they

---

12. S. Matthew ii. 1—12.

rejoiced with exceeding great joy.   And they came into
the house and saw the young child with Mary his mother; 25
and they fell down and worshipped him; and opening
their treasures they offered unto him gifts, gold and
frankincense and myrrh.   And being warned *of God*
in a dream that they should not return to Herod, they
departed into their own country another way.   30

Ps. 72. 10.
Is. 60. 6.
Jn. 19. 39.

13.   *Flight into Egypt.   Murder of the Innocents.*

Now when they were departed, behold, an angel of
the Lord appeareth to Joseph in a dream, saying, Arise
and take the young child and his mother, and flee into
Egypt, and be thou there until I tell thee: for Herod
will seek the young child to destroy him.   And he arose 5
and took the young child and his mother by night, and
departed into Egypt; and was there until the death
of Herod : that it might be fulfilled which was spoken
by the Lord through the prophet, saying, Out of Egypt
did I call my son.   Then Herod, when he saw that he 10
was mocked of the wise men, was exceeding wroth, and
sent forth, and slew all the male children that were in
Bethlehem, and in all the borders thereof, from two
years old and under, according to the time which he
had carefully learned of the wise men.   Then was ful- 15
filled that which was spoken by Jeremiah the prophet,
saying,

Hos. 11. 1.

Jer. 31. 15.

A voice was heard in Ramah,
Weeping and great mourning,
Rachel weeping for her children;   20
And she would not be comforted, because they are
not.

But when Herod was dead, behold, an angel of the
Lord appeareth in a dream to Joseph in Egypt, saying,
Arise and take the young child and his mother, and go
into the land of Israel: for they are dead that sought 25
the young child's life.   And he arose and took the young
child and his mother, and came into the land of Israel.
But when he heard that Archelaus was reigning over
Judæa in the room of his father Herod, he was afraid
to go thither; and being warned of God in a dream, he 30
withdrew into the parts of Galilee, and came and dwelt

13.   S. Matthew ii. 13—23.

in a city called Nazareth: that it might be fulfilled which
was spoken by the prophets, that he should be called a
Nazarene.

ph. נֵצֶר
Is. 11. 1.

14. *Jesus found in His Father's House.*

AND his parents went every year to Jerusalem at the
feast of the passover. And when he was twelve years
old, they went up after the custom of the feast; and
when they had fulfilled the days, as they were returning,
5 the boy Jesus tarried behind in Jerusalem; and his
parents knew it not; but supposing him to be in the
company, they went a day's journey; and they sought
for him among their kinsfolk and acquaintance: and
when they found him not, they returned to Jerusalem,
10 seeking for him. And it came to pass, after three days
they found him in the temple, sitting in the midst of the
doctors, both hearing them, and asking them questions:
and all that heard him were amazed at his understanding
and his answers. And when they saw him, they were
15 astonished: and his mother said unto him, Son, why
hast thou thus dealt with us? behold, thy father and I
sought thee sorrowing. And he said unto them, How is
it that ye sought me? wist ye not that I must be in my
Father's house? And they understood not the saying
20 which he spake unto them. And he went down with
them, and came to Nazareth; and he was subject unto
them: and his mother kept all these sayings in her heart.

　　And Jesus advanced in wisdom and stature, and in
favour with God and men.

Ex. 23. 14..
Deu. 16. 15.

Jn. 2. 16.

Dan. 7. 28.

1 Sa. 2. 26.

---

15. *Preaching of John the Baptist.*

THE beginning of the Gospel of Jesus Christ the Son
of God.

　　In the fifteenth year of the reign of Tiberius Cæsar,
Pontius Pilate being governor of Judæa, and Herod
5 being tetrarch of Galilee, and his brother Philip tetrarch
of the region of Ituræa and Trachonitis, and Lysanias
tetrarch of Abilene, in the high-priesthood of Annas and
Caiaphas, the word of God came unto John the son of

Jn. 18. 13.

14.　S. Luke ii. 41—52.
15.　S. Luke iii. 1—20; S. Matth. iii. 1—12; S. Mark i. 1—8.

Zacharias in the wilderness of Judæa. And he came
into all the region round about Jordan, preaching the 10
baptism of repentance unto remission of sins; and
saying, Repent ye, for the kingdom of heaven is at hand.
For this is he of whom it is written in the book of the
words of Isaiah the Prophet, saying,

Mal. 3. 1.   Behold I send my messenger before thy face   15
Who shall prepare thy way;

Is. 40. 3...   The voice of one crying in the wilderness,
Make ye ready the way of the Lord,
Make his paths straight.
Every valley shall be filled,   20
And every mountain and hill shall be brought low;
And the crooked shall become straight,
And the rough ways smooth;
And all flesh shall see the salvation of God.

Now John himself had his raiment of camel's hair, 25
2 Ki. 1. 8. and a leathern girdle about his loins, and his food was
locusts and wild honey. And there went out to him all
the country of Judæa, and all they of Jerusalem, and all
the region round about Jordan; and they were baptized
Acts 19.18. of him in the river Jordan, confessing their sins. But 30
Jam. 5. 16. when he saw many of the Pharisees and Sadducees
coming to his baptism, he said unto them and unto the
multitudes that went out to be baptized of him, Ye
Is. 59. 5. offspring of vipers, who warned you to flee from the
wrath to come? Bring forth therefore fruits worthy of 35
repentance, and begin not to say within yourselves, We
Jn. 8. 39. have Abraham to our father: for I say unto you that God
is able of these stones to raise up children unto Abraham.
And even now is the axe also laid to the root of the
tree: every tree therefore that bringeth not forth good fruit 40
is hewn down and cast into the fire. And the multitudes
asked him, saying, What then must we do? And he
answered and said unto them, He that hath two coats,
Job 31. 19. let him impart to him that hath none; and he that hath
— 31. 17. food, let him do likewise. And there came also publicans 45
to be baptized, and they said unto him, Master, what
Lk. 19. 8. must we do? And he said unto them, Extort no more
than that which is appointed you. And soldiers also
asked him, saying, And we, what must we do? And he
said unto them, Do violence to no man, neither exact 50
Acts 24. 29. anything wrongfully; and be content with your wages.

And as the people were in expectation, and all men
reasoned in their hearts concerning John, whether haply
he were the Christ, John answered, saying unto them all,
55 I indeed baptize you with water unto repentance; but
there cometh after me he that is mightier than I, the
latchet of whose shoes I am not worthy to stoop down
and unloose: he shall baptize you with the Holy Ghost Acts 1. 5.
and with fire: whose fan is in his hand, throughly to
60 cleanse his threshing-floor, and to gather the wheat into Amos 9. 9.
his garner; but the chaff he will burn up with unquench- Is. 66. 24.
able fire.   Mt. 13. 30.

With many other exhortations therefore preached he   **51**
good tidings unto the people; but Herod the tetrarch,
65 being reproved by him for Herodias his brother's wife,   **46. 60**
and for all the evil things which Herod had done, added
yet this above all, that he shut up John in prison.

16. *Baptism of Jesus.*

AND it came to pass in those days, when all the
people were baptized, that Jesus also came from Nazareth
of Galilee to the Jordan unto John to be baptized of him.
But John would have hindered him, saying, I have need
5 to be baptized of thee, and comest thou to me? But
Jesus answering saith unto him, Suffer it now: for thus it
becometh us to fulfil all righteousness. Then he suffered
him. And Jesus when he was baptized went up straightway out of the water and was praying: and lo, the
10 heavens were opened unto him, and he saw the Spirit of
God descending in a bodily form as a dove and coming
upon him; and lo, a voice came out of the heavens, **72. 141**
saying, This is my beloved Son; in whom I am well Ps. 2. 7.
pleased.   Is. 42. 1.

17. *Fasting and Temptation of Jesus.*

AND Jesus full of the Holy Spirit, returned from the
Jordan; and straightway the Spirit driveth him forth into
the wilderness. And he was in the wilderness forty days
tempted of Satan; and he was with the wild beasts.
5 And he did eat nothing in those days: and when they Ex. 34. 28.
were completed, he hungered. And the tempter came 1 Ki. 19. 8.

16. S. Matth. iii. 13—17; S. Mark i. 9—11; S. Luke iii. 21, 22.
17. S. Luke iv. 1—13; S. Matth. iv. 1—11; S. Mark i. 12, 13.

and said unto him, If thou art the Son of God, command
this stone that it become bread.   And Jesus answered
Deu. 8. 3.   unto him, It is written, Man shall not live by bread alone,
but by every word that proceedeth out of the mouth of 10
God.

Again the devil taketh him unto an exceeding high
mountain, and showeth him all the kingdoms of the
world, in a moment of time ; and he said unto him, To
thee will I give all these things, and the authority, and 15
Jn. 16. 11.   the glory of them : for it hath been delivered unto me,
— 14, 30.   and to whomsoever I will, I give it.   If therefore thou
Rev. 13. 7.   wilt fall down and worship before me, it shall all be thine.
And Jesus answered and said unto him, Get thee hence,
Deu. 6. 13.   Satan : for it is written, Thou shalt worship the Lord thy 20
— 10. 20.   God, and him only shalt thou serve.

Then the devil taketh him to the holy city and he set
him on the pinnacle of the temple, and said unto him, If
thou art the Son of God, cast thyself down from hence ;
for it is written,   25
Ps. 91. 11.   He shall give his angels charge concerning thee, to
guard thee :
And on their hands they shall bear thee up,
Lest haply thou dash thy foot against a stone.
And Jesus answering said unto him, Again it is written,
Deu. 6. 16.   Thou shalt not tempt the Lord thy God.   30
And when the devil had completed every temptation,
he departed from him for a season, and behold the
Lk. 22. 43.   angels came and ministered unto him.

18. *John Baptist of Jesus and of himself.*

JOHN beareth witness of him, and crieth, saying,
This was he of whom I said, He that cometh after me is
become before me : for he was before me.   For of his
Col. 1. 19.   fulness we all received, and grace for grace.   For the law
was given by Moses ; grace and truth came by Jesus 5
1 Tim 6.16.   Christ.   No man hath seen God at any time ; the only-
1 Joh. 4. 12.   begotten Son, which is in the bosom of the Father, he
hath declared him.

And this is the witness of John, when the Jews sent
unto him from Jerusalem priests and Levites to ask him, 10
Acts 13. 25.   Who art thou ?   And he confessed, and denied not ; and

18. S. John 1. 15—28.

he confessed, I am not the Christ. And they asked him,
What then? Art thou Elijah? And he saith, I am not. Mal. 4. 5.
Art thou the prophet? And he answered, No. They De. 18. 15..
15 said therefore unto him, Who art thou? that we may give
an answer to them that sent us. What sayest thou of
thyself? He said, I am the voice of one crying in the Is. 40. 3.
wilderness, Make straight the way of the Lord, as said
Isaiah the prophet. And they had been sent from the
20 Pharisees. And they asked him, and said unto him,
Why then baptizest thou, if thou art not the Christ, Eze. 36. 25.
neither Elijah, neither the prophet? John answered Is. 52. 15.
them, saying, I baptize with water: in the midst of you Zech. 13. 1.
standeth one whom ye know not, *even* he that cometh
25 after me, the latchet of whose shoe I am not worthy to
unloose. These things were done in Bethany beyond
Jordan, where John was baptizing.

19. *The Lamb of God. Andrew, Peter, Philip, Nathanael.*

ON the morrow he seeth Jesus coming unto him, and
saith, Behold, the Lamb of God, which taketh away the Is. 53. 7.
sin of the world! This is he of whom I said, After me Ex. 29. 38.
cometh a man which is become before me: for he was Ex. 12. 3.
5 before me. And I knew him not; but that he should be
made manifest to Israel, for this cause came I baptizing
with water. And John bare witness, saying, I have
beheld the Spirit descending as a dove out of heaven; 16
and it abode upon him. And I knew him not: but he
10 that sent me to baptize with water, he said unto me,
Upon whomsoever thou shalt see the Spirit descending,
and abiding upon him, the same is he that baptizeth with Acts 1. 5.
the Holy Spirit. And I have seen, and have borne
witness that this is the Son of God.
15 Again on the morrow John was standing, and two of
his disciples; and he looked upon Jesus as he walked,
and saith, Behold, the Lamb of God! And the two
disciples heard him speak, and they followed Jesus. And
Jesus turned, and beheld them following, and saith unto
20 them, What seek ye? And they said unto him, Rabbi
(which is to say, being interpreted, Master), where
abidest thou? He saith unto them, Come, and ye shall

---

19. S. John 1. 29—51.

see. They came therefore and saw where he abode;
and they abode with him that day: it was about the tenth
hour. One of the two that heard John *speak*, and 25
followed him, was Andrew, Simon Peter's brother. He
findeth first his own brother Simon, and saith unto him,
We have found the Messiah (which is, being interpreted,
Christ). He brought him unto Jesus. Jesus looked upon
him, and said, Thou art Simon the son of John: thou 30
Mt. 16. 18. shalt be called Cephas (which is by interpretation, Peter).

71   On the morrow he was minded to go forth into
Galilee, and he findeth Philip: and Jesus saith unto him,
Jn. 12. 21. Follow me. Now Philip was from Bethsaida, of the city
Jn. 21. 2. of Andrew and Peter. Philip findeth Nathanael, and 35
Gen.49.10. saith unto him, We have found him, of whom Moses in
the law, and the prophets, did write, Jesus of Nazareth,
the son of Joseph. And Nathanael said unto him, Can
Joh. 7. 52. any good thing come out of Nazareth? Philip saith
unto him, Come and see. Jesus saw Nathanael coming 40
to him, and saith of him, Behold, an Israelite indeed, in
Ps. 32. 2. whom is no guile! Nathanael saith unto him, Whence
knowest thou me? Jesus answered and said unto him,
Mic. 4. 4. Before Philip called thee, when thou wast under the fig
Zech. 3. 10. tree, I saw thee. Nathanael answered him, Rabbi, thou 45
art the Son of God; thou art King of Israel. Jesus
answered and said unto him, Because I said unto thee, I
saw thee underneath the fig tree, believest thou? thou
shalt see greater things than these. And he saith unto
him, Verily, verily, I say unto you, Ye shall see the 50
Gen.28.12. heaven opened, and the angels of God ascending and
descending upon the Son of man.

20. *Water made Wine.*

AND the third day there was a marriage in Cana of
Galilee; and the mother of Jesus was there: and Jesus
also was bidden, and his disciples, to the marriage. And
when the wine failed, the mother of Jesus saith unto him,
Jn. 19. 26. They have no wine. And Jesus saith unto her, Woman, 5
2 S. 16.10; what have I to do with thee? mine hour is not yet come.
— 19. 22. His mother saith unto the servants, Whatsoever he saith
unto you, do it. Now there were six waterpots of stone
Mk. 7. 3. set there after the Jews' manner of purifying, containing

---

20. S. John ii. 1—12.

10 two or three firkins apiece. Jesus saith unto them, Fill
the waterpots with water. And they filled them up to
the brim. And he saith unto them, Draw out now, and
bear unto the ruler of the feast. And they bare it. Ecclus.
And when the ruler of the feast tasted the water now 32. 1.
15 become wine, and knew not whence it was (but the
servants which had drawn the water knew), the ruler of
the feast calleth the bridegroom, and saith unto him,
Every man setteth on first the good wine; and when
men have drunk freely, *then* that which is worse: thou
20 hast kept the good wine until now. This beginning of
his signs did Jesus in Cana of Galilee, and manifested
his glory; and his disciples believed on him. Jn. 1. 14.
After this he went down to Capernaum, he, and his
mother, and *his* brethren, and his disciples: and there Mt. 12. 46..
25 they abode not many days.

21. *Temple cleansed. Sign.*

AND the passover of the Jews was at hand, and Jesus De. 16. 16.
went up to Jerusalem. And he found in the temple those **127**
that sold oxen and sheep and doves, and the changers of De. 14. 24..
money sitting: and he made a scourge of cords, and cast
5 all out of the temple, both the sheep and the oxen; and
he poured out the changers' money, and overthrew their
tables; and to them that sold the doves he said, Take
these things hence; make not my Father's house a house
of merchandise. His disciples remembered that it was
10 written, The zeal of thine house shall eat me up. The Ps. 69. 9.
Jews therefore answered and said unto him, What sign De. 18. 21..
shewest thou unto us, seeing that thou doest these things?
Jesus answered and said unto them, Destroy this temple, Mt. 26. 61.
and in three days I will raise it up. The Jews therefore
15 said, Forty and six years was this temple in building, and
wilt thou raise it up in three days? But he spake of the Col. 2. 9.
temple of his body. When therefore he was raised from 1 Cor. 6. 19.
the dead, his disciples remembered that he spake this; 2 Cor. 6. 16.
and they believed the scripture, and the word which
20 Jesus had said.
Now when he was in Jerusalem at the passover,
during the feast, many believed on his name, beholding
his signs which he did. But Jesus did not trust himself

---

21. S. John ii. 13—25.

Acts i. 24. unto them, for that he knew all men, and because he
1 Cor.2.11. needed not that any one should bear witness concerning 25
man; for he himself knew what was in man.

22. *Nicodemus. The New Birth.*

Jn. 7. 50;   Now there was a man of the Pharisees. named Nico-
— 19. 39. demus, a ruler of the Jews: the same came unto him by
night, and said to him, Rabbi, we know that thou art a
Jn. 9. 33. teacher come from God: for no man can do these signs
that thou doest, except God be with him.   Jesus an- 5
swered and said unto him, Verily, verily, I say unto
Jn. 1. 13. thee, Except a man be born anew, he cannot see the
Gal. 6. 15. kingdom of God.   Nicodemus saith unto him, How can
a man be born when he is old? can he enter a second
time into his mother's womb, and be born?   Jesus an- 10
swered, Verily, verily, I say unto thee, Except a man
Tit. 3. 5. be born of water and the Spirit, he cannot enter into the
1 Pet. 1.23; kingdom of God.   That which is born of the flesh is
— 3. 21. flesh; and that which is born of the Spirit is spirit.
Marvel not that I said unto thee, Ye must be born anew. 15
The wind bloweth where it listeth, and thou hearest the
voice thereof, but knowest not whence it cometh, and
whither it goeth: so is every one that is born of the
Spirit.   Nicodemus answered and said unto him, How
can these things be?   Jesus answered and said unto 20
him, Art thou the teacher of Israel, and understandest
not these things?   Verily, verily, I say unto thee, We
speak that we do know, and bear witness of that we
have seen; and ye receive not our witness.   If I told
you earthly things, and ye believe not, how shall ye 25
believe, if I tell you heavenly things?   And no man
hath ascended into heaven, but he that descended out
of heaven, even the Son of man, which is in heaven.
Num.21.8. And as Moses lifted up the serpent in the wilderness,
even so must the Son of man be lifted up: that who- 30
soever believeth may in him have eternal life.
1 Joh. 4. 9.   For God so loved the world, that he gave his only
begotten Son, that whosoever believeth on him should
not perish, but have eternal life.   For God sent not the
Jn. 12. 47. Son into the world to judge the world; but that the 35
world should be saved through him.   He that believeth

on him is not judged: he that believeth not hath been
judged already, because he hath not believed on the
name of the only begotten Son of God. And this
40 is the judgement, that the light is come into the
world, and men loved the darkness rather than the
light; for their works were evil. For every one that
doeth ill hateth the light, and cometh not to the light,
lest his works should be reproved. But he that doeth
45 the truth cometh to the light, that his works may be Eph. 5. 13.
made manifest, that they have been wrought in God.

23. *John Baptist's last testimony to Jesus. Eternal Life.*

AFTER these things came Jesus and his disciples into
the land of Judæa; and there he tarried with them, and
baptized. And John also was baptizing in Ænon near
to Salim, because there was much water there: and they
5 came, and were baptized. For John was not yet cast
into prison. There arose therefore a questioning on the
part of John's disciples with a Jew about purifying.
And they came unto John, and said to him, Rabbi, he
that was with thee beyond Jordan, to whom thou hast
10 borne witness, behold, the same baptizeth, and all men
come to him. John answered and said, A man can
receive nothing, except it have been given him from 1 Cor. 4. 7.
heaven. Ye yourselves bear me witness, that I said, I
am not the Christ, but, that I am sent before him. He
15 that hath the bride is the bridegroom: but the friend of
the bridegroom, which standeth and heareth him, rejoiceth greatly because of the bridegroom's voice: this Mt. 9. 15.
my joy therefore is fulfilled. He must increase, but I
must decrease.
20 He that cometh from above is above all: he that is
of the earth is of the earth, and of the earth he speaketh:
he that cometh from heaven is above all. What he hath
seen and heard, of that he beareth witness; and no man
receiveth his witness. He that hath received his witness
25 hath set his seal to this, that God is true. For he whom
God hath sent speaketh the words of God: for he giveth
not the Spirit by measure. The Father loveth the Son,
and hath given all things into his hand. He that be- Mt. 28. 18.
lieveth on the Son hath eternal life; but he that obeyeth Hab. 2. 4.

23. S. John iii. 22—36.

not the Son shall not see life, but the wrath of God 30
abideth on him.

24. *The Woman of Samaria. True Worship. Messiah.*

WHEN therefore the Lord knew how that the Pharisees had heard that Jesus was making and baptizing
more disciples than John (although Jesus himself baptized not, but his disciples), he left Judæa, and departed
again into Galilee. And he must needs pass through 5
Samaria. So he cometh to a city of Samaria, called
Gen. 48. 22. Sychar, near to the parcel of ground that Jacob gave to
Jos. 24. 32. his son Joseph: and Jacob's well was there. Jesus
therefore, being wearied with his journey, sat thus by
the well. It was about the sixth hour. There cometh 10
a woman of Samaria to draw water: Jesus saith unto
her, Give me to drink. For his disciples were gone
away into the city to buy food. The Samaritan woman
therefore saith unto him, How is it that thou, being a
2 Ki. 17. 24. Jew, askest drink of me, which am a Samaritan woman? 15
(For Jews have no dealings with Samaritans.) Jesus
answered and said unto her, If thou knewest the gift of
God, and who it is that saith to thee, Give me to drink;
Rev. 22. 17. thou wouldest have asked of him, and he would have
given thee living water. The woman saith unto him, 20
Sir, thou hast nothing to draw with, and the well is deep:
from whence then hast thou that living water? Art thou
greater than our father Jacob, which gave us the well,
and drank thereof himself, and his sons, and his cattle?
Jesus answered and said unto her, Every one that 25
drinketh of this water shall thirst again: but whosoever drinketh of the water that I shall give him shall
Jn. 7. 37. never thirst; but the water that I shall give him shall
become in him a well of water springing up unto eternal
life. The woman saith unto him, Sir, give me this water, 30
that I thirst not, neither come all the way hither to draw.
Jesus saith unto her, Go, call thy husband, and come
hither. The woman answered and said unto him, I have
no husband. Jesus saith unto her, Thou saidst well, I
have no husband: for thou hast had five husbands; and 35
he whom thou now hast is not thy husband: this hast
thou said truly. The woman saith unto him, Sir, I per-

ceive that thou art a prophet.   Our fathers worshipped
in this mountain; and ye say, that in Jerusalem is the Deu.12.13.
40 place where men ought to worship.   Jesus saith unto
her, Woman, believe me, the hour cometh, when neither
in this mountain, nor in Jerusalem, shall ye worship the
Father.   Ye worship that which ye know not: we worship that which we know: for salvation is from the Jews.
45 But the hour cometh, and now is, when the true worshippers shall worship the Father in spirit and truth:
for such doth the Father seek to be his worshippers.
God is a Spirit: and they that worship him must worship 2 Cor.3.17.
in spirit and truth.   The woman saith unto him, I know
50 that Messiah cometh (which is called Christ): when he
is come, he will declare unto us all things.   Jesus saith
unto her, I that speak unto thee am he.

25.   *The Samaritans.*

AND upon this came his disciples; and they marvelled that he was speaking with a woman; yet no man
said, What seekest thou? or, Why speakest thou with
her?   So the woman left her waterpot, and went away
5 into the city, and saith to the men, Come, see a man,
which told me all things that ever I did: can this be the
Christ?   They went out of the city, and were coming to
him.   In the mean while the disciples prayed him, saying, Rabbi, eat.   But he said unto them, I have meat to Rev. 2. 17.
10 eat that ye know not.   The disciples therefore said one
to another, Hath any man brought him aught to eat?
Jesus saith unto them, My meat is to do the will of him
that sent me, and to accomplish his work.   Say not ye,
There are yet four months, and then cometh the harvest?
15 behold, I say unto you, Lift up your eyes, and look on Is. 49. 18.
the fields, that they are white already unto harvest.   He
that reapeth receiveth wages, and gathereth fruit unto
life eternal; that he that soweth and he that reapeth
may rejoice together.   For herein is the saying true,
20 One soweth, and another reapeth.   I sent you to reap
that whereon ye have not laboured: others have laboured, Jos. 24. 13.
and ye are entered into their labour.

And from that city many of the Samaritans believed
on him because of the word of the woman, who testified,

He told me all things that ever I did. So when the 25
Samaritans came unto him, they besought him to abide
with them : and he abode there two days. And many
more believed because of his word ; and they said to
the woman, Now we believe, not because of thy speaking : for we have heard for ourselves, and know that this 30
1 Joh.4.14. is indeed the Saviour of the world.

26. *Nobleman's Son healed.*

AND after the two days he went forth from thence
into Galilee. For Jesus himself testified, that a prophet
Mt. 13. 57. hath no honour in his own country. So when he came
into Galilee, the Galilæans received him, having seen all
the things that he did in Jerusalem at the feast : for they 5
also went unto the feast.

20 He came therefore again unto Cana of Galilee, where
he made the water wine. And there was a certain nobleman, whose son was sick at Capernaum. When he
heard that Jesus was come out of Judæa into Galilee, 10
he went unto him, and besought him that he would
come down, and heal his son ; for he was at the point
of death. Jesus therefore said unto him, Except ye see
signs and wonders, ye will in no wise believe. The
Mk. 5. 23. nobleman saith unto him, Sir, come down ere my child 15
die. Jesus saith unto him, Go thy way : thy son liveth.
The man believed the word that Jesus spake unto him,
and he went his way. And as he was now going down,
his servants met him, saying, that his son lived. So he
inquired of them the hour when he began to amend. 20
They said therefore unto him, Yesterday at the seventh
hour the fever left him. So the father knew that it was
at that hour in which Jesus said unto him, Thy son liveth :
and himself believed, and his whole house. This is again
the second sign that Jesus did, having come out of Judæa 25
into Galilee.

27. *Teaching at Nazareth. Rejected.*

Now when Jesus had heard that John was delivered
up, he returned in the power of the Spirit into Galilee :
and a fame went out concerning him through all the

---

26. S. John iv. 43—54.
27. S. Luke iv. 14—30 ; S. Matthew iv. 12 ; S. Mark i. 14.

region round about. And he taught in their synagogues,
5 being glorified of all.

And he came to Nazareth, where he had been brought **57**
up : and he entered, as his custom was, into the synagogue on the sabbath day, and stood up to read. And Acts 13.15.
there was delivered unto him the book of the prophet
10 Isaiah. And he opened the book, and found the place
where it was written,

The Spirit of the Lord is upon me, Is. 61. 1.
Because he anointed me to preach good tidings to
the poor :
He hath sent me to proclaim release to the captives,
15 And recovering of sight to the blind,
To set at liberty them that are bruised,
To proclaim the acceptable year of the Lord.
And he closed the book, and gave it back to the attend-
ant, and sat down : and the eyes of all in the synagogue
20 were fastened on him. And he began to say unto them,
To-day hath this scripture been fulfilled in your ears.
And all bare him witness, and wondered at the words
of grace which proceeded out of his mouth : and they
said, Is not this Joseph's son ? And he said unto them, Jn. 6. 42.
25 Doubtless ye will say unto me this parable, Physician, Mk. 6. 3.
heal thyself : whatsoever we have heard done at Capernaum, do also here in thine own country. And he said,
Verily I say unto you, No prophet is acceptable in his
own country. But of a truth I say unto you, There were
30 many widows in Israel in the days of Elijah, when the
heaven was shut up three years and six months, when
there came a great famine over all the land ; and unto
none of them was Elijah sent, but only to Zarephath, in 1 Ki. 17.9.
the land of Sidon, unto a woman that was a widow.
35 And there were many lepers in Israel in the time of
Elisha the prophet ; and none of them was cleansed,
but only Naaman the Syrian. And they were all filled 2 Ki. 5. 14.
with wrath in the synagogue, as they heard these things ;
and they rose up, and cast him forth out of the city, and
40 led him unto the brow of the hill whereon their city was
built, that they might throw him down headlong. But
he passing through the midst of them went his way.

28. *Capernaum. Preaching of Repentance.*

AND leaving Nazareth, he came and dwelt in Capernaum, which is by the sea, in the borders of Zebulun and Naphtali : that it might be fulfilled which was spoken by Isaiah the Prophet, saying,

Is. 9. 1.

> The land of Zebulun and the land of Naphtali,   5
> Toward the sea, beyond Jordan,
> Galilee of the Gentiles,
> The people which sat in darkness
> Saw a great light,
> And to them which sat in the region and shadow of 10
>   death,
> To them did light spring up.

From that time began Jesus to preach the Gospel of God, and to say, The time is fulfilled, and the kingdom of God is at hand : Repent ye, and believe in the Gospel.   15

29. *Four Fishermen called.*

AND passing along by the sea of Galilee, he saw two brethren, Simon who is called Peter, and Andrew his brother, casting a net into the sea : for they were fishers. And Jesus saith unto them, Come ye after me, and I will make you to become fishers of men. And they 5 straightway left the nets and followed him.

19. 33

Mt. 13.47..

And going on from thence a little further, he saw other two brethren, James the son of Zebedee and John his brother, who also were in the boat with Zebedee their father, mending their nets. And straightway he called 10 them. And they straightway left their father Zebedee in the boat with the hired servants, and followed him.

30. *Demoniac at Capernaum.*

AND he came down to Capernaum, a city of Galilee ; and straightway on the sabbath day he entered into the synagogue and taught. And they were astonished at his teaching : for he taught them as having authority, and not as the scribes. And straightway there was in the syna- 5

Mt. 7. 28.
43*

28. S. Matthew iv. 13—17 ; S. Mark i. 14, 15.
29. S. Mark i. 16—20 ; S. Matthew iv. 18—22.
30. S. Mark i. 21—28 ; S. Luke iv. 31—37.

gogue a man which had a spirit of an unclean devil; **56. 58**
and he cried out with a loud voice, Ah, what have we to **73. 92**
do with thee, thou Jesus of Nazareth? art thou come to
destroy us? I know thee who thou art, the Holy One of Acts 19.15.
10 God. And Jesus rebuked him, saying, Hold thy peace,
and come out of him. And when the unclean spirit had
thrown him down in the midst and convulsed him he
cried out with a loud voice and came out of him, having
done him no hurt. And amazement came upon them
15 all, insomuch that they questioned among themselves,
and spake together one with another, saying, What is
this? a new teaching! for with authority and power he
commandeth even the unclean spirits, and they obey him
and come out. And the report of him went out straight-
20 way everywhere into every place of the region of Galilee
round about.

31. *Peter's Wife's Mother.   General healing.*

AND he rose up from the synagogue, and came into
the house of Simon and Andrew, with James and John.
Now Simon's wife's mother lay sick, holden with a great 1 Cor. 9. 5.
fever, and straightway they tell him of her and beseech
5 him for her. And when he saw her he came and stood
over her and rebuked the fever; and he took her by the
hand and raised her up: and the fever left her; and
immediately she rose up and ministered unto them.
And at even, when the sun was setting, all they that
10 had any sick with divers diseases brought them unto him, **41. 46.**
and them that were possessed with devils. And all the **67**
city was gathered together at the door. And he laid his
hands upon every one of them that were sick, and healed Acts 10.38.
them: that it might be fulfilled which was spoken by
15 Isaiah the prophet, saying, Himself took our infirmities, Is. 53. 4.
and bare our diseases. And he cast out the spirits with
a word, and they came forth from many, crying out and
saying, Thou art the Son of God. And rebuking them, he
suffered them not to speak, because they knew that he Mk. 3. 12.
20 was the Christ. Acts 15.17.

---

31. S. Mark i. 29—34; S. Luke iv. 38—41; S. Matthew viii. 14—17.

32. *Circuit of Galilee. Effect.*

AND in the morning, a great while before day, he rose
42   up, and went out, and departed into a desert place, and
there prayed. And Simon and they that were with him
followed after him ; and they found him, and say unto
him, All are seeking thee. *For* the multitudes sought 5
after him and came unto him, and would have stayed
him, that he should not go from them. But he said
unto them, Let us go elsewhere into the next towns, for I
must preach the good tidings of the kingdom of God to
Is. 61. 1... the other cities also, for to this end came I forth.   10

And Jesus went about in all Galilee, teaching in their
synagogues, and preaching the gospel of the kingdom,
and casting out devils, and healing all manner of disease
and all manner of sickness among the people. And the
report of him went forth into all Syria : and they brought 15
unto him all that were sick, holden with divers diseases
and torments, possessed with devils, and epileptic, and
palsied ; and he healed them. And there followed him
great multitudes from Galilee and Decapolis and Jerusalem and Judæa and from beyond Jordan.   20

33. *First Draught of Fishes.*

Now it came to pass, while the multitude pressed
upon him and heard the word of God, that he was
standing by the lake of Gennesaret; and he saw two
boats standing by the lake : but the fishermen had gone
out of them, and were washing their nets. And he 5
Mk. 4. 1.   entered into one of the boats, which was Simon's, and
49   asked him to put out a little from the land. And he sat
down and taught the multitudes out of the boat. And
when he had left speaking, he said unto Simon, Put out
Jn. 21. 6.   into the deep, and let down your nets for a draught. 10
And Simon answered and said, Master, we toiled all
night, and took nothing : but at thy word I will let down
182   the nets. And when they had this done, they inclosed a
great multitude of fishes ; and their nets were breaking ;
and they beckoned unto their partners in the other boat, 15
that they should come and help them. And they came,

---

32. S. Mark i. 35—39 ; S. Luke iv. 42—44 ; S. Matthew iv. 23—25.
33. S. Luke v. 1—11.

and filled both the boats, so that they began to sink.
But Simon Peter, when he saw it, fell down at Jesus' 2 Sam. 6. 9.
knees, saying, Depart from me; for I am a sinful man, Is. 6. 5.
20 O Lord. For he was amazed, and all that were with him,
at the draught of the fishes which they had taken; and so
were also James and John, sons of Zebedee, which were
partners with Simon. And Jesus said unto Simon, Fear   29
not; from henceforth thou shalt catch men. And when 2 Ti. 2. 26.
25 they had brought their boats to land, they left all, and   Gr.
followed him.

34. *The Leper healed.*

AND it came to pass, while he was in one of the cities,
behold there cometh unto him a man full of leprosy: 114
and when he saw Jesus he fell on his face and besought
him, kneeling down to him and worshipping him, and
5 saying unto him, Lord, if thou wilt, thou canst make me
clean. And being moved with compassion, he stretched
forth his hand, and touched him, saying, I will: be thou
made clean. And straightway his leprosy departed from
him, and he was made clean. And he strictly charged
10 him, and straightway sent him out, and saith unto him, See
thou say nothing to any man: but go thy way, and shew
thyself to the priest, and offer for thy cleansing the things Le. 13. 2...
which Moses commanded, for a testimony unto them. — 14. 2...
But he went out and began to publish it much, and to
15 spread abroad the matter, insomuch that Jesus could no
more openly enter into a city, but was without in desert
places; and great multitudes came together from every
quarter to hear, and to be healed of their infirmities. But   32
he withdrew himself in the deserts, and prayed.

35. *Paralytic at Capernaum.*

AND he entered into a boat and crossed over, and
came unto his own city. And when he entered again
into Capernaum after some days, it came to pass that he
was teaching, and there were Pharisees and doctors of
5 the law sitting by, which were come out of every village
of Galilee and Judæa and Jerusalem: and the power of
the Lord was with him to heal. And it was noised that he

---

34. S. Mark i. 40—45; S. Luke v. 12—16; S. Matthew viii. 2—4.
35. S. Mark ii. 1—12; S. Luke v. 17—26; S. Matthew ix. 1—8.

was in the house: and many were gathered together so
that there was no longer room for them, no, not even
about the door, and he spake the word unto them.   And 10
behold men bring unto him a man sick of the palsy lying
on a bed, borne of four; and they sought to bring him in
and to lay him before him.   And not finding by what
way they might come nigh unto him or bring him in
Mk. 13.15. because of the multitude, they went up to the housetop 15
and uncovered the roof where he was; and when they
had broken it up, they let down through the tiles the bed
whereon the sick of the palsy lay into the midst before
Jesus.   And Jesus seeing their faith saith unto the sick
of the palsy, Son, be of good cheer, thy sins are forgiven 20
thee.   But the Scribes and the Pharisees that were sitting
47   there began to reason in their hearts, and to say within
themselves, Why doth this man thus speak? Who is this
Job 14. 4. that speaketh blasphemies? Who can forgive sins but one,
Is. 43. 25. even God?   And straightway Jesus perceiving in his 25
Ps. 139. 2. spirit that they so reasoned within themselves, answered
Acts 1. 24. and said unto them, Why reason ye these things? wherefore think ye evil in your hearts?   For whether is easier,
to say to the sick of the palsy, Thy sins are forgiven thee,
or to say, Arise, and take up thy bed, and walk?   But 30
that ye may know that the Son of man hath power on
earth to forgive sins (he saith to the sick of the palsy) I
Jn. 5. 8. say unto thee, arise and take up thy bed, and go unto
37   thy house.   And immediately he rose up before them,
and took up that whereon he lay, and went forth before 35
them all, and departed to his house, glorifying God.   And
amazement took hold on all, and they glorified God
which had given such power unto men, and they were
filled with fear, saying, We have seen strange things to-
day.   We never saw it on this fashion.   40

36.   *Levi (or Matthew) called.   Of Fasting.*

AND after these things he went forth again by the
sea side; and all the multitude resorted unto him, and
he taught them.   And as he passed by, he beheld a
publican, Levi the son of Alphæus, sitting at the place of
toll; and he saith unto him, Follow me.   And he forsook 5
all and rose up, and followed him.   And Levi made him

36. S. Mark ii. 13—22; S. Luke v. 27—39; S. Matthew ix. 9—17.

a great feast in his house, and as he sat at meat, many
publicans and sinners came and sat down with Jesus and Lk. 15. 1...
his disciples; for there were many, and they followed
10 him. And when the Pharisees and their Scribes saw that
he was eating with publicans and sinners, they murmured
against his disciples, saying, He eateth and drinketh with **110**
publicans and sinners! And when Jesus heard it, he said
unto them, They that are whole have no need of a
15 physician, but they that are sick. But go ye and learn Hos. 6. 6.
what this meaneth, I desire mercy and not sacrifice : Mic. 6. 6...
for I came not to call the righteous, but sinners to 1 Tim. 1. 16.
repentance. Lk. 19. 10.

And John's disciples and the Pharisees were fasting :
20 and they come and say unto him, Why do John's
disciples fast often and make supplications, likewise also
the disciples of the Pharisees, but thy disciples fast not? Lk. 18. 12.
And Jesus said unto them, Can ye make the sons of the
bridechamber fast while the bridegroom is with them? as Jn. 3. 29.
25 long as they have the bridegroom with them they cannot
fast. But the days will come, when the bridegroom shall
be taken away from them, and then will they fast in Acts 13. 2..
that day. — 14. 23.

And he spake also a parable unto them. No man 1 Cor. 7. 5.
30 seweth a piece of undressed cloth on an old garment ;
else that which should fill it up taketh from it, the new
from the old, and a worse rent is made. And no man
putteth new wine into old wine-skins ; else the new wine Job 32. 19.
will burst the skins, and itself will be spilled and the
35 skins perish : but new wine must be put into fresh wine-
skins, and both are preserved. And no man having
drunk old wine desireth new, for he saith, The old is good.

37. *Bethesda. Sabbath.*

AFTER these things there was a feast of the Jews ;
and Jesus went up to Jerusalem.

Now there is in Jerusalem by the sheep gate a pool, Neh. 3. 1.
which is called in Hebrew Bethesda, having five porches.
5 In these lay a multitude of them that were sick, blind,
halt, withered. And a certain man was there, which had
been thirty and eight years in his infirmity. When Jesus
saw him lying, and knew that he had been now a long

time in that case, he saith unto him, Wouldest thou be
made whole? The sick man answered him, Sir, I have 10
no man, when the water is troubled, to put me into the
pool: but while I am coming, another steppeth down
Mt. 9. 6. before me. Jesus saith unto him, Arise, take up thy
35 bed, and walk. And straightway the man was made
whole, and took up his bed and walked.   15
Jn. 9. 14.   Now it was the sabbath on that day. So the Jews
80 said unto him that was cured, It is the sabbath, and it is
Neh. 13. 19. not lawful for thee to take up thy bed. But he answered
Jer. 17. 22. them, He that made me whole, the same said unto me,
Take up thy bed, and walk. They asked him, Who is 20
the man that said unto thee, Take up thy bed, and walk?
But he that was healed wist not who it was: for Jesus
had conveyed himself away, a multitude being in the
Acts 3. 8. place. Afterward Jesus findeth him in the temple, and
Jn. 8. 11. said unto him, Behold, thou art made whole: sin no 25
Mt. 12. 45. more, lest a worse thing befall thee. The man went
away, and told the Jews that it was Jesus which had
made him whole. And for this cause did the Jews
persecute Jesus, because he did these things on the
sabbath. But Jesus answered them, My Father worketh 30
even until now, and I work. For this cause therefore
Jn. 7. 19. the Jews sought the more to kill him, because he not only
brake the sabbath, but also called God his own Father,
Jn. 10. 30. making himself equal with God.
Phil. 2. 5.

38. *Jesus' defence. He is the Son of God, and Judge of
the world. Witness of John, of His Father, of His
works, and of Moses.*

JESUS therefore answered and said unto them,
Jn. 8. 28;   Verily, verily, I say unto you, The Son can do nothing
— 14. 10. of himself, but what he seeth the Father doing: for what
things soever he doeth, these the Son also doeth in like
2 Pet. 1. 17. manner. For the Father loveth the Son, and sheweth 5
him all things that himself doeth: and greater works than
these will he shew him, that ye may marvel. For as the
Father raiseth the dead and quickeneth them, even so
the Son also quickeneth whom he will. For neither doth
the Father judge any man, but he hath given all judge- 10
Mt. 25. 31. ment unto the Son; that all may honour the Son, even

as they honour the Father. He that honoureth not the
Son honoureth not the Father which sent him. Verily, 1 Jn. 2. 23.
verily, I say unto you, He that heareth my word, and
15 believeth him that sent me, hath eternal life, and cometh Jn. 6. 47.
not into judgement, but hath passed out of death into life. 1 Jn. 3. 14.
Verily, verily, I say unto you, The hour cometh, and now
is, when the dead shall hear the voice of the Son of Eph. 2. 5;
God ; and they that hear shall live. For as the Father — 5. 14.
20 hath life in himself, even so gave he to the Son also to
have life in himself : and he gave him authority to execute Acts 10.42.
judgement, because he is the Son of man. Marvel not Dan. 12. 2.
at this : for the hour cometh, in which all that are in the
tombs shall hear his voice, and shall come forth ; they that Is. 26. 19.
25 have done good, unto the resurrection of life ; and they 1 Co. 15.52.
that have done ill, unto the resurrection of judgement. Dan. 12. 2.
    I can of myself do nothing : as I hear, I judge : and
my judgement is righteous ; because I seek not mine own Mt. 26. 39.
will, but the will of him that sent me. If I bear witness Jn. 6. 38.
30 of myself, my witness is not true. It is another that
beareth witness of me ; and I know that the witness Jn. 8. 13...
which he witnesseth of me is true. Ye have sent unto
John, and he hath borne witness unto the truth. But the Jn. 1. 19...
witness which I receive is not from man : howbeit I say **18. 23**
35 these things, that ye may be saved. He was the lamp
that burneth and shineth : and ye were willing to rejoice 2 Pet. 1. 19.
for a season in his light. But the witness which I have
is greater than that of John : for the works which the 1 Jn. 5. 9.
Father hath given me to accomplish, the very works that Jn. 10. 25.
40 I do, bear witness of me, that the Father hath sent me. **82**
And the Father which sent me, he hath borne witness of Mt. 3. 17.
me. Ye have neither heard his voice at any time, nor Deu. 4. 12.
seen his form. And ye have not his word abiding in 1 Tim.6.16.
you : for whom he sent, him ye believe not. Ye search
45 the scriptures, because ye think that in them ye have Is. 34. 16.
eternal life ; and these are they which bear witness of me ; Lk. 24. 27.
and ye will not come to me, that ye may have life. I Jn. 3. 19.
receive not glory from men. But I know you, that ye
have not the love of God in yourselves. I am come in
50 my Father's name, and ye receive me not : if another
shall come in his own name, him ye will receive. How Mt. 24. 24.
can ye believe, which receive glory one of another, and Mt. 23. 6.
the glory that cometh from the only God ye seek not ?
Think not that I will accuse you to the Father : there is

J. H.   3

one that accuseth you, even Moses, on whom ye have set 55
Deu.18.15. your hope.   For if ye believed Moses, ye would believe
me ; for he wrote of me.   But if ye believe not his
writings, how shall ye believe my words ?

39. *Sabbath.   Ears of Corn.*

AND it came to pass at that season that Jesus was
going on the sabbath day through the cornfields ; and
his disciples were an hungred, and began as they went to
Deu.23.25. pluck the ears of corn, and to eat, rubbing them in their
hands.   But certain of the Pharisees, when they saw it, 5
said unto him, Behold, why do thy disciples that which
Ex.16.22... it is not lawful to do on the sabbath day ?   And
Jesus answering them said, Have ye not read even this,
what David did, when he had need, and was an hungred,
1 Sa. 21. 6. he and they that were with him ; how he entered into 10
the house of God when Abiathar was high priest, and
Lev. 24. 8. did take and eat the shewbread, which it was not lawful
for him to eat, neither for them that were with him, but
only for the priests, and gave also to them that were with
him?   Or have ye not read in the law, how that on the 15
Num.28.9. sabbath day the priests in the temple profane the sabbath
and are guiltless ?   But I say unto you that one greater
1 Ch.6.18. than the temple is here.   But if ye had known what this
Hos. 6. 6. meaneth, I desire mercy and not sacrifice, ye would not
have condemned the guiltless.   And he said unto them, 20
The sabbath was made for man, and not man for the
sabbath : so that the Son of Man is lord even of the
sabbath.

40. *Sabbath.   The Withered Hand.*

AND it came to pass on another sabbath, that he
entered again into their synagogue and taught : and
behold there was a man there and his right hand was
withered.   And the scribes and the Pharisees watched him
whether he would heal him on the sabbath day, that they 5
might find how to accuse him.   But he knew their

39. S. Matthew xii. 1—8 ; S. Mark ii. 23—28 ; S. Luke vi. 1—5.
40. S. Luke vi. 6—11 ; S. Mark iii. 1—6 ; S. Matthew xii. 9—14.

thoughts; and he said unto the man that had his hand
withered, Rise up and stand forth in the midst.   And he
arose and stood forth.   And Jesus said unto them, I ask
10 you, Is it lawful on the sabbath to do good or to do   Lk. 14. 3...
harm? to save a life or to destroy it?   But they held   Jas. 4. 17.
their peace.   And he said unto them, What man shall
there be of you that shall have one sheep, and if this fall   **106**
into a pit on the sabbath day, will he not lay hold on it
15 and lift it out?   How much then is a man of more value   Mt. 5. 26.
than a sheep!   Wherefore it is lawful to do good on the
sabbath day.   And when he had looked round about on
them all with anger, being grieved at the hardening of
their heart, he saith unto the man, Stretch forth thy hand.
20 And he stretched it forth; and his hand was restored,
whole, as the other.   But the Pharisees were filled with
madness, and communed with one another what they
might do to Jesus.   And they went out, and straightway
with the Herodians took counsel against him how they   Mt. 22. 16.
25 might destroy him.

41. *Jesus withdraws to the Sea of Galilee.   Many miracles.*

AND Jesus perceiving it withdrew from thence with
his disciples to the sea, and a great multitude from
Galilee followed, and he healed them all: and from   **31. 46.**
Judæa, and from Jerusalem, and from Idumæa, and   **67**
5 beyond Jordan, and about Tyre and Sidon, a great
multitude, hearing what great things he did, came unto
him.   And he spake to his disciples, that a little boat
should wait on him because of the crowd, lest they should
throng him: for he had healed many; insomuch that as
10 many as had plagues pressed upon him that they might
touch him.   And the unclean spirits, whensoever they
beheld him, fell down before him, and cried, saying, Thou
art the Son of God.   And he charged them much that
they should not make him known: that it might be
15 fulfilled which was spoken by Isaiah the prophet, saying,
Behold, my servant whom I have chosen;   Is. 42. 1...
My beloved in whom my soul is well pleased:

41. S. Mark iii. 7—12; S. Matthew xii. 15—21.

I will put my Spirit upon him,
And he shall declare judgement to the Gentiles.
He shall not strive, nor cry aloud;   20
Neither shall any one hear his voice in the streets.
A bruised reed shall he not break,
And smoking flax shall he not quench,
Till he send forth judgement unto victory.
Gr.   And in his name shall the Gentiles hope.   25

42. *Appointment of twelve Apostles.*

Mt. 14. 23.   AND it came to pass in these days that he went out
Lk. 9. 28. into the mountain to pray, and he continued all night in
63. 72. prayer to God.   And when it was day, he called unto
him his disciples, whom he himself would, and they went
Mt. 10. 2... unto him : and he chose from them twelve, whom he also 5
59 named Apostles, that they might be with him, and that
he might send them forth to preach, and to have
Acts 1. 13. authority to cast out devils : Simon whom he also sur-
Jn. 1. 42. named Peter, and Andrew his brother, and James the son
of Zebedee and John the brother of James, and them he 10
surnamed Boanerges, which is Sons of thunder : and Philip
and Bartholomew, Thomas and Matthew the publican, and
James the son of Alphæus, and Simon which was called
Acts 22. 3. the Zealot, and Judas the son of James, and Judas Iscariot
Jos. 15. 25. which was the traitor.   And he came down with them and 15
stood on a level place, and a great multitude of his
disciples, and a great number of the people from all
Judæa and Jerusalem, and the sea coast of Tyre and
Sidon, which came to hear him, and to be healed of
their diseases : and they that were troubled with unclean 20
spirits were healed.   And all the multitude sought to
touch him : for power came forth from him and healed
them all.

43. *Sermon on the Mount.   St Luke.*

AND he lifted up his eyes on his disciples, and said,
Jas. 2. 5. Blessed are ye poor : for yours is the kingdom of God.
Is. 55. 1... Blessed are ye that hunger now : for ye shall be filled.
Is. 61. 3. Blessed are ye that weep now : for ye shall laugh.
1 Pe. 2. 20. Blessed are ye, when men shall hate you, and when 5

42. S. Luke vi. 12—19 ; S. Mark iii. 13—19.
43. S. Luke vi. 20—49.

they shall separate you from their company, and reproach Jn. 16. 2;
you, and cast out your name as evil, for the Son of man's — 9. 34.
sake. Rejoice in that day, and leap *for joy* : for behold, Acts 5. 41.
your reward is great in heaven : for in the same manner Jas. 1. 2...
10 did their fathers unto the prophets. But woe unto you Amos 6. 1..
that are rich ! for ye have received your consolation. Lk. 16. 25.
Woe unto you, ye that are full now ! for ye shall hunger. Is. 65. 13.
Woe unto you, ye that laugh now ! for ye shall mourn Pro. 14. 13.
and weep. Woe unto you, when all men shall speak Jn. 15. 19.
15 well of you ! for in the same manner did their fathers to
the false prophets.

But I say unto you which hear, Love your enemies, Ex. 23. 4.
do good to them that hate you, bless them that curse Pro. 25. 21.
you, pray for them that despitefully use you. To him Acts 7. 60.
20 that smiteth thee on the one cheek offer also the other ;
and from him that taketh away thy cloke withhold not 1 Cor. 6. 7.
thy coat also. Give to every one that asketh thee ; and Pro. 21. 26.
of him that taketh away thy goods ask them not again.
And as ye would that men should do to you, do ye also Tob. 4. 15.
25 to them likewise. And if ye love them that love you,
what thank have ye ? for even sinners love those that
love them. And if ye do good to them that do good to
you, what thank have ye ? for even sinners do the same.
And if ye lend to them of whom ye hope to receive,
30 what thank have ye ? even sinners lend to sinners, to
receive again as much. But love your enemies, and do
them good, and lend, never despairing ; and your reward Ps. 37. 26.
shall be great, and ye shall be sons of the Most High :
for he is kind toward the unthankful and evil. Be ye
35 merciful, even as your Father is merciful. And judge Jas. 4. 11.
not, and ye shall not be judged : and condemn not, and Rom. 14. 4.
ye shall not be condemned : release, and ye shall be
released : give, and it shall be given unto you ; good Pro. 19. 17.
measure, pressed down, shaken together, running over,
40 shall they give into your bosom. For with what measure Ps. 79. 12.
ye mete it shall be measured to you again. Jas. 2. 13.

And he spake also a parable unto them, Can the Mt. 15. 14.
blind guide the blind ? shall they not both fall into a
pit ? The disciple is not above his master : but every Mt. 10. 24.
45 one when he is perfected shall be as his master. And
why beholdest thou the mote that is in thy brother's eye,
but considerest not the beam that is in thine own eye ?
Or how canst thou say to thy brother, Brother, let me

cast out the mote that is in thine eye, when thou thyself
beholdest not the beam that is in thine own eye? Thou 50
hypocrite, cast out first the beam out of thine own eye,
and then shalt thou see clearly to cast out the mote that
Mt. 12. 33. is in thy brother's eye.   For there is no good tree that
92   bringeth forth corrupt fruit; nor again a corrupt tree
that bringeth forth good fruit.   For each tree is known 55
by its own fruit.   For of thorns men do not gather figs,
nor of a bramble bush gather they grapes.   The good
Mt. 12. 35. man out of the good treasure of his heart bringeth forth
that which is good; and the evil man out of the evil
treasure bringeth forth that which is evil: for out of the 60
abundance of the heart his mouth speaketh.

And why call ye me, Lord, Lord, and do not the
things which I say? Every one that cometh unto me,
and heareth my words, and doeth them, I will shew you
to whom he is like: he is like a man building a house, 65
who digged and went deep, and laid a foundation upon
the rock: and when a flood arose, the stream brake
against that house, and could not shake it: because it
had been well builded.   But he that heareth, and doeth
not, is like a man that built a house upon the earth 70
without a foundation; against which the stream brake,
and straightway it fell in; and the ruin of that house was
great.

43*.   *Sermon on the Mount. St Matthew.*

AND seeing the multitudes, he went up into the
mountain: and when he had sat down, his disciples
came unto him: and he opened his mouth and taught
them, saying,
Is. 57. 15;   Blessed are the poor in spirit: for theirs is the king- 5
— 66. 2. dom of heaven.
Is. 61. 2.   Blessed are they that mourn: for they shall be comforted.
Ps. 37. 11.   Blessed are the meek: for they shall inherit the earth.
Is. 65. 13.   Blessed are they that hunger and thirst after right- 10
eousness: for they shall be filled.
Jas. 2. 13.   Blessed are the merciful: for they shall obtain mercy.
Ps. 24. 4.   Blessed are the pure in heart: for they shall see God.

Blessed are the peacemakers : for they shall be called Ps. 34. 14.
15 sons of God.

Blessed are they that have been persecuted for rig'it- 1 Pet. 3. 14.
eousness' sake : for theirs is the kingdom of heaven. 2 Tim. 2. 12.
Blessed are ye when men shall reproach you, and per-
secute you, and say all manner of evil against you falsely, 1 Pet. 4. 14.
20 for my sake.   Rejoice, and be exceeding glad : for great
is your reward in heaven : for so persecuted they the 1 Th. 2. 15.
prophets which were before you.

Ye are the salt of the earth : but if the salt have lost Lk. 14. 34.
its savour, wherewith shall it be salted ? it is thenceforth Mk. 9. 50.
25 good for nothing, but to be cast out and trodden under **75. 109**
foot of men.   Ye are the light of the world.   A city set Pro. 4. 18.
on a hill cannot be hid.   Neither do men light a lamp, Lk. 11. 33.
and put it under the bushel, but on the stand ; and it
shineth unto all that are in the house.   Even so let your
30 light shine before men, that they may see your good 1 Pet. 2. 12.
works, and glorify your Father which is in heaven. 1 Co. 14. 25.

Think not that I came to destroy the law or the Is. 42. 21.
prophets : I came not to destroy, but to fulfil.   For
verily I say unto you, Till heaven and earth pass away, Lk. 16. 17.
35 one jot or one tittle shall in no wise pass away from the
law, till all things be accomplished.   Whosoever there- Jas. 2. 10.
fore shall break one of these least commandments, and
shall teach men so, shall be called least in the kingdom
of heaven : but whosoever shall do and teach them, he
40 shall be called great in the kingdom of heaven.   For I
say unto you, that except your righteousness shall exceed
the righteousness of the scribes and Pharisees, ye shall in Ro. 9. 31..
no wise enter into the kingdom of heaven. — 10. 3.

Ye have heard that it was said to them of old time, Ex. 20. 13.
45 Thou shalt not kill ; and whosoever shall kill shall be in Deu. 5. 17.
danger of the judgement : but I say unto you, that every
one who is angry with his brother shall be in danger of Jas. 1. 19..
the judgement ; and whosoever shall say to his brother,
Raca, shall be in danger of the council ; and whosoever
50 shall say, Thou fool, shall be in danger of the hell of fire. or מורה
If therefore thou art offering thy gift at the altar, and Nu. 20. 10.
there rememberest that thy brother hath aught against
thee, leave there thy gift before the altar, and go thy
way, first be reconciled to thy brother, and then come Mk. 11. 25.
55 and offer thy gift.   Agree with thine adversary quickly, Lk. 12. 58.
whiles thou art with him in the way ; lest haply the ad-

Pro. 25. 8. versary deliver thee to the judge, and the judge deliver thee to the officer, and thou be cast into prison. Verily I say unto thee, Thou shalt by no means come out thence, till thou have paid the last farthing.   60

Ex. 20. 14.
Deu. 5. 18.
Job 31. 1.
Pro. 6. 25.
Mt. 19. 12.

Ye have heard that it was said, Thou shalt not commit adultery: but I say unto you, that every one that looketh on a woman to lust after her hath committed adultery with her already in his heart. And if thy right eye causeth thee to stumble, pluck it out, and cast it 65 from thee: for it is profitable for thee that one of thy members should perish, and not thy whole body be cast into hell. And if thy right hand causeth thee to stumble, cut it off, and cast it from thee: for it is profitable for thee that one of thy members should perish, and not thy 70 whole body go into hell. It was said also, Whosoever

Deu. 24. 1.
Lk. 16. 18.
1Co. 7. 10.

shall put away his wife, let him give her a writing of divorcement: but I say unto you, that every one that putteth away his wife, saving for the cause of fornication, maketh her an adulteress: and whosoever shall marry 75 her when she is put away committeth adultery.

Ex. 20. 7.
Lev. 19. 12.
Num. 30. 2.
De. 23. 21.
Is. 66. 1.
Ps. 48. 2.

Again, ye have heard that it was said to them of old time, Thou shalt not forswear thyself, but shalt perform unto the Lord thine oaths: but I say unto you, Swear not at all; neither by the heaven, for it is the throne of 80 God; nor by the earth, for it is the footstool of his feet; nor by Jerusalem, for it is the city of the great King. Neither shalt thou swear by thy head, for thou canst not make one hair white or black. But let your speech be,

Jas. 5. 12. Yea, yea; Nay, nay: and whatsoever is more than these 85 is of the evil one.

Ex. 21. 24.
Lev. 24. 20.
Deu. 19. 21.

Ye have heard that it was said, An eye for an eye, and a tooth for a tooth: but I say unto you, Resist not him that is evil: but whosoever smiteth thee on thy right cheek, turn to him the other also. And if any man 90

1 Cor. 6. 7. would go to law with thee, and take away thy coat, let him have thy cloke also. And whosoever shall compel thee to go one mile, go with him twain. Give to him

Deu. 15. 8. that asketh thee, and from him that would borrow of thee turn not thou away.   95

Lev. 19. 18. Ye have heard that it was said, Thou shalt love thy neighbour, and hate thine enemy: but I say unto you,

Acts 7. 60. Love your enemies, and pray for them that persecute you; that ye may be sons of your Father which is in

75

100 heaven : for he maketh his sun to rise on the evil and Job 25. 3.
the good, and sendeth rain on the just and the unjust.
For if ye love them that love you, what reward have ye?
do not even the publicans the same? And if ye salute
your brethren only, what do ye more than others? do not
110 even the Gentiles the same? Ye therefore shall be per- De. 18. 13.
fect, as your heavenly Father is perfect. Jas. 1. 4.

Take heed that ye do not your righteousness before
men, to be seen of them : else ye have no reward with
your Father which is in heaven.

115 When therefore thou doest alms, sound not a trumpet He. 13. 16.
before thee, as the hypocrites do in the synagogues and
in the streets, that they may have glory of men. Verily
I say unto you, They have received their reward. But
when thou doest alms, let not thy left hand know what
120 thy right hand doeth : that thine alms may be in secret :
and thy Father which seeth in secret shall recompense 2 Co. 9. 6.
thee.

And when ye pray, ye shall not be as the hypocrites :
for they love to stand and pray in the synagogues and in
125 the corners of the streets, that they may be seen of men.
Verily I say unto you, They have received their reward.
But thou, when thou prayest, enter into thine inner Is. 26. 20.
chamber, and having shut thy door, pray to thy Father 2 Ki. 4. 33.
which is in secret, and thy Father which seeth in secret
130 shall recompense thee. And in praying use not vain
repetitions, as the Gentiles do : for they think that they 1 Ki. 18. 27.
shall be heard for their much speaking. Be not there- Ecclus.
fore like unto them : for your Father knoweth what things 7. 14.
ye have need of, before ye ask him. After this manner
135 therefore pray ye : Our Father which art in heaven, Lk. 11. 2.
Hallowed be thy name. Thy kingdom come. Thy will 91
be done, as in heaven, so on earth. Give us this day
our daily bread. And forgive us our debts, as we also Pro. 30. 8.
have forgiven our debtors. And bring us not into temp-
140 tation, but deliver us from the evil one. For if ye forgive
men their trespasses, your heavenly Father will also for- Mk. 11. 25.
give you. But if ye forgive not men their trespasses, Mt. 18. 35.
neither will your Father forgive your trespasses. Jas. 2. 13.

Moreover when ye fast, be not, as the hypocrites, of 36
145 a sad countenance : for they disfigure their faces, that Is. 58. 3...
they may be seen of men to fast. Verily I say unto
you, They have received their reward. But thou, when

thou fastest, anoint thy head, and wash thy face; that thou be not seen of men to fast, but of thy Father which is in secret: and thy Father, which seeth in secret, shall 150 recompense thee.

Lk. 12. 33.   Lay not up for yourselves treasures upon the earth,
Jas. 5. 1... where moth and rust doth consume, and where thieves
1 Tim.6.19. break through and steal: but lay up for yourselves treasures in heaven, where neither moth nor rust doth 155 consume, and where thieves do not break through nor steal: for where thy treasure is, there will thy heart be
Lk. 11. 34. also. The lamp of the body is the eye: if therefore
96   thine eye be single, thy whole body shall be full of light. But if thine eye be evil, thy whole body shall be full of 160 darkness. If therefore the light that is in thee be dark-
Lk. 16. 13. ness, how great is the darkness! No man can serve two
111   masters: for either he will hate the one, and love the other; or else he will hold to one, and despise the other.
1 Co.10.21. Ye cannot serve God and mammon. Therefore I say 165
Lk. 12.22.. unto you, Be not anxious for your life, what ye shall eat,
99   or what ye shall drink; nor yet for your body, what ye shall put on. Is not the life more than the food, and
Job 38. 41. the body than the raiment? Behold the birds of the
Ps. 147. 9. heaven, that they sow not, neither do they reap, nor 170 gather into barns; and your heavenly Father feedeth them. Are not ye of much more value than they? And which of you by being anxious can add one cubit unto
Lk. 19. 3. his stature? And why are ye anxious concerning rai-
Gr.   ment? Consider the lilies of the field, how they grow; 175 they toil not, neither do they spin: yet I say unto you, that even Solomon in all his glory was not arrayed like
Ps. 104. 14. one of these. But if God doth so clothe the grass of the
Jas. 1. 10. field, which to-day is, and to-morrow is cast into the oven, shall he not much more clothe you, O ye of little 180
Ps. 55. 22. faith? Be not therefore anxious, saying, What shall we
1 Pet. 5. 7. eat? or, What shall we drink? or, Wherewithal shall we
Phil. 4. 6. be clothed? For after all these things do the Gentiles seek; for your heavenly Father knoweth that ye have need of all these things. But seek ye first his kingdom, 185
1 Ki. 3. 13. and his righteousness; and all these things shall be added
1 Tim. 4. 8. unto you. Be not therefore anxious for the morrow: for the morrow will be anxious for itself. Sufficient unto the day is the evil thereof.

Rom. 2. 1.   Judge not, that ye be not judged. For with what 190

judgement ye judge, ye shall be judged: and with what Mk. 4. 24.
measure ye mete, it shall be measured unto you.   And Ro. 14. 3...
why beholdest thou the mote that is in thy brother's Jas. 2. 13.
eye, but considerest not the beam that is in thine own
195 eye?   Or how wilt thou say to thy brother, Let me cast
out the mote out of thine eye; and lo, the beam is in
thine own eye?   Thou hypocrite, cast out first the beam
out of thine own eye; and then shalt thou see clearly to
cast out the mote out of thy brother's eye.

200   Give not that which is holy unto the dogs, neither Pro. 9. 7...
cast your pearls before the swine, lest haply they trample ─ 23. 9.
them under their feet, and turn and rend you.

         Ask, and it shall be given you; seek, and ye shall Lk. 11. 9...
find; knock, and it shall be opened unto you: for every   **91**
205 one that asketh receiveth; and he that seeketh findeth; Jas. 1. 5.
and to him that knocketh it shall be opened.   Or what 1 Jn. 5. 14..
man is there of you, who, if his son shall ask him for a
loaf, will give him a stone; or if he shall ask for a fish,
will give him a serpent?   If ye then, being evil, know Gen. 6. 5.
210 how to give good gifts unto your children, how much
more shall your Father which is in heaven give good Lk. 11. 13.
things to them that ask him?   All things therefore whatsoever ye would that men should do unto you, even Jas. 2. 8.
so do ye also unto them: for this is the law and the   **133**
215 prophets.

         Enter ye in by the narrow gate: for wide is the gate, Lk. 13. 24.
and broad is the way, that leadeth to destruction, and   **104**
many be they that enter in thereby.   For narrow is the
gate, and straitened the way, that leadeth unto life, and
220 few be they that find it.

         Beware of false prophets, which come to you in Deu. 13. 2..
sheep's clothing, but inwardly are ravening wolves.   By Acts 20. 29.
their fruits ye shall know them.   Do men gather grapes
of thorns, or figs of thistles?   Even so every good tree
225 bringeth forth good fruit; but the corrupt tree bringeth Mt. 12. 33..
forth evil fruit.   A good tree cannot bring forth evil   **92**
fruit, neither can a corrupt tree bring forth good fruit.
Every tree that bringeth not forth good fruit is hewn Mt. 3. 10.
down, and cast into the fire.   Therefore by their fruits Jn. 15. 2...
230 ye shall know them.   Not every one that saith unto me,   **151**
Lord, Lord, shall enter into the kingdom of heaven; but Hos. 8. 2...
he that doeth the will of my Father which is in heaven. Rom. 2. 13.
Many will say to me in that day, Lord, Lord, did we not Jas. 1. 22..

Jer. 27. 15. prophesy by thy name, and by thy name cast out devils,
— 14. 14. and by thy name do many mighty works? And then 235
Lk. 13. 27. will I profess unto them, I never knew you: depart from
Ps. 6. 8. me, ye that work iniquity. Every one therefore which
heareth these words of mine, and doeth them, shall be
likened unto a wise man, which built his house upon the
rock: and the rain descended, and the floods came, and 240
the winds blew, and beat upon that house; and it fell
not: for it was founded upon the rock. And every one
Jas. 1. 23.. that heareth these words of mine, and doeth them not,
shall be likened unto a foolish man, which built his house
upon the sand: and the rain descended, and the floods 245
came, and the winds blew, and smote upon that house;
and it fell: and great was the fall thereof.

And it came to pass, when Jesus ended these words,
the multitudes were astonished at his teaching: for he
Jn. 7. 46. taught them as one having authority, and not as their 250
scribes.

And when he was come down from the mountain,
great multitudes followed him.

44. *Centurion's Servant healed.*

AFTER he had ended all his sayings in the ears of
the people, he entered into Capernaum.
Mk. 15. 39. And a certain centurion's servant, who was dear unto
Acts 10. 2. him, was lying in the house sick of the palsy, grievously
tormented, and at the point of death. And when he heard 5
concerning Jesus, he sent unto him elders of the Jews,
asking that he would come and save his servant. And
they, when they came to Jesus, besought him earnestly,
saying, He is worthy that thou shouldest do this for him:
for he loveth our nation, and himself built us our syna- 10
gogue. And Jesus saith, I will come and heal him. And
he went with them. And when he was now not far from
the house, the centurion sent friends to him, saying unto
him, Lord, trouble not thyself: for I am not worthy that
thou shouldest come under my roof: wherefore neither 15
thought I myself worthy to come unto thee: but only
Ps. 107. 20. say the word, and my servant shall be healed. For I
also am a man set under authority, having under myself
soldiers: and I say to this one, Go, and he goeth; and

---

44.   **S. Luke vii. 1—10.**   **S. Matthew viii. 5—13.**

20 to another, Come, and he cometh; and to my servant,
Do this, and he doeth it. And when Jesus heard these
things, he marvelled at him, and turned and said to the
multitude that followed him, Verily I say unto you, I Mt. 15. 28.
have not found so great faith, no, not in Israel. And **66**
25 I say unto you, that many shall come from the east and Mal. 1. 11.
the west, and shall sit down with Abraham, Isaac and Is. 59. 19.
Jacob in the kingdom of heaven: but the sons of the
kingdom shall be cast forth into the outer darkness: Mt. 21. 43.
there shall be the weeping and the gnashing of teeth. 2 Pet. 2. 17.
30 And Jesus said unto the centurion, Go thy way; as thou Jude 13.
hast believed, so be it done unto thee. And the servant
was healed in that hour. And they that were sent, returning to the house, found the servant whole.

45. *Widow's Son raised.*

AND it came to pass soon afterwards, that he went to
a city called Nain; and his disciples went with him, and
a great multitude. Now when he drew near to the gate
of the city, behold, there was carried out one that was
5 dead, the only son of his mother, and she was a widow:
and much people of the city was with her. And when
the Lord saw her, he had compassion on her, and said
unto her, Weep not. And he came nigh and touched
the bier: and the bearers stood still. And he said, Mk. 5. 41.
10 Young man, I say unto thee, Arise. And he that was Jn. 11. 43.
dead sat up, and began to speak. And he gave him to **57. 83.**
his mother. And fear took hold on all: and they glorified God, saying, A great prophet is arisen among us:
and, God hath visited his people. And this report went Lk. 1. 68.
15 forth concerning him in the whole of Judæa, and all the
region round about.

46. *John Baptist's question. Jesus' Testimony to him.*

AND the disciples of John told him of all these things.
And when John heard in the prison the works of the Lk. 3. 20.
Christ, he called unto him two of his disciples, and sent **15**
them unto the Lord, saying, Art thou he that cometh, or
5 look we for another? And when the men were come
unto him, they said, John the Baptist hath sent us unto
thee, saying, Art thou he that cometh, or look we for

---

45. S. Luke vii. 11—17.
46. S. Luke vii. 18—35. S. Matthew xi. 2—19.

31. 41.
67   another? In that hour he cured many of diseases and plagues and evil spirits; and on many that were blind he bestowed sight. And he answered and said unto 10 them, Go your way, and tell John what things ye have
Is. 35. 5..; seen and heard: the blind receive their sight, the lame
— 29. 18. walk, the lepers are cleansed, and the deaf hear, the dead
Is. 61. 1. are raised up, and the poor have good tidings preached
Jas. 2. 5. unto them. And blessed is he whosoever shall find none 15
1 Pet. 2. 8. occasion of stumbling in me.

And when the messengers of John were departed, as they went their way, Jesus began to say unto the multitudes concerning John, What went ye out into the wil-
Eph. 4. 14. derness to behold? a reed shaken with the wind? But 20 what went ye out to see? a man clothed in soft raiment? Behold, they which are gorgeously apparelled, and live delicately, are in kings' courts. But what went ye out to see? a prophet? Yea, I say unto you, and much more than a prophet. This is he of whom it is written, 25
Mal. 3. 1.   Behold, I send my messenger before thy face,
Who shall prepare thy way before thee.
Verily I say unto you, among them that are born of women there hath not arisen a greater than John the Baptist: yet he that is but little in the kingdom of God 30 is greater than he. And from the days of John until
Lk. 16. 16. now the kingdom of heaven suffereth violence, and men
111   of violence take it by force. For all the prophets and the law prophesied until John. And if ye are willing to
Mal. 4. 5. receive it, this is Elijah, which is to come. He that 35 hath ears to hear, let him hear. And all the people
Mt. 21. 31. when they heard, and the publicans, justified God, being
128   baptized with the baptism of John. But the Pharisees
1 Tim. 2. 4. and the lawyers rejected for themselves the counsel of God, being not baptized of him. Whereunto then shall 40 I liken the men of this generation, and to what are they like? They are like unto children that sit in the market-
Lk. 15. 25. place and call one to another; which say, We piped unto
Mk. 5. 38. you, and ye did not dance; we wailed, and ye did not weep. For John the Baptist is come eating no bread 45 nor drinking wine; and ye say, He hath a devil. The
Jn. 2. 2. Son of man is come eating and drinking; and ye say,
Lk. 14. 1. Behold a gluttonous man and a winebibber, a friend of
Jn. 12. 2. publicans and sinners! And Wisdom is justified of all her children. 50

47. *Jesus' feet anointed. The sinner forgiven.*

AND one of the Pharisees desired him that he would
eat with him. And he entered into the Pharisee's house,
and sat down to meat. And behold, a woman which
was in the city, a sinner; and when she knew that he
5 was sitting at meat in the Pharisee's house, she brought
an alabaster cruse of ointment, and standing behind at Mk. 14. 3.
his feet, weeping, she began to wet his feet with her **125**
tears, and wiped them with the hair of her head, and
kissed his feet, and anointed them with the ointment.
10 Now when the Pharisee which had bidden him saw it,
he spake within himself, saying, This man, if he were a Lk. 15. 2.
prophet, would have perceived who and what manner of Is. 65. 5.
woman this is which toucheth him, that she is a sinner.
And Jesus answering said unto him, Simon, I have some-
15 what to say unto thee. And he saith, Master, say on.
A certain lender had two debtors: the one owed five
hundred pence, and the other fifty. When they had not
wherewith to pay, he forgave them both. Which of Mt. 18. 23.
them therefore will love him most? Simon answered
20 and said, He, I suppose, to whom he forgave the most.
And he said unto him, Thou hast rightly judged. And
turning to the woman, he said unto Simon, Seest thou
this woman? I entered into thine house, thou gavest
me no water for my feet: but she hath wetted my feet Gen. 18. 4.
25 with her tears, and wiped them with her hair. Thou
gavest me no kiss: but she, since the time I came in, Ex. 18. 7.
hath not ceased to kiss my feet. My head with oil thou
didst not anoint: but she hath anointed my feet with Ps. 23. 5.
ointment. Wherefore I say unto thee, Her sins, which
30 are many, are forgiven; for she loved much: but to
whom little is forgiven, the same loveth little. And he
said unto her, Thy sins are forgiven. And they that sat
at meat with him began to say within themselves, Who Mk. 2. 7.
is this that even forgiveth sins? And he said unto the **35**
35 woman, Thy faith hath saved thee; go in peace.

48. *Circuit in Galilee. Ministering women.*

AND it came to pass soon afterwards, that he went
about through cities and villages, preaching and bringing

---

47. S. Luke vii. 36—50.　　　　**48. S. Luke viii. 1—3.**

the good tidings of the kingdom of God, and with him
the twelve, and certain women which had been healed
of evil spirits and infirmities, Mary that was called Mag- 5
Mk. 16. 9. dalene, from whom seven devils had gone out, and Joanna the wife of Chuza Herod's steward, and Susanna,
and many others, which ministered unto them of their
substance.

49. *Parable of the Sower.*

ON that day went Jesus out of the house and sat by the
sea side: and he began to teach by the sea side. And
there were gathered unto him great multitudes, and they
of every city resorted unto him, so that he entered into a
Lk. 5. 3. boat and sat in the sea, and all the multitude were 5
33 standing by the sea on the land. And he taught them
Ps. 78. 2. many things in parables, and said unto them in his
teaching, Hearken: Behold the sower went forth to sow
his seed: and it came to pass, as he sowed, some fell by
the way side; and it was trodden under foot, and the 10
birds of the heaven came and devoured it: and other
fell on the rocky ground, where it had not much earth;
and straightway it sprang up, because it had no deepness
Jas. 1. 11. of earth: and when the sun was risen it was scorched,
and because it had no root, it withered away. And other 15
Jer. 4. 3. fell among the thorns, and the thorns grew up with it, and
choked it, and it yielded no fruit. And others fell into
Jn. 15. 5. the good ground, and yielded fruit, growing up and
Col. 1. 6. increasing, and brought forth some a hundredfold, some
sixtyfold, some thirtyfold. As he said these things, he 20
cried, He that hath ears to hear, let him hear.

50. *Of teaching by parables. The Sower explained.*

AND when he was alone, they that were about him
with the twelve came, and said unto him, Why speakest
thou unto them in parables? And he said unto them,
Mt. 11. 25. Unto you it is given to know the mysteries of the
kingdom of God: but unto the rest that are without, it 5
is not given, but all things are done in parables. For
Mt. 25. 28.. whosoever hath, to him shall be given, and he shall have
abundance: but whosoever hath not, from him shall be

49. S. Mark iv. 1—9; S. Matthew xiii. 1—9; S. Luke viii. 4—8.
50. S. Matthew xiii. 10—23; S. Mark iv. 10—20; S. Luke viii.
9—15.

taken away even that which he hath. Therefore speak I Lk. 19. 24.
10 unto them in parables; because seeing they see not and
hearing they hear not, neither do they understand. And
unto them is fulfilled the prophecy of Isaiah, which saith,
> By hearing ye shall hear, and shall in no wise Is. 6. 9.
> understand; Jn. 12. 40.
> And seeing ye shall see and shall in no wise perceive: Acts 28. 26.
15 > For this people's heart is waxed gross,
> And their ears are dull of hearing, Heb. 5. 11.
> And their eyes they have closed;
> Lest haply they should perceive with their eyes,
> And hear with their ears,
20 > And understand with their heart,
> And should turn again,
> And I should heal them.

But blessed are your eyes, for they see, and your ears, Lk. 10. 24.
for they hear. For verily I say unto you, that many
25 prophets and righteous men desired to see the things Heb. 11. 13.
which ye see, and saw them not; and to hear the things 1 Pet. 1. 10.
which ye hear, and heard them not. And he saith unto
them, Know ye not this parable? And how shall ye know
all the parables? Hear then ye the parable of the sower.
30 Now the parable is this: The sower soweth the word; the 1 Cor. 3. 6...
seed is the word of God. When any one heareth the
word of the kingdom and understandeth it not, straightway cometh Satan, and snatcheth away the word which Eph. 2. 2.
hath been sown in his heart, that he may not believe and
35 be saved. This is he that was sown by the way side.
And in like manner he that was sown upon the rocky
places, this is he that heareth the word, and straightway
with joy receiveth it; yet hath he no root in himself, but Eph. 3. 17.
endureth for a while: then when tribulation or persecution
40 ariseth because of the word, straightway he stumbleth. Mt. 24. 12.
And he that was sown among the thorns, this is he that
heareth the word: and the cares of the world, and the Mt. 6. 25.
deceitfulness of riches, and the lusts of other things Mk. 10. 23.
entering in, and the pleasures of this life choke the word, 1 Tim. 6. 9.
45 and he bringeth no fruit to perfection. And he that was
sown upon the good ground, this is he that in an honest Jn. 8. 47.
and good heart, having heard the word, understandeth it Prov. 16. 1.
and holdeth it fast; who verily beareth fruit with patience,
and bringeth forth, some a hundredfold, some sixty, some
50 thirty.

51. *Parable of the Lamp.   The Tares.   The Seed.*
The Mustard Seed.   The Leaven.

Mt. 5. 16.   AND he said unto them, Is the lamp brought to be
Psalm   put under the bushel, or under the bed, and not to be
119.105.   put on the stand, that they which enter in may see the
Pro. 20. 27.   light?   For nothing is hid that shall not be made
Mt. 10. 26. manifest, nor anything secret, that shall not be known 5
Lk. 12. 2. and come to light.   If any man hath ears to hear, let him
59. 98   hear.   And he said unto them, Take heed what ye hear:
Mt. 7. 2.   with what measure ye mete it shall be measured unto
43*   you: and more shall be given unto you.   Take heed
therefore how ye hear: for whosoever hath, to him shall 10
Mt. 25. 29. be given; and whosoever hath not, from him shall be
123. 139 taken away even that which he thinketh he hath.

Another parable set he before them, saying, The
kingdom of God is likened unto a man that sowed
Hos. 2. 23. good seed in his field: but while men slept, his enemy 15
came and sowed tares also among the wheat, and went
away.   But when the blade sprang up, and brought forth
fruit, then appeared the tares also.   And the servants of
the householder came and said unto him, Sir, didst thou
not sow good seed in thy field? whence then hath it tares? 20
And he said unto them, An enemy hath done this.   And
the servants say unto him, Wilt thou then that we go and
gather them up?   But he saith, Nay; lest haply while ye
gather up the tares, ye root up the wheat with them.
Let both grow together until the harvest: and in the 25
time of the harvest I will say to the reapers, Gather up
Mt. 3. 12. first the tares, and bind them in bundles to burn them:
Amos 9. 9. but gather the wheat into my barn.

And he said, So is the kingdom of God, as if a man
should cast seed upon the earth; and should sleep and 30
rise night and day, and the seed should spring up and
grow, he knoweth not how.   The earth beareth fruit of
herself; first the blade, then the ear, then the full corn in
Joel 3. 13. the ear.   But when the fruit is ripe, straightway he
Rev. 14. 15. putteth forth the sickle, because the harvest is come.   35
And he said, How shall we liken the kingdom of
heaven? or in what parable shall we set it forth?   It is

---

51. S. Mark iv. 21—34; S. Matthew xiii. 24—35; S. Luke viii.
16—18.

like a grain of mustard seed which a man took and sowed **103**
in his field : which indeed is less than all the seeds that
40 are upon the earth, yet when it is sown, groweth up and
becometh greater than all the herbs, and becometh a
tree, and putteth forth great branches; so that the birds Dan. 4. 12.
of the heaven come and lodge under the shadow thereof. Ez.17.22...

Another parable he spake unto them : The kingdom
45 of heaven is like unto leaven, which a woman took, and **103**
hid in three measures of meal, till it was all leavened. Ex. 16. 36.

And with many such parables spake he the word unto cp.Gr.&H.
the multitudes, as they were able to hear it : and without
a parable spake he not unto them : but privately to his
50 own disciples he expounded all things: that it might be
fulfilled which was spoken by the prophet, saying,

  I will open my mouth in parables : Ps. 78. 2.
  I will utter things hidden from the foundation of the
    world.

52. *Parable of Tares explained. Hidden Treasure. Pearl. Net.*

THEN he left the multitudes, and went into the house:
and his disciples came unto him, saying, Explain unto us
the parable of the tares of the field. And he answered
and said, He that soweth the good seed is the Son of
5 man; and the field is the world; and the good seed, Ro. 10. 18.
these are the sons of the kingdom ; and the tares are the
sons of the evil *one*; and the enemy that sowed them is Jn. 8. 44.
the devil : and the harvest is the end of the world ; and 1 Jn. 3. 8.
the reapers are angels. As therefore the tares are Re.14.15...
10 gathered up and burned with fire; so shall it be in the
end of the world. The Son of man shall send forth his **140**
angels, and they shall gather out of his kingdom all
things that cause stumbling, and them that do iniquity,
and shall cast them into the furnace of fire : there shall Is. 66. 24.
15 be the weeping and gnashing of teeth. Then shall the
righteous shine forth as the sun in the kingdom of their Dan. 12. 3.
Father. He that hath ears, let him hear. Rev. 7. 9.

The kingdom of heaven is like unto a treasure hidden
in the field; which a man found, and hid ; and in his
20 joy he goeth and selleth all that he hath, and buyeth that Phil. 3. 7..
field. Is. 55. 1.
Rev. 3. 18.

52. S. Matthew xiii. 36—52.

Again, the kingdom of heaven is like unto a man that
is a merchant seeking goodly pearls: and having found
Pro. 3. 13.. one pearl of great price, he went and sold all that he
had, and bought it.   25

Again, the kingdom of heaven is like unto a net, that
Mt. 22. 10. was cast into the sea, and gathered of every kind: which,
when it was filled, they drew up on the beach; and they
sat down, and gathered the good into vessels, but the
bad they cast away.   So shall it be in the end of the 30
Mt. 25. 32. world: the angels shall come forth, and sever the wicked
140   from among the righteous, and shall cast them into the
furnace of fire: there shall be the weeping and gnashing
of teeth.

Have ye understood all these things? They say 35
unto him, Yea.   And he said unto them, Therefore
every scribe who hath been made a disciple to the
kingdom of heaven is like unto a man that is a householder, which bringeth forth out of his treasure things
new and old.   40

53. *His Mother and Brethren.*

WHILE he was yet speaking unto the multitudes,
54   behold, his mother and his brethren came, seeking to
speak with him; and they could not come at him for the
crowd; and standing without, they sent unto him,
calling him.   And a multitude was sitting about him: 5
and one said unto him, Behold thy mother and thy
brethren stand without seeking to speak to thee.   But
he answered and said unto him that told him, Who is
my mother? and who are my brethren?   And looking
round on them which sat round about him, he stretched 10
forth his hand towards his disciples, and said, Behold
my mother and my brethren! *even* these which hear
Jn. 15. 10. the word of God and do it.   For whosoever shall do
the will of my Father which is in heaven, the same is
my brother and sister and mother.   15

53. S. Matthew xii. 46—50 ; S. Mark iii. 31—35 ; S. Luke viii.
19—21.

54. *His own received Him not.*

AND it came to pass, when Jesus had finished these
parables, he departed thence ; and he cometh into his
own country, and his disciples follow him. And when
the sabbath was come, he began to teach in the synagogue,
5 insomuch that many hearing him were astonished, saying, Lk. 4.16...
Whence hath this man these things? and what is the 27. 64
wisdom that is given unto this man, and what mean
such mighty works wrought by his hands? Is not this
the carpenter? Is not his mother called Mary? and his
10 brethren, James and Joseph and Simon and Judas? Gal. 1. 19.
And his sisters, are they not all here with us? And they Jude 1.
were offended in him. But Jesus said unto them, A
prophet is not without honour save in his own country, Jn. 4. 44.
and among his own kin, and in his own house. And he
15 could there do no mighty work because of their un- Gen.19.22.
belief, save that he laid his hands upon a few sick folk, Mk. 9. 23...
and healed them. And he marvelled because of their Acts 14. 9.
unbelief.

55. *He stilleth the Storm.*

Now it came to pass on one of those days when even
was come, he entered into a boat, and his disciples
followed him ; and he said unto them, Let us go over
unto the other side of the lake : and leaving the multi-
5 tude, they take him with them even as he was in the
boat, and they launched forth. And other boats were
with him. But as they sailed, he fell asleep. And there
came down a great storm of wind on the lake, and the
waves beat into the boat, insomuch that the boat was
10 now filling, and they were in jeopardy. But he himself
was in the stern, asleep on the cushion. And they came
to him and awoke him, saying, Save, Lord, we perish.
And he saith unto them, Why are ye fearful, O ye of little
faith? Then he arose and rebuked the wind, and the
15 raging of the water ; and said unto the sea, Peace, be Ps. 89. 9.
still. And the wind ceased, and there was a great calm. Ps. 107. 29.

---

54. S. Mark vi. 1—6 ; S. Matthew xiii. 53—58.
55. S. Mark iv. 35—41 ; S. Luke viii. 22—25 ;
S. Matthew viii. 18, 23—27.

63   And he saith unto them, Why are ye fearful? Where is
your faith? Have ye not yet faith? And being exceedingly afraid they marvelled, and said one to another,
Who then is this, that he commandeth even the winds 20
and the sea, and they obey him?

56. *Demoniacs healed. The Swine.*

AND they came to the other side of the sea into the
country of the Gerasenes, which is over against Galilee.
And when he was come out of the boat upon the land,

two. Mt.   straightway there met him out of the tombs a certain man
out of the city, with an unclean spirit. And for a long 5
time he had worn no clothes, and abode not in any house,
but had his dwelling in the tombs, and was exceeding
fierce, so that no man could pass by that way. And no man
could any more bind him, no, not with a chain; because that
he had often been bound with fetters and chains, and the 10
chains had been rent asunder by him, and the fetters
broken in pieces: and no man had strength to tame him;
but breaking the bands asunder, he was driven of the
devil into the deserts. And always night and day, in
the tombs and in the mountains, he was crying out, and 15
cutting himself with stones. And when he saw Jesus
from afar, he cried out, and ran, and fell down before him,
and worshipped him; and crying out with a loud voice

Mk. 1. 24.   said, What have I to do with thee, Jesus, thou Son of the
30   Most High God? I adjure thee by God, torment me 20
not. Art thou come hither to torment us before the
time? For he said unto him, Come forth, thou unclean
spirit, out of the man. And he asked him, What is thy
name? And he saith unto him, My name is Legion, for
we are many; for many devils had entered into him. 25
And he besought him much that he would not send
them away out of the country, or command them to

Rev. 20. 1..   depart into the abyss. Now there was afar off from them
Is. 65. 4.   on the mountain side a great herd of swine feeding:
and they intreated him that he would give them leave to 30
enter into them. And he gave them leave. And the
unclean spirits came out from the man and entered into
the swine: and behold, the whole herd rushed down the

56. S. Mark v. 1—20; S. Luke viii. 26—39;
S. Matthew viii. 28—34.

steep place into the sea, in number about two thousand,
35 and perished in the waters. And when they that fed
them saw what was come to pass, they fled and went
away into the city, and told everything, and what was
befallen him that was possessed with devils. And behold
all the city came out to see what it was that had come to
40 pass. And they come to Jesus, and found the man from
whom the devils were gone out, sitting, clothed and in
his right mind, at the feet of Jesus; even him that had Lk. 10. 39.
the legion; and they were afraid. And they that saw it
told them how he that was possessed with devils was
45 made whole, and concerning the swine. And all the
people of the country of the Gerasenes round about
began to beseech him to depart from their borders, for Acts 16. 39.
they were holden with great fear: and he entered into a
boat and returned. And as he was entering into the
50 boat, the man from whom the devils were gone out
prayed him that he might be with him. And he suffered
him not, but sent him away, saying, Return to thy house
unto thy friends, and declare unto them how great things
God hath done for thee, and how he had mercy upon
55 thee. And he went his way, and began to publish
throughout the whole city and in Decapolis how great
things Jesus had done for him: and all men did marvel.

57. *Jairus' Daughter. Issue of Blood.*

AND as Jesus returned, when he had crossed over
again in the boat unto the other side, a great multitude
was gathered unto him, and they welcomed him, for they
were all waiting for him: and he was by the sea. And
5 behold, there cometh one of the rulers of the synagogue,
Jaïrus by name, and seeing him, he falleth at his feet,
and worshippeth him, and beseecheth him much to come
into his house; saying, My little daughter is at the point
of death: but come and lay thy hands upon her, that she
10 may be made whole, and live. And Jesus arose and followed him, and so did his disciples. And as he went with
him, a great multitude followed him and thronged him.
And behold, a woman who had an issue of blood Le. 15. 19...
twelve years, and had suffered many things of many
15 physicians, and could not be healed of any; and had

---

57. S. Mark v. 21—43; S. Luke viii. 40—56; S. Matthew ix. 18—26.

spent all that she had, and was nothing bettered, but
rather grew worse, having heard the things concerning
Jesus, came in the crowd behind him, and touched
Nu. 15. 38. the border of his garment.   For she said within her-
Deu.22.12. self, If I do but touch his garment I shall be made 20
Mt. 23. 5. whole.   And immediately the fountain of her blood was
dried up; and she felt in her body that she was healed
of her plague.   And straightway Jesus, perceiving in
Lk. 6. 19. himself that the power proceeding from him had gone
forth, turned him about in the crowd, and said, Who 25
touched my garments?   And when all denied, Peter said,
and they that were with him, Master thou seest the
multitude thronging and pressing thee, and sayest thou
who touched me?   But Jesus said, Some one did touch
me: for I perceived that power had gone forth from me. 30
And he looked round about to see her that had done
this thing.   But the woman fearing and trembling,
knowing what had been done to her, when she saw that
she was not hid, came and fell down before him, and
told him all the truth: and declared in the presence of 35
all the people for what cause she touched him, and how she
was healed immediately.   And he said unto her, Daughter,
Mk.10.52. be of good cheer: thy faith hath made thee whole; go
Acts 3. 16. in peace, and be whole of thy plague.   And the woman
was made whole from that hour.   40
          While he yet spake, there cometh one from the ruler
of the synagogue's house, saying, Thy daughter is dead:
why troublest thou the Master any further?   But Jesus
not heeding the word spoken, saith unto the ruler of the
synagogue, Fear not, only believe, and she shall be made 45
whole.   And when they came to the house of the ruler
of the synagogue, he suffered not any man to enter in
72. 156 with him save Peter and James and John the brother of
James, and the father of the maiden, and her mother.
And when he was entered in, he beholdeth the flute- 50
players and the crowd making a tumult, and many
Lk. 7. 32. weeping and wailing greatly.   But he saith unto them,
Give place: why make ye a tumult and weep? the child
Jn. 11. 11. is not dead but sleepeth.   And they laughed him to
scorn, knowing that she was dead.   But he having put 55
them all forth, taketh the father of the child and her
mother, and them that were with him, and goeth in where
the child was.   And taking the child by the hand, he

saith unto her, Talitha cumi; which is, being interpreted,
60 Damsel, I say unto thee, Arise. And her spirit returned,   **45. 83**
and she rose up immediately, and walked, for she was
twelve years old; and he commanded that something
should be given her to eat. And her parents were
amazed straightway with a great amazement; but he
65 charged them much to tell no man what had been done. Mk. 7. 36.
But the fame hereof went forth into all that land.

58. *Two Blind Men. A Dumb Demoniac.*

AND as Jesus passed by from thence, two blind men
followed him, crying out, and saying, Have mercy on us,
thou son of David. And when he was come into the Mt. 15. 22.
house, the blind men came to him : and Jesus saith unto Mk. 10. 47.
5 them, Believe ye that I am able to do this? They say
unto him, Yea, Lord. Then touched he their eyes,
saying, According to your faith be it done unto you. Acts 14. 9.
And their eyes were opened. And Jesus strictly charged
them, saying, See that no man know it. But they went
10 forth, and spread abroad his fame in all that land.

And as they went forth, behold, there was brought to
him a dumb man possessed with a devil. And when the
devil was cast out, the dumb man spake : and the multi-   **73. 92**
tudes marvelled, saying, It was never so seen in Israel.
15 But the Pharisees said, By the prince of the devils casteth
he out devils.

59. *Mission of the Twelve. Instructions.*

AND Jesus went round about all the cities and the
villages, teaching in their synagogues, and preaching the
gospel of the kingdom, and healing all manner of disease Acts 10. 38.
and all manner of sickness. But when he saw the
5 multitudes, he was moved with compassion for them,
because they were distressed and scattered, as sheep not Nu. 27. 17.
having a shepherd. Then saith he unto his disciples, Eze. 34. 5.
The harvest truly is plenteous, but the labourers are few. Jn. 4. 35.
Pray ye therefore the Lord of the harvest, that he send
10 forth labourers into his harvest. And he called unto him Mk. 4. 29.
his twelve disciples, and began to send them forth by two
and two ; and he gave them authority over the unclean

---

58. S. Matthew ix. 27—34.
59. S. Matthew ix. 35—xi. 1 ; S. Mark vi. 6—13 ; S. Luke ix. 1—6.

spirits, to cast them out; and to heal all manner of
disease and all manner of sickness.

42   Now the names of the twelve apostles are these: The 15
Acts 1. 13. first, Simon, who is called Peter, and Andrew his brother;
Jn. 1. 42. James the *son* of Zebedee, and John his brother; Philip,
and Bartholomew; Thomas, and Matthew the publican;
James the *son* of Alphæus, and Thaddæus; Simon the
Acts 22. 3. Cananæan, and Judas Iscariot, who also betrayed him. 20
Jos. 15. 25. These twelve Jesus sent forth to preach the kingdom of
God and to heal the sick. And he charged them, saying,
Go not into *any* way of the Gentiles, and enter not
Mt. 15. 24. into any city of the Samaritans: but go rather to the lost
Acts 13.46. sheep of the house of Israel. And as ye go, preach, 25
saying, The kingdom of heaven is at hand. Heal the
sick, raise the dead, cleanse the lepers, cast out devils:
Acts 8.18.. freely ye received, freely give. Get you no gold nor
Lk. 10. 4. silver nor brass in your purses. Take nothing for your
85   journey, no wallet, neither two coats, nor shoes, nor 30
1 Cor. 9.7.. staff, nor bread; for the labourer is worthy of his food.
1 Ti. 5. 18. And into whatsoever city or village ye shall enter, search
out in it who is worthy, and there abide till ye go forth.
And as ye enter into the house, salute it. And if the
house be worthy, let your peace come upon it: but if it 35
be not worthy, let your peace return to you. And whosoever shall not receive you, nor hear your words, as ye
Neh. 5. 13. go forth out of that house or that city, shake off the dust
Acts 13.51. that is under your feet for a testimony against them.
Verily I say unto you, It shall be more tolerable for the 40
86   land of Sodom and Gomorrah in the day of judgement,
than for that city.
Behold, I send you forth as sheep in the midst of
Ro. 16. 19. wolves: be ye therefore wise as serpents, and harm-
1Co.14.20. less as doves. But beware of men: for they will deliver 45
Acts 22.19. you up to councils, and in their synagogues they will
Mk. 13. 9.. scourge you; yea and before governors and kings shall
137   ye be brought for my sake, for a testimony to them and to
the Gentiles. But when they deliver you up, be not
anxious how or what ye shall speak: for it shall be given 50
you in that hour what ye shall speak. For it is not ye
1 Cor. 2.13. that speak, but the Spirit of your Father that speaketh in
you. And brother shall deliver up brother to death, and
Mic. 7. 6. the father his child: and children shall rise up against
parents, and cause them to be put to death. And ye 55

shall be hated of all men for my name's sake : but he
that endureth to the end, the same shall be saved. But Jas. 1. 12.
when they persecute you in this city, flee into the next : Acts 8. 4.
for verily I say unto you, Ye shall not have gone through
60 the cities of Israel, till the Son of man be come.

A disciple is not above his master, nor a servant Lk. 6. 40.
above his lord. It is enough for the disciple that he be Jn. 13. 16.
as his master, and the servant as his lord. If they have
called the master of the house Beelzebub, how much
65 more shall they call them of his household ! Fear them
not therefore : for there is nothing covered, that shall not Mk. 4. 22.
be revealed ; and hid, that shall not be known. What I Lk. 12. 2.
tell you in the darkness, speak ye in the light : and what **51. 98**
ye hear in the ear, proclaim upon the housetops. And
70 be not afraid of them which kill the body, but are not Is. 8. 12..
able to kill the soul : but rather fear him which is able to Lk. 12. 4...
destroy both soul and body in hell. Are not two Jas. 4. 12.
sparrows sold for a farthing ? and not one of them shall
fall on the ground without your Father : but the very
75 hairs of your head are all numbered. Fear not there- 2Sa. 14. 11.
fore ; ye are of more value than many sparrows. Every one
therefore who shall confess me before men, him will I Rev. 3. 5.
also confess before my Father which is in heaven. But
whosoever shall deny me before men, him will I also Lk. 9. 26.
80 deny before my Father which is in heaven. 2Tim.2.12.

Think not that I came to send peace on the earth :
I came not to send peace, but a sword. For I came to Lk.12.51...
set a man at variance against his father, and the daughter Mic. 7. 6.
against her mother, and the daughter in law against her
85 mother in law : and a man's foes shall be they of his own
household. He that loveth father or mother more than Lk.14.26...
me is not worthy of me : and he that loveth son or
daughter more than me is not worthy of me. And he
that doth not take up his cross and follow after me, is Lk. 9. 24.
90 not worthy of me. He that findeth his life shall lose it ; **71**
and he that loseth his life for my sake shall find it. Jn. 12. 25.

He that receiveth you receiveth you receiveth me, Mt. 18. 5.
and he that receiveth me receiveth him that sent me. Jn. 13. 20.
He that receiveth a prophet in the name of a prophet
95 shall receive a prophet's reward ; and he that receiveth a 1Ki.17.10..
righteous man in the name of a righteous man shall re- 2 Ki. 4. 8..
ceive a righteous man's reward. And whosoever shall Mk. 9. 41.
give to drink unto one of these little ones a cup of cold **75**

Ge. 24. 18.. water only, in the name of a disciple, verily I say unto
you, he shall in no wise lose his reward.   100

And they departed, and went throughout the villages,
preaching the gospel, and healing everywhere.   And
they preached that men should repent.   And they cast
Lk. 10. 34. out many devils, and anointed with oil many that were
Jas. 5. 14. sick, and healed them.   105

And it came to pass when Jesus had made an end of
commanding his twelve disciples, he departed thence to
teach and preach in their cities.

60.   *Herod's opinion of Jesus.   His Murder of*
John Baptist.

AT that season Herod the tetrarch heard the report
concerning Jesus, and all that was done ; for his name
had become known : and he was much perplexed,
because that it was said by some that John was risen
71   from the dead ; and by some that Elijah had appeared ; 5
and by others that one of the old prophets was risen
again.   But Herod when he heard thereof said unto his
servants, This is John the Baptist whom I beheaded :
he is risen from the dead, and therefore do these powers
work in him.   And he sought to see him.   For Herod 10
Lk. 3. 20. himself had sent forth and laid hold upon John and
15   bound him and put him in prison for the sake of
Ex. 20. 14. Herodias, his brother Philip's wife : for he had married
Le. 18. 16; her.   For John said unto Herod, It is not lawful for
— 20. 21. thee to have thy brother's wife.   And when he would 15
have put him to death, he feared the multitude, because
they counted him as a prophet.   And Herodias set herself against him, and desired to kill him ; and she could
not ; for Herod feared John, knowing that he was a
righteous man, and holy, and kept him safe.   And when 20
he heard him, he was much perplexed; and he heard him
gladly.   And when a convenient day was come, that
Gen.40. 20. Herod on his birthday made a supper to his lords, and
the high captains, and the chief men of Galilee, and when
the daughter of Herodias herself came in and danced in 25
the midst, she pleased Herod and them that sat at meat
with him ; and the king said unto the damsel, Ask of me
whatsoever thou wilt, and I will give it thee.   And he

---

60. S. Mark vi. 14—29 ; S. Matthew xiv. 1—12 ; S. Luke ix. 7—9.

sware unto her, Whatsoever thou shalt ask of me, I will Est. 5. 3..;
30 give it thee, unto the half of my kingdom. And she — 7. 2.
went out, and said unto her mother, What shall I ask?
And she said, The head of John the Baptist. And she
came in straightway with haste unto the king, and asked,
saying, I will that thou forthwith give me in a charger the
35 head of John the Baptist. And the king was exceeding
sorry; but for the sake of his oaths and of them that Jud. 11.3;.
sat at meat with him, he would not reject her. And cf. 1 Sam.
straightway the king sent forth a soldier of his guard, and 25. 22, 33.
commanded to bring his head: and he went and be-
40 headed him in the prison, and brought his head in a
charger, and gave it to the damsel, and the damsel brought
it and gave it to her mother. And when his disciples
heard *thereof*, they came and took up his corpse, and Acts 8. 2.
laid it in a tomb; and they went and told Jesus.

61. *Jesus withdraws. Passover at hand.*

AND the apostles when they were returned, gather
themselves together unto Jesus; and declared unto him
all things, whatsoever they had done and whatsoever they
had taught. And he saith unto them, Come ye your-
5 selves apart into a desert place, and rest awhile. For
there were many coming and going, and they had no Mk. 3. 20.
leisure so much as to eat. And he took them, and they Jn. 4. 32..
withdrew in the boat to a desert place apart; to a city
called Bethsaida, on the other side of the sea of Galilee,
10 which is the sea of Tiberias. And the people saw them
going, and many knew them and they ran there together
on foot from all the cities, and outwent them; because
they beheld the signs which he did on them that were
sick. And he came forth and saw a great multitude, and
15 he had compassion on them because they were as sheep Nu. 27. 17.
not having a shepherd; and he welcomed them, and Ezek. 34.5.
began to teach them many things, and spake to them of
the kingdom of God, and them that had need of healing Acts 10.38.
he healed. And Jesus went up into the mountain, and
20 there he sat with his disciples. Now the passover, the
feast of the Jews, was at hand.
And when the day was now far spent, his disciples

---

61. S. Mark vi. 30—37; S. Luke ix. 10—13; S. Matthew xiv. 13 --16;
S. John vi. 1—4.

came unto him, and said, The place is desert, and the
day is now far spent: send the multitudes away, that
they may go into the country and villages round about 25
and lodge and buy themselves somewhat to eat.   But
Jesus answered and said unto them, They have no need
to go away; give ye them to eat.

62.   *Five Thousand Men fed.*

68   JESUS therefore lifting up his eyes and seeing that a
great multitude cometh unto him, saith unto Philip,
Whence are we to buy bread that these may eat?   And
this he said to prove him; for he himself knew what he
would do.   Philip answered him, Two hundred penny- 5
Nu. 11. 22. worth of bread is not sufficient for them, that every one
may take a little.   One of his disciples, Andrew, Simon
Peter's brother, saith unto him; There is a lad here
which hath five barley loaves, and two fishes: but what
2 Ki. 4. 43. are they among so many?   And he said, Bring them 10
hither unto me.   Now there was much grass in the place.
And he said unto his disciples, Make them all sit down
by companies upon the green grass.   So the men sat
down in ranks, by hundreds and by fifties, in number
about five thousand.   Jesus therefore took the five 15
loaves and the two fishes; and looking up to heaven, he
1 Sa. 9. 13. blessed, and gave thanks, and brake the loaves, and gave
Lk. 24. 30.. to the disciples to distribute to them that were set down:
Rom.14.6. likewise also the two fishes divided he among them all,
as much as they would.   And they did all eat and were 20
filled.   And when they were filled, he saith unto his
disciples, Gather up the broken pieces which remain over,
that nothing be lost.   So they gathered them up, and
filled twelve baskets with broken pieces from the five
barley loaves, and also from the fishes, which remained 25
over unto them that had eaten.   And they that did eat
were about five thousand men, besides women and
children.   When therefore the people saw the sign which
De. 18.18.. he did, they said, This is of a truth the prophet that
cometh into the world.   30

62. S. John vi. 5—14; S. Mark vi. 37—44; S. Luke ix. 13—17;
S. Matthew xiv. 17—21.

63. *Jesus walketh on the Sea. Peter.*

JESUS therefore, perceiving that they were about to
come and take him by force, to make him king, straight- Jn. 18. 36.
way constrained his disciples to enter into the boat, and
to go before him unto the other side to Bethsaida, while
5 he himself sendeth the multitudes away.   And after he
had taken leave of them he went up into the mountain
apart to pray: and when even was come, he was there Lk. 6. 12.
alone.   But his disciples were going over the sea, unto — 9. 28.
Capernaum : and it was now dark, and Jesus had not
10 yet come unto them.   And the sea was rising, by reason
of a great wind that blew : and the boat was now in the
midst of the sea, distressed by the waves, for the wind
was contrary.   And in the fourth watch of the night,
when they had rowed about five and twenty or thirty
15 furlongs, seeing them distressed in rowing, he cometh
unto them, walking upon the sea, and he would have
passed by them.   But when they beheld Jesus walking Job 9. 8.
on the sea, and drawing nigh unto the boat, they were
afraid, and supposed that it was an apparition, and cried Lk. 24. 37.
20 out for fear, for they all saw him and were troubled.   **180**
But Jesus straightway spake unto them, and saith unto
them, Be of good cheer; it is I; be not afraid.   And
Peter answered him and said, Lord, if it be thou, bid me Jn. 21. 7.
come unto thee upon the waters.   And he said, Come.
25 And Peter went down from the boat, and walked upon
the waters, to come to Jesus.   But when he saw the
wind, he was afraid ; and beginning to sink, he cried out,
saying, Lord, save me.   And immediately Jesus stretched Mt. 8. 25.
forth his hand, and took hold of him, and saith unto
30 him, O thou of little faith, wherefore didst thou doubt?
They were willing therefore to receive him into the boat;
and when they were gone up into the boat, the wind   **55**
ceased.   And they that were in the boat worshipped Ps. 89. 9.
him, saying, Of a truth thou art the Son of God.   And Mt. 16. 16.
35 they were sore amazed in themselves, for they understood not concerning the loaves, but their heart was
hardened.   And straightway the boat was at the land
whither they were going.   Ps. 107. 30.

---

63. S. Matthew xiv. 22 — 36 ; S. Mark vi. 45 — 56 ; S. John vi.
15—21.

And when they had crossed over, they came to the land, unto Gennesaret, and moored to the shore. And 40 when they were come out of the boat, straightway the men of that place knew him, and ran and sent into all that region round about, and began to carry about on their beds and to bring unto him all those that were sick, where they heard he was. And wheresoever he entered, into villages, 45 Acts 5. 15... or into cities, or into the country, they laid the sick in the market places, and besought him that they might Acts 19. 12. touch if it were but the border of his garment: and as — 10. 3ʰ· many as touched him were made whole.

64. *The Bread of Life.*

ON the morrow the multitude which stood on the other side of the sea saw that there was none other boat there, save one, and that Jesus entered not with his disciples into the boat, but that his disciples went away alone (howbeit there came boats from Tiberias nigh unto 5 the place where they ate the bread after the Lord had given thanks): when the multitude therefore saw that Jesus was not there, neither his disciples, they themselves got into the boats, and came to Capernaum, seeking Jesus. And when they found him on the other side of 10 the sea, they said unto him, Rabbi, when camest thou hither? Jesus answered them and said, Verily, verily, I say unto you, Ye seek me, not because ye saw signs, but Is. 55. 1... because ye ate of the loaves, and were filled. Work not for the meat which perisheth, but for the meat which 15 Mt. 5. 6. abideth unto eternal life, which the Son of man shall give unto you: for him the Father, even God, hath Jn. 3. 33. sealed. They said therefore unto him, What must we do, that we may work the works of God? Jesus answered and said unto them, This is the work of God, 20 1 Jn. 3. 23. that ye believe on him whom he hath sent. They said therefore unto him, What then doest thou for a sign, that we may see, and believe thee? what workest thou? Our Ex. 16. 4... fathers ate the manna in the wilderness; as it is written, Ps. 78. 24. He gave them bread out of heaven to eat. Jesus there- 25 fore said unto them, Verily, verily, I say unto you, It was not Moses that gave you the bread out of heaven; but Deu. 8. 3. my Father giveth you the true bread out of heaven. For

64. S. John vi. 22—71.

the bread of God is that which cometh down out of
30 heaven, and giveth life unto the world. They said therefore unto him, Lord, evermore give us this bread. Jesus
said unto them, I am the bread of life : he that cometh
to me shall not hunger, and he that believeth on me Jn. 4. 14.
shall never thirst. But I said unto you, that ye have
35 seen me, and yet believe not. All that which the Father
giveth me shall come unto me ; and him that cometh to Ro. 10. 11..
me I will in no wise cast out. For I am come down 1 Jn. 2. 19.
from heaven, not to do mine own will, but the will of
him that sent me. And this is the will of him that sent
40 me, that of all that which he hath given me I should lose Jn. 17. 12.
nothing, but should raise it up at the last day. For this
is the will of my Father, that every one that beholdeth
the Son, and believeth on him, should have eternal life ; Jn. 5. 24.
and I will raise him up at the last day.
45 The Jews therefore murmured concerning him,
because he said, I am the bread which came down out
of heaven. And they said, Is not this Jesus, the son Lk. 4. 22.
of Joseph, whose father and mother we know? how Mt. 13. 55.
doth he now say, I am come down out of heaven? **27. 54**
50 Jesus answered and said unto them, Murmur not among
yourselves. No man can come to me, except the Father
which sent me draw him : and I will raise him up in the
last day. It is written in the prophets, And they shall Is. 54. 13.
all be taught of God. Every one that hath heard from Jer.31.33...
55 the Father, and hath learned, cometh unto me. Not Heb.8.10..
that any man hath seen the Father, save he which is Jn. 1. 18.
from God, he hath seen the Father. Verily, verily, I say
unto you, He that believeth hath eternal life. I am the Jn. 3. 16.
bread of life. Your fathers did eat the manna in the
60 wilderness, and they died. This is the bread which
cometh down out of heaven, that a man may eat thereof, Rev. 2. 17.
and not die. I am the living bread which came down out Jn. 3. 13.
of heaven : if any man eat of this bread, he shall live for Jn. 8. 51...
ever : yea and the bread which I will give is my flesh, for
65 the life of the world.
The Jews therefore strove one with another, saying,
How can this man give us his flesh to eat? Jesus there- 1Co.11.24.
fore said unto them, Verily, verily, I say unto you, Mt.26.26..
Except ye eat the flesh of the Son of man and drink his **148**
70 blood, ye have not life in yourselves. He that eateth my
flesh and drinketh my blood hath eternal life ; and I will

1Co.10.16. raise him up at the last day. For my flesh is meat
indeed, and my blood is drink indeed. He that eateth
1Jn. 3. 24. my flesh and drinketh my blood abideth in me, and I in
him. As the living Father sent me, and I live because 75
of the Father; so he that eateth me, he also shall live
because of me. This is the bread which came down out
of heaven: not as the fathers did eat, and died: he that
Rev. 2. 17. eateth this bread shall live for ever. These things said
he in the synagogue, as he taught in Capernaum.   80
     Many therefore of his disciples, when they heard this,
said, This is a hard saying; who can hear it? But Jesus
knowing in himself that his disciples murmured at this,
Mt. 11. 6. said unto them, Doth this cause you to stumble? What
then if ye should behold the Son of man ascending where 85
2 Cor. 3. 6. he was before? It is the spirit that quickeneth; the
flesh profiteth nothing: the words that I have spoken
unto you are spirit, and are life. But there are some of
Jn. 2. 24... you that believe not. For Jesus knew from the beginning
who they were that believed not, and who it was that 90
Jn. 13. 11. should betray him. And he said, For this cause have I
said unto you, that no man can come unto me, except it
be given unto him of the Father.
     Upon this many of his disciples went back, and
walked no more with him. Jesus said therefore unto the 95
twelve, Would ye also go away? Simon Peter answered
him, Lord, to whom shall we go? thou hast the words of
Mt. 16. 16. eternal life. And we have believed and know that thou
   71   art the Holy One of God. Jesus answered them, Did
not I choose you the twelve, and one of you is a devil? 100
Jn. 13. 27. Now he spake of Judas the son of Simon Iscariot, for he
it was that should betray him, being one of the twelve.

65.   *The Unwashen Hands.*

     AND there are gathered together unto him the Phari-
sees, and certain of the scribes, which had come from
Jerusalem, and had seen that some of his disciples ate
their bread with defiled, that is, unwashen, hands. For
the Pharisees, and all the Jews, except they wash their 5
Col. 2. 8. hands diligently, eat not, holding the tradition of the
elders; and when they come from the marketplace,
except they wash themselves, they eat not: and many

---

65. S. Mark vii. 1—23 ; S. Matthew xv. 1—20.

other things there be, which they have received to hold,
10 washings of cups, and pots, and brasen vessels. And the Jn. 2. 6.
Pharisees and the scribes ask him, saying, Why walk not
tny disciples according to the tradition of the elders, but
transgress it, *and* eat their bread with defiled hands?
And he answered and said unto them, Why do ye also
15 transgress the commandment of God, because of your
tradition? Ye leave the commandment of God, and hold Ex. 20. 12.
fast the tradition of men. For God said, Honour thy Deu. 5. 16.
father and thy mother; and, He that speaketh evil of Ex. 21. 17.
father or mother, let him die the death. But ye say, If Lev. 20. 9.
20 a man shall say to his father or his mother, that where- Pro. 20. 20.
with thou mightest have been profited by me is Corban,
that is to say, given to God; he shall not honour his
father; *and* ye no longer suffer him to do aught for his
father or his mother; making void the word of God by
25 your tradition which ye have delivered: and many other
such like things ye do. Ye hypocrites, well did Isaiah
prophesy of you, as it is written,

This people honoureth me with their lips,   Is. 29. 13.
But their heart is far from me.   Gr.
30 But in vain do they worship me,   Eze. 33. 31.
Teaching as their doctrines the precepts of men.   Tit. 1. 14.

Full well do ye reject the commandment of God, that 2 Cor. 11. 4.
ye may keep your tradition. And he called unto (ironice.)
him the multitude again, and said unto them, Hear me
35 all of you and understand: There is nothing from with- Acts 10. 15.
out the man that going into him can defile him: but Ro. 14. 14..
the things that proceed out of the man are those that 1 Tim. 4. 4.
defile the man. And when he was entered into the
house from the multitude, his disciples came and said
40 unto him, Knowest thou that the Pharisees were offended, when they heard this saying? But he answered
and said, Every plant which my heavenly Father planted Jn. 15. 2.
not, shall be rooted up. Let them alone: they are
blind guides. And if the blind guide the blind, both Is. 9. 16.
45 shall fall into a pit! And Peter answered and said unto
him, Declare unto us the parable. And he said, Are ye
also even yet without understanding? Perceive ye not,
that whatsoever from without goeth into the man, it
cannot defile him; because it goeth not into his heart, 1 Cor. 6. 13.
50 but into his belly, and is cast out into the draught?
This he said, making all meats clean. But the things Acts 10. 15.

Jas. 3. 6. which proceed out of the mouth, come forth out of the
Gen. 6. 5; heart; and they defile the man.   For from within, out
— 8. 21. of the heart of men, come forth evil thoughts, murders,
Gal.5.19... adulteries, fornications, thefts, false witness, covetings, 55
wickednesses, deceit, lasciviousness, an evil eye, railing,
pride, foolishness: all these evil things proceed from
within, and these are the things which defile the man:
but to eat with unwashen hands defileth not the man.

66. *The Syrophœnician Woman.*

AND Jesus arose from thence, and went away into
the borders of Tyre and Sidon.   And he entered into a
house, and would have no man know it: and he could
not be hid.   But behold, a Canaanitish woman from
those borders, whose little daughter had an unclean 5
Ro. 10. 12. spirit, heard of him.   Now the woman was a Greek, a
Syrophœnician by race.   And she besought him, and
cried, saying, Have mercy on me, O Lord, thou Son of
David; my daughter is grievously vexed with a devil.
But he answered her not a word.   And his disciples 10
came and besought him, saying, Send her away, for she
Mt. 10. 6. crieth after us.   But he answered and said, I was not
Acts 3. 26. sent but unto the lost sheep of the house of Israel.
But she came and worshipped him, and fell down at his
feet, saying, Lord, help me !   And he answered and said 15
unto her, Let the children first be filled: for it is not
meet to take the children's bread and cast it unto the
Mt. 7. 6. dogs.   But she answered and said unto him, Yea, Lord:
for even the dogs under the table eat of the children's
crumbs.   Then Jesus answered and said unto her, O 20
Lk. 7. 9. woman, great is thy faith: for this saying go thy way ; be
44 it done unto thee even as thou wilt: the devil is gone
out of thy daughter.   And she went away unto her house,
and found the child laid upon the bed, and the devil
gone out.   25

67. *Deaf and Dumb Man, and many others, healed.*

AND again he went out from the borders of Tyre,
and came through Sidon unto the sea of Galilee, through

66. S. Mark vii. 24—30 ; S. Matthew xv. 21—28.
67. S. Mark vii. 31—37 ; S. Matthew xv. 29—31.

the midst of the borders of Decapolis. And they bring
unto him one that was deaf, and had an impediment in
5 his speech ; and they beseech him to lay his hand upon
him.   And he took him aside from the multitude Mk. 8. 23.
privately, and put his fingers into his ears, and he spat, Jn. 9. 6.
and touched his tongue ; and looking up to heaven, he   **70. 80**
sighed, and saith unto him, Ephphatha, that is, Be Jn. 11. 33..
10 opened.   And his ears were opened, and the bond of
his tongue was loosed, and he spake plain.   And he
charged them that they should tell no man : but the Mk. 5. 43.
more he charged them, so much the more a great deal
they published it.   And they were beyond measure
15 astonished, saying, He hath done all things well : he
maketh even the deaf to hear, and the dumb to speak.   Is. 35. 5...

And he went up into the mountain and sat there.
And there came unto him great multitudes, having with
them the lame, blind, dumb, maimed, and many others,   **31. 41**
20 and they cast them down at his feet; and he healed   **46**
them : insomuch that the multitude wondered, when they
saw the dumb speaking, the maimed whole, and the
lame walking, and the blind seeing : and they glorified
the God of Israel.

68.   *Four Thousand Men fed.*

IN those days, when there was again a great multitude,   **62**
and they had nothing to eat, he called unto him his
disciples, and saith unto them, I have compassion on
the multitude, because they continue with me now three
5 days, and have nothing to eat, and I would not send
them away fasting to their home, lest haply they faint in
the way ; and some of them are come from far.   And
his disciples answered him, Whence shall one be able to 2 Ki. 4. 43.
fill so great a multitude with bread here in a desert
10 place?   And Jesus said unto them, How many loaves Mt. 14. 17..
have ye?   And they said, Seven.   And he commandeth
the multitude to sit down on the ground : and he took
the seven loaves, and having given thanks, he brake, and 1 Sa. 9. 13.
gave to his disciples to set before them; and they set Lk. 22. 19.
15 them before the multitude.   And they had a few small
fishes : and having blessed them, he commanded to set
these also before them.   And they did all eat and were

68. S. Mark viii. 1—10 ; S. Matthew xv. 32—39.

filled : and they took up of the broken pieces that
Acts 9. 25. remained over, seven baskets full.　And they that did
eat were about four thousand men, besides women and 20
children.　And he sent them away.　And straightway he
entered into the boat with his disciples, and came into
the parts of Dalmanutha.

69. *Sign from Heaven.　Leaven of Pharisees.*

Jn. 6. 30.　　　AND the Pharisees and Sadducees came forth, and
1 Cor.1.22. began to question with him, and asked him to shew them
Mt. 12. 38. a sign from heaven, tempting him.　But he answered
95　and said unto them, When it is evening, ye say it will
be fair weather : for the heaven is red.　And in the 5
morning, It will be foul weather to day : for the heaven
Lk. 12. 56. is red and lowring.　Ye know how to discern the face of
100　the heaven ; but ye cannot discern the signs of the times.
And he sighed deeply in his spirit, and saith, Why doth this
generation seek a sign ?　An evil and adulterous genera- 10
tion seeketh after a sign : verily I say unto you, there
shall no sign be given unto this generation, but the sign
of Jonah.　And he left them, and again entering into
the boat, departed to the other side.

And they forgot to take bread; and they had not in 15
the boat with them more than one loaf.　And he charged
Lk. 12. 1. them, saying, Take heed and beware of the leaven of the
Pharisees and the leaven of Herod.　And they reasoned
one with another, saying, We have no bread.　And
Jesus perceiving it saith unto them, O ye of little faith, 20
why reason ye among yourselves, because ye have no
bread ?　Do ye not yet perceive, neither understand?
Jer. 5. 21. Having eyes, see ye not, and having ears, hear ye not ?
Ezek.12.2. and do ye not remember ?　When I brake the five loaves
62　among the five thousand, how many baskets full of 25
broken pieces took ye up ?　They say unto him, Twelve.
68　And when the seven among the four thousand, how many
baskets full of broken pieces took ye up ?　And they say
unto him, Seven.　And he said unto them, Do ye not
yet understand ?　How is it that ye do not perceive that 30
I spake not to you concerning bread ?　But beware of
the leaven of the Pharisees and Sadducees.　Then understood they how that he bade them not beware of the

---

69. S. Mark viii. 11—21 ; S. Matthew xvi. 1—12.

leaven of bread, but of the teaching of the Pharisees and 1Cor.5.6...
35 Sadducees.

70. *Blind Man healed gradually.*

AND they come unto Bethsaida. And they bring to
him a blind man, and beseech him to touch him. And
he took hold of the blind man by the hand, and brought
him out of the village ; and when he had spit on his eyes, Mk. 7. 33.
5 and laid his hands upon him, he asked him, Seest thou Jn. 9. 6.
aught? And he looked up, and said, I see men ; for I 67. 80
behold them as trees, walking. Then again he laid his
hands upon his eyes ; and he looked stedfastly, and was
restored, and saw all things clearly. And he sent him
10 away to his home, saying, Do not even enter into the
village.

71. *The great Confession. Passion foretold.*

AND Jesus went forth and his disciples, into the
villages of Cæsarea Philippi ; and in the way, as he was
praying alone, he asked them, saying, Who do men say
that I, the Son of man, am? And they answering, told
5 him, saying, Some say John the Baptist ; but others say 60
Elijah ; and others Jeremiah, or that one of the old
prophets is risen again. And he asked them, But who
say ye that I am? Simon Peter answereth and saith
unto him, Thou art the Christ, the Son of the living God. Jn. 6. 69.
10 And Jesus answered and said unto him, Blessed art thou, — 11. 27.
Simon Bar-Jonah : for flesh and blood hath not revealed 1Cor.2.10.
it unto thee, but my Father which is in heaven. And I
also say unto thee, that thou art Peter, and upon this Jn. 1. 42.
rock I will build my church ; and the gates of Hades Eph. 2. 20.
15 shall not prevail against it. I will give unto thee the Rev.21.14.
keys of the kingdom of heaven : and whatsoever thou Is. 22. 22.
shalt bind on earth shall be bound in heaven : and Mt. 18. 18.
whatsoever thou shalt loose on earth shall be loosed in 76
heaven. Then charged he the disciples, and commanded
20 them to tell no man that he was the Christ.
From that time began Jesus to shew unto his dis- Mt. 20. 17.
ciples how that he must go unto Jerusalem and suffer 121

---

70. S. Mark viii. 22—26.
71. S. Matthew xvi. 13—28; S. Mark viii. 27—ix. 1;
S. Luke ix. 18—27.

many things, and be rejected of the elders and the chief
priests and the scribes, and be killed, and the third day
be raised up.   And he spake the saying openly.   But 25
Peter took him and began to rebuke him, saying, Be it
Gen.43.22. far from thee, Lord : this shall never be unto thee.   But
Gr.   he turning about and seeing his disciples, rebuked Peter
Mt. 4. 10. and said unto him, Get thee behind me, Satan : thou art
a stumblingblock unto me : for thou mindest not the 30
things of God, but the things of men.   And he called
unto him the multitude with his disciples, and said unto
them all, If any man would come after me, let him deny
Mt. 10. 38. himself, and take up his cross daily and follow me.   For
59. 71 whosoever would save his life shall lose it ; and whoso- 35
Jn. 12. 25. ever shall lose his life for my sake and the gospel's, the
same shall find it.   For what shall a man be profited, if
Ps. 49. 7.. he shall gain the whole world, and lose or forfeit his own
self? or what shall a man give in exchange for his life?
Ro. 1. 16. For whosoever shall be ashamed of me and of my words 40
2 Tim. 1.8. in this adulterous and sinful generation, of him shall the
— 2. 12. Son of man also be ashamed when he cometh in his own
glory, and in the glory of his Father, and of the holy
Ps. 62. 12. angels ; and then shall he render unto every man
Rom. 2. 6. according to his deeds.   And he said unto them, Verily 45
Pro. 24. 12. I say unto you, there be some here of them that stand
Jn. 21. 22. by, which shall in no wise taste of death till they see the
Mt. 24. 30. Son of man coming in his kingdom.
137

72. *The Transfiguration.   Elijah.*

Mk. 5. 37.   AND it came to pass about eight days after these
Mt. 26.37. sayings, he took with him Peter and James and John
57. 156 his brother, and bringeth them up into a high mountain
apart by themselves, to pray.   And as he was praying,
he was transfigured before them, and the fashion of his 5
Rev. 1.13... countenance was altered, and his face did shine as the

72. S. Mark ix. 2—13; S. Matthew xvii. 1—13;
S. Luke ix. 28—36.

sun, and his raiment became dazzling, exceeding white, Dan. 7. 9.
so as no fuller on earth can whiten them.   And behold,
there talked with him two men, which were Moses and
10 Elijah ; who appeared in glory, and spake of his decease
which he was about to accomplish at Jerusalem.   Now
Peter and they that were with him were heavy with sleep: Mt. 26. 43.
but when they were fully awake, they saw his glory, and Jn. 1. 14.
the two men that stood with him.   And it came to pass, 1 Jn. 1. 1...
15 as they were parting from him, Peter answered and said
unto Jesus, Rabbi, it is good for us to be here : if thou
wilt, I will make here three tabernacles ; one for thee,
and one for Moses, and one for Elijah.   For he wist not
what to answer, for they became sore afraid.   While he
20 was yet speaking, there came a cloud and overshadowed
them : and they feared as they entered into the cloud.
And behold, a voice came out of the cloud, saying, This 2 Pet. 1. 17.
is my beloved Son, my chosen, in whom I am well Mt. 3. 17.
pleased ; hear ye him.   And when the voice came, Jesus   **16**
25 was found alone.   And when the disciples heard it, they
fell on their face and were sore afraid.   And Jesus came Dan. 10. 18.
and touched them and said, Arise, be not afraid.   And
suddenly looking round about, they saw no one any
more, save Jesus only with themselves.
30   And as they were coming down from the mountain,
he charged them that they should tell no man what
things they had seen, save when the Son of man should
have risen again from the dead.   And they held their
peace, and told no man in those days any of the things
35 which they had seen.   And they kept the saying, questioning among themselves what the rising again from the
dead should mean.   And his disciples asked him, saying,
Why then say the scribes that Elijah must first come? Mal. 4. 5.
And he answered and said unto them, Elijah indeed
40 cometh first, and restoreth all things : and how is it Acts 3. 21.
written of the Son of man, that he should suffer many Is. 53. 2...
things and be set at nought?   But I say unto you that Ps. 22. 6..
Elijah is come already, and they knew him not, but have
done to him whatsoever they listed, even as it is written Mt. 14. 3...
45 of him.   Even so shall the Son of man also suffer of   **60**
them.   Then understood the disciples that he spake unto
them of John the Baptist.

73. *The Boy with a Deaf and Dumb Spirit.*
Passion foretold.

AND it came to pass, on the next day, when they were come down from the mountain, they came to the disciples and saw a great multitude about them, and scribes questioning with them. And straightway all the multitude when they saw him were greatly amazed, and 5 running to him saluted him. And behold, there came to him a man from the multitude, kneeling unto him; and he cried, saying, Lord, I beseech thee to look upon my son, *and* have mercy on. him; for he is my only child. I have brought him unto thee, for he hath 10 a dumb spirit, and suffereth grievously. And wheresoever it taketh him, he suddenly crieth out, and it dasheth him down, and teareth him, that he foameth and grindeth his teeth and pineth away, and it hardly departeth from him, bruising him sorely. And I brought 15 him to thy disciples, and spake to them, and besought them to cast it out, and they were not able to cure him. And Jesus answereth them and saith, O faithless and perverse generation, how long shall I be with you? how long shall I bear with you? bring thy son hither to me. 20 And they brought him unto him. And as he was yet a coming, when he saw him, straightway the spirit dashed Mk. 1. 26. him down, and tare him grievously, and he fell on the ground, and wallowed foaming. And he asked his father, How long time is it since this hath come unto 25 him? And he said, From a child. And oft-times it hath cast him both into the fire and into the waters, to destroy him : but if thou canst do anything, have compassion on us, and help us. And Jesus said unto him, Mk.11.23. If thou canst! All things are possible to him that be- 30 Jn. 11. 40. lieveth. Straightway the father of the child cried out, and said, I believe; help thou mine unbelief. And when Jesus saw that a multitude came running together, **58. 92** he rebuked the unclean spirit, saying unto him, Thou dumb and deaf spirit, I command thee, come out of him, 35 and enter no more into him. And having cried out, and torn him much, the devil came out from him : and the child became as one dead; insomuch that the more

---

73. S. Mark ix. 14—32; S. Luke ix. 37—45;
S. Matthew xvii. 14—23.

part said, He is dead. But Jesus took him by the hand,
40 and raised him up, and he arose; and he gave him back Lk. 7. 15.
to his father. And the boy was cured from that hour.
And they were all astonished at the majesty of God.
And when he was come into the house, his disciples
came unto him apart, and asked him privately, saying,
45 Why could not we cast it out? And he said unto them,
Because of your little faith: for verily I say unto you, if Mt. 21. 21.
ye have faith as a grain of mustard seed, ye shall say **127**
unto this mountain, Remove hence to yonder place; and 1 Cor.13.2.
it shall remove; and nothing shall be impossible unto you.
50 But this kind can come out by nothing save by prayer.

And they went forth from thence, and passed through
Galilee, and he would not that any man should know it.
For while they abode in Galilee, while all were marvelling at all the things which he did, he taught his dis-
55 ciples and said unto them, Let these words sink into your
ears: for the Son of man shall be delivered up into the Lk. 24. 6.
hands of men, and they shall kill him: and when he is **175**
killed, after three days he shall rise again. But they
understood not this saying, and it was concealed from Lk. 18. 34.
60 them, that they should not perceive it: and they were **121**
afraid to ask him about this saying. And they were exceeding sorry.

74. *The Temple Tax supplied.*

AND when they were come to Capernaum, they that Ex. 30. 13;
received the half-shekel came to Peter, and said, Doth — 38. 26.
not your master pay the half-shekel? He saith, Yea.
And when he came into the house, Jesus spake first to
5 him, saying, What thinkest thou, Simon? the kings of
the earth, from whom do they receive toll or tribute? Rom.13.6.
from their sons, or from strangers? And when he said,
From strangers, Jesus said unto him, Therefore the sons
are free. But, lest we cause them to stumble, go thou
10 to the sea, and cast a hook, and take up the fish that Hab. 1. 15.
first cometh up; and when thou hast opened his mouth,
thou shalt find a shekel: that take, and give unto them
for me and thee.

---

74. S. Matthew xvii. 24—27.

75. *Of little Children.   Our duties towards them.*

AND they came to Capernaum, and when he was in
the house, he asked them, What were ye reasoning in
the way? But they held their peace: for they had dis-
Lk. 22. 24. puted one with another in the way, who was the greatest.
145 But when Jesus saw the reasoning of their heart he sat 5
down and called the twelve, and he saith unto them,
Mt. 20. 21. If any man would be first he shall be last of all, and
121 minister of all. And they say unto him, Who then is
greatest in the kingdom of heaven? And he called unto
Mk. 10.15. him a little child, and took him and set him by his side 10
Mt. 19. 14. in the midst of them, and said, Verily I say unto you,
118 Except ye turn and become as little children, ye shall in
Ps. 131. 2. no wise enter into the kingdom of heaven. Whosoever
1Co.14.20. therefore shall humble himself as this little child, the
same is the greatest in the kingdom of heaven. And 15
taking him in his arms, he said unto them, Whosoever
Mt. 10.40.. shall receive one of such little children in my name, re-
59 ceiveth me: and whosoever receiveth me, receiveth not
Jn. 13. 20. me, but him that sent me: for he that is least among you
all, the same is great. And John answered and said, 20
Nu. 11. 28. Master, we saw one casting out devils in thy name, and
Mt. 12. 27. we forbade him, because he followeth not with us. But
Acts 19.13. Jesus said unto him, Forbid him not: for there is no
Phil. i. 18. man which shall do a mighty work in my name, and
Cp. be able quickly to speak evil of me. For he that is 25
Mt. 12. 30. not against us is for us. For whosoever shall give
Mt. 10. 42. you a cup of water to drink because ye are Christ's,
59 verily I say unto you, he shall in no wise lose his reward.
Lk. 17. 1... But whosoever shall cause one of these little ones
113 which believe on me to stumble, it were better for him 30
if a great millstone were hanged about his neck, and
he were sunk in the depth of the sea. Woe unto the
world because of occasions of stumbling! for it must
1Co.11.19. needs be that the occasions come; but woe to that man
through whom the occasion cometh! And if thy hand 35
Mt.5. 29... cause thee to stumble, cut it off and cast it from thee:
43* it is good for thee to enter into life maimed, rather than
Deu. 13. 6. having thy two hands to go into hell, into the unquench-

able fire.   And if thy foot cause thee to stumble, cut it
40 off: it is good for thee to enter into life halt, rather than
having thy two feet to be cast into hell.   And if thine
eye cause thee to stumble, pluck it out, and cast it from
thee: it is good for thee to enter into the kingdom of
God with one eye, rather than having two eyes to be cast
45 into hell; where their worm dieth not, and the fire is not Is. 66. 24.
quenched.   For every one shall be salted with fire. Salt Lev. 2. 13.
is good: but if the salt have lost its saltness, wherewith Mt. 5. 13.
will ye season it?   Have salt in yourselves, and be at Lk. 14. 34.
peace one with another.   See that ye despise not one of **43*. 109**
50 these little ones; for I say unto you, that in heaven their Col. 4. 6.
angels do always behold the face of my Father which is Ps. 91. 11.
in heaven.   How think ye? if any man have a hundred Heb. 1. 13.
sheep, and one of them be gone astray, doth he not Lk. 15. 3...
leave the ninety and nine, and go unto the mountains, **110**
55 and seek that which goeth astray?   And if so be that he Ezek. 34. 6.
find it, verily I say unto you, he rejoiceth over it more Ps. 119.
than over the ninety and nine which have not gone   176.
astray.   Even so it is not the will of your Father which 2 Pet. 3. 9.
is in heaven, that one of these little ones should perish. 1 Tim. 2. 4.

76. *Of offences against ourselves.   The Unmerciful*
Servant.

AND if thy brother sin against thee, go, shew him his Lev. 19. 17.
fault between thee and him alone: if he hear thee, thou Lk. 17. 3..
hast gained thy brother.   But if he hear *thee* not, take **113**
with thee one or two more, that at the mouth of two Deu. 19. 15.
5 witnesses or three every word may be established.   And
if he refuse to hear them, tell it unto the church: and if 2 Cor. 13. 1.
he refuse to hear the church also, let him be unto thee 1 Cor. 5. 11.
as the Gentile and the publican.   Verily I say unto you, 2 Th. 3. 14.
What things soever ye shall bind on earth shall be bound
10 in heaven: and what things soever ye shall loose on earth Mt. 16. 19.
shall be loosed in heaven.   Again I say unto you, that if **71**
two of you shall agree on earth as touching anything that
they shall ask, it shall be done for them of my Father 1 Jn. 3. 22;
which is in heaven.   For where two or three are gathered — 5. 14.
15 together in my name, there am I in the midst of them. 1 Cor. 5. 4.
Then came Peter, and said to him, Lord, how oft
shall my brother sin against me, and I forgive him?

76. S. Matthew xviii. 15—35.

Amo.1.3... until seven times? Jesus saith unto him, I say not unto
Gen.4. 24. thee, Until seven times; but, Until seventy times seven.
Gr.   Therefore is the kingdom of heaven likened unto a 20
certain king, which would make a reckoning with his
servants. And when he had begun to reckon, one was
brought unto him, which owed him ten thousand talents.
But forasmuch as he had not *wherewith* to pay, his lord
Le.25.39... commanded him to be sold, and his wife, and children, 25
Deu.15.12. and all that he had, and payment to be made. The
2 Ki. 4. 1. servant therefore fell down and worshipped him, saying,
Lord, have patience with me, and I will pay thee all.
Lk. 7. 42. And the lord of that servant, being moved with com-
47   passion, released him, and forgave him the debt. But 30
that servant went out, and found one of his fellow-
servants, which owed him a hundred pence: and he
laid hold on him, and took *him* by the throat, saying,
Pay what thou owest. So his fellow-servant fell down
and besought him, saying, Have patience with me, and 35
I will pay thee. And he would not: but went and cast
him into prison, till he should pay that which was due.
So when his fellow-servants saw what was done, they
were exceeding sorry, and came and told unto their lord
all that was done. Then his lord called him unto him, 40
and saith to him, Thou wicked servant, I forgave thee
Mt.6.12... all that debt, because thou besoughtest me: shouldest
Eph.4.32. not thou also have had mercy on thy fellow-servant, even
Col. 3. 13. as I had mercy on thee? And his lord was wroth, and
delivered him to the tormentors, till he should pay all 45
Jas. 2. 13. that was due. So shall also my heavenly Father do unto
Mk.11.25. you, if ye forgive not every one his brother from your
hearts.

77. *The Feast of Tabernacles.*

AND after these things Jesus walked in Galilee: for
Jn. 5. 16. he would not walk in Judæa, because the Jews sought
to kill him. Now the feast of the Jews, the feast of
Le. 23. 34... tabernacles, was at hand. His brethren therefore said
unto him, Depart hence, and go into Judæa, that thy 5
disciples also may behold thy works which thou doest.
For no man doeth anything in secret, and himself
seeketh to be known openly. If thou doest these things,

---

77. S. John vii. 1—52.

manifest thyself to the world. For even his brethren did
10 not believe on him. Jesus therefore saith unto them,
My time is not yet come; but your time is alway ready. Jn. 8. 20.
The world cannot hate you; but me it hateth, because I Jn. 15. 19.
testify of it, that its works are evil. Go ye up unto the
feast: I go not up yet unto this feast; because my time
15 is not yet fulfilled. And having said these things unto
them, he abode *still* in Galilee.

But when his brethren were gone up unto the feast,
then went he also up, not publicly, but as it were in
secret. The Jews therefore sought him at the feast, and Jn. 11. 56.
20 said, Where is he? And there was much murmuring **124**
among the multitudes concerning him: some said, He
is a good man: others said, Not so, but he leadeth the
multitude astray. Howbeit no man spake openly of him
for fear of the Jews. Jn. 9. 22.

25 But when it was now the midst of the feast Jesus
went up into the temple, and taught. The Jews therefore marvelled, saying, How knoweth this man letters,
having never learned? Jesus therefore answered them, Acts 4. 13.
and said, My teaching is not mine, but his that sent me. Jn. 8. 28.
30 If any man willeth to do his will, he shall know of the
teaching, whether it be of God, or *whether* I speak from
myself. He that speaketh from himself seeketh his own Jn. 5. 41;
glory: but he that seeketh the glory of him that sent — 8. 50.
him, the same is true, and no unrighteousness is in him.
35 Did not Moses give you the law, and *yet* none of you Acts 7. 38.
doeth the law? Why seek ye to kill me? The multi- Jn. 5. 8...
tude answered, Thou hast a devil: who seeketh to kill **39**
thee? Jesus answered and said unto them, I did one
work, and ye all marvel. For this cause hath Moses Lev. 12. 3.
40 given you circumcision (not that it is of Moses, but of Gen.17.10.
the fathers); and on the sabbath ye circumcise a man.
If a man receiveth circumcision on the sabbath, that the
law of Moses may not be broken; are ye wroth with me,
because I made a man every whit whole on the sabbath?
45 Judge not according to appearance, but judge righteous Deu.1.16..
judgement. Is. 11. 3..

Some therefore of them of Jerusalem said, Is not
this he whom they seek to kill? And lo, he speaketh
openly, and they say nothing unto him. Can it be that
50 the rulers indeed know that this is the Christ? Howbeit we know this man whence he is: but when the Mt. 13. 55.

Christ cometh, no one knoweth whence he is. Jesus
therefore cried in the temple, teaching and saying, Ye
Jn. 8. 14.   both know me, and know whence I am; and I am not
come of myself, but he that sent me is true, whom ye 55
know not. I know him; because I am from him, and
Jn. 8. 42.   he sent me. They sought therefore to take him: and
Lk. 22. 53. no man laid his hand on him, because his hour was not
Jn. 8. 20.   yet come. But of the multitude many believed on him;
and they said, When the Christ shall come, will he do 60
more signs than those which this man hath done? The
Pharisees heard the multitude murmuring these things
concerning him; and the chief priests and the Pharisees
Jn. 13. 33. sent officers to take him. Jesus therefore said, Yet a
Jn. 16. 16. little while am I with you, and I go unto him that sent 65
Lk. 17. 22. me. Ye shall seek me, and shall not find me: and
Jn. 8. 21.   where I am, ye cannot come. The Jews therefore said
79   among themselves, Whither will this man go that we
Jas. 1. 1.   shall not find him? will he go unto the Dispersion
among the Greeks, and teach the Greeks? What is this 70
word that he said, Ye shall seek me, and shall not find
me: and where I am, ye cannot come?
Lev. 23. 36.   Now on the last day, the great day of the feast, Jesus
stood and cried, saying, If any man thirst, let him come
Is. 12. 3;   unto me, and drink. He that believeth on me, as the 75
— 58. 11.   scripture hath said, out of his belly shall flow rivers of
Zech. 14. 8. living water. But this spake he of the Spirit, which they
Is. 44. 3.   that believed on him were to receive: for the Spirit was
Joel 2. 28. not yet given; because Jesus was not yet glorified. Some
of the multitude therefore, when they heard these words, 80
said, This is of a truth the prophet. Others said, This is
the Christ. But some said, What, doth the Christ come
Ps. 89. 3.   out of Galilee? Hath not the scripture said that the
Is. 11. 1.   Christ cometh of the seed of David, and from Bethlehem,
Mic. 5. 2.   the village where David was? So there arose a division 85
in the multitude because of him. And some of them
would have taken him; but no man laid hands on him.
        The officers therefore came to the chief priests and
Pharisees; and they said unto them, Why did ye not
bring him? The officers answered, Never man so spake. 90
The Pharisees therefore answered them, Are ye also led
astray? Hath any of the rulers believed on him, or of
the Pharisees? But this multitude which knoweth not
Jn. 3. 1.   the law are accursed. Nicodemus saith unto them (he

95 that came to him before, being one of them), Doth our
law judge a man, except it first hear from himself and Deu. 1. 17.
know what he doeth? They answered and said unto — 19.15.
him, Art thou also of Galilee? Search, and see that out
of Galilee ariseth no prophet. Jn. 1. 45.

78. *The Adulteress.*

[AND they went every man unto his own house: but
Jesus went unto the mount of Olives. And early in the Lk. 21. 37.
morning he came again into the temple, and all the
people came unto him; and he sat down, and taught
5 them. And the scribes and the Pharisees bring a woman
taken in adultery; and having set her in the midst, they
say unto him, Master, this woman hath been taken in
adultery, in the very act. Now in the law Moses com- Lev. 20. 10.
manded us to stone such: what then sayest thou of her? De. 22. 22;
10 And this they said, tempting him, that they might have 24.
whereof to accuse him. But Jesus stooped down, and Mt. 22. 18.
with his finger wrote on the ground. But when they
continued asking him, he lifted up himself, and said unto
them, He that is without sin among you, let him first Deu. 17. 7.
15 cast a stone at her. And again he stooped down, and Ro. 2. 22.
with his finger wrote on the ground. And they, when
they heard it, went out one by one, beginning from the
eldest, even unto the last: and Jesus was left alone, and
the woman, where she was, in the midst. And Jesus
20 lifted up himself, and said unto her, Woman, where are
they? did no man condemn thee? And she said, No
man, Lord. And Jesus said, Neither do I condemn Jn. 3. 17.
thee: go thy way; from henceforth sin no more.] Lk. 12. 14.
Ro. 5. 20...
1 Tim. 1. 15...

79. *Jesus the Son of God, Himself God.*

AGAIN therefore Jesus spake unto them, saying, I am Jn. 1. 9;
the light of the world: he that followeth me shall not — 9. 5;
walk in the darkness, but shall have the light of life. —12. 35...
The Pharisees therefore said unto him, Thou bearest **141**
5 witness of thyself; thy witness is not true. Jesus an- Jn. 5. 31.
swered and said unto them, Even if I bear witness of **38**
myself, my witness is true; for I know whence I came,
and whither I go; but ye know not whence I come, or Jn. 9. 29...

---

78. S. John vii. 53—viii. 11.   79. S. John viii. 12—59.

Jn. 8. 11. whither I go. Ye judge after the flesh ; I judge no man.
— 12. 47. Yea and if I judge, my judgement is true ; for I am not 10
alone, but I and the Father that sent me. Yea and in
Deu. 17. 6. your law it is written, that the witness of two men is
true. I am he that beareth witness of myself, and the
Mt. 3. 17; Father that sent me beareth witness of me. They said
— 17. 5. therefore unto him, Where is thy Father ? Jesus an- 15
16. 72 swered, Ye know neither me, nor my Father : if ye knew
Jn. 14. 7 ... me, ye would know my Father also. These words spake
he in the treasury, as he taught in the temple : and no
Jn. 7. 30; man took him ; because his hour was not yet come.
44. He said therefore again unto them, I go away, and 20
Jn. 7. 34... ye shall seek me, and shall die in your sin : whither I go,
77 ye cannot come. The Jews therefore said, Will he kill
himself, that he saith, Whither I go, ye cannot come ?
And he said unto them, Ye are from beneath ; I am from
above : ye are of this world ; I am not of this world. 25
I said therefore unto you, that ye shall die in your sins :
Mk. 16. 16. for except ye believe that I am he, ye shall die in your
Heb. 2. 3. sins. They said therefore unto him, . Who art thou ?
Jesus said unto them, Even that which I have also spoken
unto you from the beginning. I have many things to 30
speak and to judge concerning you : howbeit he that
sent me is true ; and the things which I heard from him,
Jn. 1. 18. these speak I unto the world. They perceived not that
he spake to them of the Father. Jesus therefore said,
Jn. 3. 14. When ye have lifted up the Son of man, then shall ye 35
Jn. 5. 30. know that I am he, and that I do nothing of myself, but
as the Father taught me, I speak these things. And he
Jn. 14. 11. that sent me is with me ; he hath not left me alone ;
Jn. 4. 34; for I do always the things that are pleasing to him.
— 6. 38. As he spake these things, many believed on him.   40
Jesus therefore said to those Jews which had believed
Jn. 15. 10. him, If ye abide in my word, then are ye truly my
disciples ; and ye shall know the truth, and the truth
Jas. 1. 25. shall make you free. They answered unto him, We be
Abraham's seed, and have never yet been in bondage to 45
any man : how sayest thou, Ye shall be made free ?
Ro. 6. 16... Jesus answered them, Verily, verily, I say unto you,
Gal. 4. 3... Every one that committeth sin is the bondservant of sin.
2 Pet. 2. 19. And the bondservant abideth not in the house for ever :
Rom. 8. 2. the son abideth for ever. If therefore the Son shall make 50
Gal. 5. 1. you free, ye shall be free indeed. I know that ye are

Abraham's seed; yet ye seek to kill me, because my word Jn. 5. 18.
hath not free course in you.   I speak the things which I
have seen with my Father: and ye also do the things which Jn. 14. 10.
55 ye heard from your father.   They answered and said
unto him, Our father is Abraham.   Jesus saith unto Mt. 3. 9.
them, If ye were Abraham's children, ye would do the Gal. 3. 7;
works of Abraham.   But now ye seek to kill me, a man   29.
that hath told you the truth, which I heard from God:
60 this did not Abraham.   Ye do the works of your father.
They said unto him, We were not born of fornication;
we have one Father, even God.   Jesus said unto them,
If God were your Father, ye would love me: for I came 1 Jn. 5. 1.
forth and am come from God; for neither have I come
65 of myself, but he sent me.   Why do ye not understand
my speech?   Even because ye cannot hear my word. Jn. 7. 17.
Ye are of your father the devil, and the lusts of your 1 Jn. 3. 8.
father it is your will to do.   He was a murderer from the
beginning, and stood not in the truth, because there is
70 no truth in him.   When he speaketh a lie, he speaketh
of his own: for he is a liar, and the father thereof.   But
because I say the truth, ye believe me not.   Which of
you convicteth me of sin?   If I say truth, why do ye
not believe me?   He that is of God heareth the words 1 Jn. 4. 6.
75 of God: for this cause ye hear them not, because ye are
not of God.   The Jews answered and said unto him,
Say we not well that thou art a Samaritan, and hast a Jn. 4. 9.
devil?   Jesus answered, I have not a devil; but I honour
my Father, and ye dishonour me.   But I seek not mine Jn. 5. 41;
80 own glory: there is one that seeketh and judgeth. — 7. 18.
Verily, verily, I say unto you, If a man keep my word, Jn. 5. 24;
he shall never see death.   The Jews said unto him, Now — 11. 26.
we know that thou hast a devil.   Abraham is dead, and Zech. 1. 5.
the prophets; and thou sayest, If a man keep my word,
85 he shall never taste of death.   Art thou greater than our
father Abraham, which is dead? and the prophets are
dead: whom makest thou thyself?   Jesus answered, If
I glorify myself, my glory is nothing: it is my Father Jn. 12. 28.
that glorifieth me; of whom ye say, that he is your God;
90 and ye have not known him: but I know him; and if I
should say, I know him not, I shall be like unto you, a
liar: but I know him, and keep his word.   Your father Lk. 10. 24.
Abraham rejoiced to see my day; and he saw it, and was He. 11. 13.
glad.   The Jews therefore said unto him, Thou art not

yet fifty years old, and hast thou seen Abraham? Jesus 95
Is. 43. 13. said unto them, Verily, verily, I say unto you, Before
Jn. 10. 30. Abraham was, I am. They took up stones therefore to
cast at him : but Jesus hid himself, and went out of the
Lk. 4. 30. temple.

80. *The Man Blind from his Birth.*

AND as he passed by, he saw a man blind from his
birth. And his disciples asked him, saying, Rabbi, who
did sin, this man, or his parents, that he should be born
blind? Jesus answered, Neither did this man sin, nor
Jn. 11. 4. his parents : but that the works of God should be made 5
manifest in him. We must work the works of him that
Jn. 12. 35. sent me, while it is day : the night cometh, when no man
Jn. 1. 9. can work. When I am in the world, I am the light of
Mk. 7. 33; the world. When he had thus spoken, he spat on the
— 8. 23. ground, and made clay of the spittle, and anointed his 10
67. 70 eyes with the clay, and said unto him, Go, wash in the
Is. 8. 6. pool of Siloam (which is by interpretation, Sent). He
Neh. 3. 15. went away therefore, and washed, and came seeing.
The neighbours therefore, and they which saw him aforetime, that he was a beggar, said, Is not this he that sat 15
and begged? Others said, It is he: others said, No,
but he is like him. He said, I am he. They said therefore unto him, How then were thine eyes opened? He
answered, The man that is called Jesus made clay, and
anointed mine eyes, and said unto me, Go to Siloam, 20
and wash : so I went away and washed, and I received
sight. And they said unto him, Where is he? He saith,
I know not.
They bring to the Pharisees him that aforetime was
Jn. 5. 10. blind. Now it was the sabbath on the day when Jesus 25
37 made the clay, and opened his eyes. Again therefore
the Pharisees also asked him how he received his sight.
And he said unto them, He put clay upon mine eyes,
and I washed, and do see. Some therefore of the
Pharisees said, This man is not from God, because he 30
keepeth not the sabbath. But others said, How can a
Jn. 3. 2. man that is a sinner do such signs? And there was a
Jn. 7. 33. division among them. They say therefore unto the blind
man again, What sayest thou of him, in that he opened

35 thine eyes? And he said, He is a prophet. The Jews Jn. 4. 19;
therefore did not believe concerning him, that he had — 6. 14.
been blind, and had received his sight, until they called
the parents of him that had received his sight, and asked
them, saying, Is this your son, who ye say was born
40 blind? how then doth he now see? His parents answered and said, We know that this is our son, and that
he was born blind: but how he now seeth, we know not;
or who opened his eyes, we know not: ask him; he is
of age; he shall speak for himself. These things said
45 his parents, because they feared the Jews: for the Jews
had agreed already, that if any man should confess him
to be Christ, he should be put out of the synagogue. Jn. 12. 42;
Therefore said his parents, He is of age; ask him. So — 16. 2.
they called a second time the man that was blind, and
50 said unto him, Give glory to God: we know that this Jos. 7. 19.
man is a sinner. He therefore answered, Whether he be
a sinner, I know not: one thing I know, that, whereas I
was blind, now I see. They said therefore unto him,
What did he to thee? how opened he thine eyes? He
55 answered them, I told you even now, and ye did not
hear: wherefore would ye hear it again? would ye also
become his disciples? And they reviled him, and said,
Thou art his disciple; but we are disciples of Moses.
We know that God hath spoken unto Moses: but as for
60 this man, we know not whence he is. The man an- Jn. 8. 14.
swered and said unto them, Why, herein is the marvel,
that ye know not whence he is, and yet he opened mine
eyes. We know that God heareth not sinners: but if Ps. 66. 18.
any man be a worshipper of God, and do his will, him Is. 1. 15.
65 he heareth. Since the world began it was never heard Ps. 34. 15.
that any one opened the eyes of a man born blind. If
this man were not from God, he could do nothing.
They answered and said unto him, Thou wast altogether
born in sins, and dost thou teach us? And they cast
70 him out.

Jesus heard that they had cast him out; and finding
him, he said, Dost thou believe on the Son of God?
He answered and said, And who is he, Lord, that I may
believe on him? Jesus said unto him, Thou hast both
75 seen him, and he it is that speaketh with thee. And he Jn. 4. 26.
said, Lord, I believe. And he worshipped him. And
Jesus said, For judgement came I into this world, that Jn. 5. 27.

Lk. 10. 21. they which see not may see; and that they which see
88   may become blind. Those of the Pharisees which were
            with him heard these things, and said unto him, Are we 80
            also blind? Jesus said unto them, If ye were blind, ye
Jn. 15. 24. would have no sin: but now ye say, We see: your sin
            remaineth.

81. *Jesus the Good Shepherd.*

VERILY, verily, I say unto you, He that entereth not
by the door into the fold of the sheep, but climbeth up
some other way, the same is a thief and a robber. But
he that entereth in by the door is the shepherd of the
sheep. To him the porter openeth; and the sheep hear 5
his voice: and he calleth his own sheep by name, and
leadeth them out. When he hath put forth all his own,
he goeth before them, and the sheep follow him: for
they know his voice. And a stranger will they not
follow, but will flee from him: for they know not the 10
voice of strangers. This parable spake Jesus unto them:
but they understood not what things they were which he
spake unto them.

Jesus therefore said unto them again, Verily, verily, I
Eph. 2. 18. say unto you, I am the door of the sheep. All that 15
Eze. 34. 2.. came before me are thieves and robbers: but the sheep
Jer. 23. 1.. did not hear them. I am the door: by me if any man
Zec. 11. 3.. enter in, he shall be saved, and shall go in and go out,
            and shall find pasture. The thief cometh not, but that
            he may steal, and kill, and destroy: I came that they 20
Is. 40. 11. may have life, and may have it abundantly. I am the
Eze. 34. 23. good shepherd: the good shepherd layeth down his life
            for the sheep. He that is a hireling, and not a shepherd,
            whose own the sheep are not, beholdeth the wolf coming,
Zec. 11. 16. and leaveth the sheep, and fleeth, and the wolf snatcheth 25
            them, and scattereth them: he fleeth because he is a
            hireling, and careth not for the sheep. I am the good
2 Ti. 2. 19. shepherd; and I know mine own, and mine own know
            me, even as the Father knoweth me, and I know the
Jn. 15. 13. Father; and I lay down my life for the sheep. And 30
Is. 56. 8. other sheep I have, which are not of this fold: them also
Ez. 34. 23; I must bring, and they shall hear my voice; and they
— 37. 24. shall become one flock, one shepherd. Therefore doth

81. S. John x. 1—21.

the Father love me, because I lay down my life, that I Is. 53. 12.
35 may take it again. No one taketh it away from me, but
I lay it down of myself. I have power to lay it down,
and I have power to take it again. This commandment Jn.12.49..;
received I from my Father. — 14. 31.
There arose a division again among the Jews because
40 of these words. And many of them said, He hath a
devil, and is mad; why hear ye him? Others said,
These are not the sayings of one possessed with a devil.
Can a devil open the eyes of the blind? 80

82. *Feast of Dedication. Jesus one with the Father.*

AND it was the feast of the dedication at Jerusalem : 1Mac.4.59.
it was winter; and Jesus was walking in the temple in
Solomon's porch. The Jews therefore came round about Acts 3. 11;
him, and said unto him, How long dost thou hold us in — 5. 12.
5 suspense? If thou art the Christ, tell us plainly. Jesus
answered them, I told you, and ye believe not: the Jn. 8. 42.
works that I do in my Father's name, these bear witness Jn. 5. 36.
of me. But ye believe not, because ye are not of my 38
sheep. My sheep hear my voice, and I know them, and
10 they follow me : and I give unto them eternal life ; and
they shall never perish, and no one shall snatch them out Jn. 18. 9.
of my hand. My Father, which hath given them unto
me, is greater than all; and no one is able to snatch
them out of the Father's hand. I and the Father are
15 one. The Jews took up stones again to stone him. Jn. 8. 59.
Jesus answered them, Many good works have I shewed
you from the Father; for which of those works do ye
stone me? The Jews answered him, For a good work
we stone thee not, but for blasphemy; and because that Jn. 5. 18.
20 thou, being a man, makest thyself God. Jesus answered
them, Is it not written in your law, I said, Ye are gods? Ps. 82. 6.
If he called them gods, unto whom the word of God
came (and the scripture cannot be broken), say ye of Mt. 5. 18.
him, whom the Father sanctified and sent into the world,
25 Thou blasphemest; because I said, I am the Son of
God? If I do not the works of my Father, believe me Jn. 15. 24.
not. But if I do them, though ye believe not me, 150
believe the works : that ye may know and understand
that the Father is in me, and I in the Father. They

Jn. 7. 30;   sought again to take him : and he went forth out of their 30
— 8. 59.   hand.

Mk. 10. 1.   And he went away again beyond Jordan into the
117   place where John was at the first baptizing ; and there he
abode.   And many came unto him ; and they said,
John indeed did no sign : but all things whatsoever John 35
spake of this man were true.   And many believed on him
there.

83.   *Raising of Lazarus.*

Now a certain man was sick, Lazarus of Bethany, of
the village of Mary and her sister Martha.   And it was
Jn. 12. 3.   that Mary which anointed the Lord with ointment, and
125   wiped his feet with her hair, whose brother Lazarus was
sick.   The sisters therefore sent unto him, saying, Lord, 5
behold, he whom thou lovest is sick.   But when Jesus
Jn. 9. 3.   heard it, he said, This sickness is not unto death, but for
Jn. 12. 23;   the glory of God, that the Son of God may be glorified
— 13. 31.   thereby.   Now Jesus loved Martha, and her sister, and
Lazarus.   When therefore he heard that he was sick, he 10
abode at that time two days in the place where he was.
Then after this he saith to the disciples, Let us go into
Jn. 10. 33.   Judæa again.   The disciples say unto him, Rabbi, the
82   Jews were but now seeking to stone thee; and goest thou
thither again?   Jesus answered, Are there not twelve 15
hours in the day?   If a man walk in the day, he
stumbleth not, because he seeth the light of this world.
Jn. 12. 35.   But if a man walk in the night, he stumbleth, because
the light is not in him.   These things spake he : and
after this he saith unto them, Our friend Lazarus is 20
1 Th. 4. 13.   fallen asleep ; but I go, that I may awake him out of sleep.
The disciples therefore said unto him, Lord, if he is
fallen asleep, he will recover.   Now Jesus had spoken of
his death : but they thought that he spake of taking rest
in sleep.   Then Jesus therefore said unto them plainly, 25
Lazarus is dead.   And I am glad for your sakes that I
was not there, to the intent ye may believe; nevertheless
let us go unto him.   Thomas therefore, who is called
Didymus, said unto his fellow-disciples, Let us also go,
Lk. 22. 33.   that we may die with him.   30
So when Jesus came, he found that he had been in

83.   S. John xi. 1—54.

the tomb four days already. Now Bethany was nigh
unto Jerusalem, about fifteen furlongs off; and many of
the Jews had come to Martha and Mary, to console them Job 2. 11..
35 concerning their brother. Martha therefore, when she
heard that Jesus was coming, went and met him : but Lk.10.38..
Mary still sat in the house. Martha therefore said unto   **90**
Jesus, Lord, if thou hadst been here, my brother had not
died. And even now I know that, whatsoever thou
40 shalt ask of God, God will give thee. Jesus saith unto
her, Thy brother shall rise again. Martha saith unto
him, I know that he shall rise again in the resurrection Acts 24.15.
at the last day. Jesus said unto her, I am the resur- Jn. 5. 28...
rection, and the life : he that believeth on me, though he
45 die, yet shall he live : and whosoever liveth and believeth Jn. 6. 39.
on me shall never die. Believest thou this ? She saith
unto him, Yea, Lord : I have believed that thou art the Mt. 16. 16.
Christ, the Son of God, even he that cometh into the Jn. 6. 69.
world. And when she had said this, she went away, and
50 called Mary her sister secretly, saying, The Master is
here, and calleth thee. And she, when she heard it,
arose quickly, and went unto him. (Now Jesus was not
yet come into the village, but was still in the place where
Martha met him.) The Jews then which were with her
55 in the house, and were comforting her, when they saw
Mary, that she rose up quickly and went out, followed
her, supposing that she was going unto the tomb to weep Mt. 28. 1.
there. Mary therefore, when she came where Jesus was,
and saw him, fell down at his feet, saying unto him,
60 Lord, if thou hadst been here, my brother had not died.
When Jesus therefore saw her weeping, and the Jews
also weeping which came with her, he groaned in the
spirit, and was troubled, and said, Where have ye laid
him ? They say unto him, Lord, come and see. Jesus
65 wept. The Jews therefore said, Behold how he loved Lk. 19. 41.
him ! But some of them said, Could not this man,
which opened the eyes of him that was blind, have Jn. 9. 6.
caused that this man also should not die ? Jesus therefore again groaning in himself cometh to the tomb.
70 Now it was a cave, and a stone lay against it. Jesus Mt. 27. 60.
saith, Take ye away the stone. Martha, the sister of him
that was dead, saith unto him, Lord, by this time he
stinketh : for he hath been dead four days. Jesus saith
unto her, Said I not unto thee, that, if thou believedst,

thou shouldest see the glory of God? So they took 75
away the stone. And Jesus lifted up his eyes, and said,
Father, I thank thee that thou heardest me. And I

Jn. 12. 30. knew that thou hearest me always : but because of the
multitude which standeth around I said it, that they may

Lk. 7. 14. believe that thou didst send me. And when he had 80

Mt. 9. 26. thus spoken, he cried with a loud voice, Lazarus, come

45. 57 forth. He that was dead came forth, bound hand and

Jn. 20. 7. foot with grave-clothes ; and his face was bound about
with a napkin. Jesus saith unto them, Loose him, and
let him go.   85

Many therefore of the Jews, which came to Mary and
beheld that which he did, believed on him. But some
of them went away to the Pharisees, and told them the
things which Jesus had done.

The chief priests therefore and the Pharisees gathered 90
a council, and said, What do we? for this man doeth

Acts 4. 16. many signs. If we let him thus alone, all men will
believe on him : and the Romans will come and take
away both our place and our nation. But a certain one

Jn. 18. 14. of them, Caiaphas, being high priest that year, said unto 95
them, Ye know nothing at all, nor do ye take account
that it is expedient for you that one man should die for
the people, and that the whole nation perish not. Now
this he said not of himself: but being high priest that
year, he prophesied that Jesus should die for the nation ; 100

Is. 49. 6. and not for the nation only, but that he might also

1 Jn. 2. 2. gather together into one the children of God that are

Ep. 2. 14.. scattered abroad. So from that day forth they took
counsel that they might put him to death.

Jesus therefore walked no more openly among the 105
Jews, but departed thence into the country near to the
wilderness, into a city called Ephraim ; and there he
tarried with the disciples.

84. *Samaritan Villagers.   Three Answers to Disciples.*

AND it came to pass, when the days were well-nigh

Acts 1. 2. come that he should be received up, he stedfastly set his
face to go to Jerusalem, and sent messengers before his
face : and they went, and entered into a village of the
Samaritans, to make ready for him. And they did not 5

---

84. S. Luke ix. 51—62 ; S. Matthew viii. 19—22.

receive him, because his face was as though he were Jn. 4. 9.
going to Jerusalem.   And when his disciples James and
John saw this, they said, Lord, wilt thou that we bid fire
to come down from heaven, and consume them?   But 2 Ki. 1. 10.
10 he turned, and rebuked them.   And they went to another
village.

And as they went in the way, a certain man said unto
him, I will follow thee whithersoever thou goest.   And
Jesus said unto him, The foxes have holes, and the birds
15 of the heaven have nests; but the Son of man hath not 1 Co. 4. 11.
where to lay his head.   And he said unto another,
Follow me.   But he said, Lord, suffer me first to go and
bury my father.   But he said unto him, Leave the dead
to bury their own dead; but go thou and publish abroad
20 the kingdom of God.   And another also said, I will
follow thee, Lord; but first suffer me to bid farewell to 1 Ki.19.20.
them that are at my house.   But Jesus said unto him,
No man, having put his hand to the plough, and looking
back, is fit for the kingdom of God.

85. *Mission of the Seventy.*

Now after these things the Lord appointed seventy
others, and sent them two and two before his face into
every city and place, whither he himself was about to
come.   And he said unto them, The harvest is plenteous, Mt. 9.37...
5 but the labourers are few : pray ye therefore the Lord of   **59**
the harvest, that he send forth labourers into his harvest.
Go your ways : behold, I send you forth as lambs in the
midst of wolves.   Carry no purse, no wallet, no shoes :
and salute no man on the way.   And into whatsoever 2 Ki. 4. 29.
10 house ye shall enter, first say, Peace be to this house.
And if a son of peace be there, your peace shall rest upon
him : but if not, it shall turn to you again.   And in that
same house remain, eating and drinking such things as 1 Co. 9. 7.
they give : for the labourer is worthy of his hire.   Go not 1Tim.5.18.
15 from house to house.   And into whatsoever city ye enter,
and they receive you, eat such things as are set before
you : and heal the sick that are therein, and say unto
them, The kingdom of God is come nigh unto you.   But Mt. 4. 17.
into whatsoever city ye shall enter, and they receive you
20 not, go out into the streets thereof and say, Even the

85. S. Luke x. 1—12.

Acts 13.51. dust from your city, that cleaveth to our feet, we do wipe
off against you : howbeit know this, that the kingdom of
God is come nigh. I say unto you, It shall be more
tolerable in that day for Sodom, than for that city.

86. *Of those who reject Him.*

THEN began he to upbraid the cities wherein most
of his mighty works were done, because they repented
not. Woe unto thee, Chorazin ! woe unto thee Bethsaida ! for if the mighty works had been done in Tyre
Ezek. 3. 6. and Sidon which were done in you, they would have 5
Is. 23. repented long ago in sackcloth and ashes. Howbeit I
Ezek. 27, say unto you, it shall be more tolerable for Tyre and
& 28. Sidon in the day of judgement, than for you. And thou,
Is. 14. 13.. Capernaum, shalt thou be exalted unto heaven? thou
shalt be brought down unto Hades : for if the mighty 10
works had been done in Sodom which were done in
thee, it would have remained until this day. Howbeit,
I say unto you, that it shall be more tolerable for the
Gen. 19. land of Sodom in the day of judgement, than for thee.
Jn. 13. 20. He that heareth you heareth me, and he that rejecteth 15
you rejecteth me: and he that rejecteth me rejecteth him
Jn. 5. 23. that sent me.

87. *Return of the Seventy.*

AND the seventy returned with joy, saying, Lord,
even the devils are subject unto us in thy name. And
Rev. 12. 9. he said unto them, I beheld Satan fallen as lightning
from heaven. Behold, I have given you authority to
Ps. 91. 13. tread upon serpents and scorpions, and over all the 5
Mk. 16. 18. power of the enemy: and nothing shall in any wise hurt
you. Howbeit in this rejoice not, that the spirits are
Phil. 4. 3. subject unto you ; but rejoice that your names are
Rev. 20. 12. written in heaven.

88. *Of those who receive Him.*

IN that same hour he rejoiced in the Holy Spirit, and
said, I thank thee, O Father, Lord of heaven and earth,
Rom. 6. 17. that thou didst hide these things from the wise and un-
(constr.)

---

86. S. Matthew xi. 20—24; S. Luke x. 13—16.
87. S. Luke x. 17—20.
88. S. Luke x. 21—24; S. Matthew xi. 25—30.

derstanding, and didst reveal them unto babes : yea, 1 Co. 1. 26..
5 Father, for so it was well-pleasing in thy sight. All things
have been delivered unto me of my Father : and no one Mt. 28. 18;
knoweth who the Son is, save the Father : neither doth any — 16. 17.
know who the Father is, save the Son, and he to whomso- Jn. 6. 46.
ever the Son willeth to reveal him. Come unto me, all
10 ye that labour and are heavy laden, and I will give you
rest. Take my yoke upon you, and learn of me ; for I
am meek and lowly in heart : and ye shall find rest unto Zec. 9. 9.
your souls. For my yoke is easy, and my burden is Jer. 6. 16.
light. And turning to the disciples, he said privately,
15 Blessed are the eyes which see the things that ye see : Mt. 13. 16.
for I say unto you that many prophets and kings desired **50**
to see the things which ye see, and saw them not ; and He. 11. 13.
to hear the things which ye hear, and heard them not.

89. *The Good Samaritan.*

AND behold, a certain lawyer stood up and tempted
him, saying, Master, what shall I do to inherit eternal Lk. 18. 18..
life ? And he said unto him, What is written in the law? **119**
how readest thou ? And he answering said, Thou shalt
5 love the Lord thy God with all thy heart, and with all Deut. 6. 5.
thy soul, and with all thy strength, and with all thy mind; **133**
and thy neighbour as thyself. And he said unto him, Lev. 19. 18.
Thou hast answered right : this do, and thou shalt live. Lev. 18. 5.
But he, desiring to justify himself, said unto Jesus, And Lk. 16. 15.
10 who is my neighbour ? Jesus made answer and said, A
certain man was going down from Jerusalem to Jericho ;
and he fell among robbers, which both stripped him and
beat him, and departed, leaving him half dead. And
by chance a certain priest was going down that way :
15 and when he saw him, he passed by on the other side. Ps. 38. 11.
And in like manner a Levite also, when he came to the
place, and saw him, passed by on the other side. But a
certain Samaritan, as he journeyed, came where he was : Jn. 4. 9.
and when he saw him, he was moved with compassion,
20 and came to him, and bound up his wounds, pouring on Is. 1. 6.
them oil and wine ; and he set him on his own beast, Mk. 6. 13.
and brought him to an inn, and took care of him. And Jas. 5. 14.
on the morrow he took out two pence, and gave them to Mt. 20. 2.
the host, and said, Take care of him ; and whatsoever

89. S. Luke x. 25—37.

thou spendest more, I, when I come back again, will 25
repay thee. Which of these three, thinkest thou, proved
neighbour unto him that fell among the robbers? And
he said, He that shewed mercy on him. And Jesus said
unto him, Go, and do thou likewise.

90. *Martha and Mary. The good part.*

Now as they went on their way, he entered into a
certain village: and a certain woman named Martha
Jn. 11.20... received him into her house. And she had a sister
83   called Mary, which also sat at the Lord's feet, and heard
Jn. 12. 2... his word. But Martha was cumbered about much serv- 5
125   ing; and she came up to him, and said, Lord, dost thou
not care that my sister did leave me to serve alone? bid
her therefore that she help me. But the Lord answered
and said unto her, Martha, Martha, thou art anxious and
Ps. 27. 4. troubled about many things: but one thing is needful: 10
for Mary hath chosen the good part, which shall not be
taken away from her.

91. *The Lord's Prayer. The Importunate Friend.*
The Father.

AND it came to pass, as he was praying in a certain
place, that when he ceased, one of his disciples said unto
him, Lord, teach us to pray, even as John also taught his
disciples. And he said unto them, When ye pray, say,
Mt. 6. 9... Father, Hallowed be thy name. Thy kingdom come. 5
43*   Give us day by day our daily bread. And forgive us our
sins; for we ourselves also forgive every one that is
indebted to us. And bring us not into temptation.
And he said unto them, Which of you shall have a
friend, and shall go unto him at midnight, and say to 10
him, Friend, lend me three loaves; for a friend of mine
is come to me from a journey, and I have nothing to set
before him; and he from within shall answer and say,
Trouble me not: the door is now shut, and my children
are with me in bed; I cannot rise and give thee? I say 15
unto you, Though he will not rise and give him, because
Lk. 18. 1... he is his friend, yet because of his importunity he will
116   arise and give him as many as he needeth. And I say

---

90. S. Luke x. 38—42.   91. S. Luke xi. 1—13.

unto you, Ask, and it shall be given you; seek, and ye
20 shall find; knock, and it shall be opened unto you. Mt. 7. 7...
For every one that asketh receiveth; and he that seeketh **43***
findeth; and to him that knocketh it shall be opened. 1 Jn. 3. 22.
And of which of you that is a father shall his son ask
a loaf, and he give him a stone? or a fish, and he for
25 a fish give him a serpent? Or if he shall ask an egg,
will he give him a scorpion? If ye then, being evil,
know how to give good gifts unto your children, how
much more shall your heavenly Father give the Holy Jas. 1. 5.
Spirit to them that ask him?

92. *Beelzebub. Of Blasphemy, and of Words.*

AND he cometh into an house. And the multitude
cometh together again, so that they could not so much
as eat bread. And when his friends heard it, they went
out to lay hold on him, for they said, He is beside him-
5 self. Then was brought unto him one possessed with a
devil, blind and dumb: and he healed him. And it **58. 73**
came to pass, when the devil was gone out, the dumb
man spake and saw. And all the multitudes were
amazed, and said, Is this the Son of David? But when
10 the Pharisees and scribes which came down from Jerusalem heard it, they said, He hath Beelzebub: and, By
the prince of the devils casteth he out the devils. And Mt. 9. 34.
others, tempting him, sought of him a sign from heaven.
But he, knowing their thoughts, called them unto him,
15 and said unto them in parables, How can Satan cast out
Satan? Every kingdom divided against itself is brought
to desolation; and every city or house divided against
itself will not be able to stand. And if Satan casteth
out Satan, and hath risen up against himself and is
20 divided, he cannot stand, but hath an end; how then
shall his kingdom stand? because ye say that I cast out
devils by Beelzebub. And if I by Beelzebub cast out Lk. 9. 49.
devils, by whom do your sons cast them out? therefore Acts 19. 13.
shall they be your judges. But if I by the finger of God Ex. 8. 19.
25 cast out devils, then is the kingdom of God come upon
you. When the strong man fully armed guardeth his
own court, his goods are in peace: but when a stronger

92. S. Matthew xii. 22—37; S. Mark iii. 20—30;
S. Luke xi. 14—23.

than he shall come upon him and overcome him, he
taketh from him his whole armour wherein he trusted
cp. and divideth his spoils. He that is not with me is 30
Mk. 9. 40. against me; and he that gathereth not with me scat-
tereth. Therefore I say unto you, All their sins shall
be forgiven unto the sons of men, and their blasphemies
wherewithsoever they shall blaspheme; but the blasphemy against the Spirit shall not be forgiven. And 35
1 Tim. 1. 13. whosoever shall speak a word against the Son of Man,
it shall be forgiven him; but whosoever shall blaspheme
Heb. 6. 4... against the Holy Spirit, it shall not be forgiven him,
1 Jn. 5. 16. neither in this world, nor in that which is to come; but
he is guilty of an eternal sin: because they said, He 40
Lk. 6. 43. hath an unclean spirit. Either make the tree good, and
Mt. 7. 16... its fruit good; or make the tree corrupt, and its fruit
43. 43* corrupt: for the tree is known by its fruit. Ye offspring
Mt. 23. 33. of vipers, how can ye, being evil, speak good things? for
out of the abundance of the heart the mouth speaketh. 45
Lk. 6. 45. The good man out of his good treasure bringeth forth
good things: and the evil man out of his evil treasure
bringeth forth evil things. And I say unto you, that
every idle word that men shall speak, they shall give
account thereof in the day of judgement. For by thy 50
words thou shalt be justified, and by thy words thou
shalt be condemned.

93. *The Unclean Spirit returning.*

BUT the unclean spirit, when he is gone out of the
Job 1. 7. man, passeth through waterless places, seeking rest, and
1 Pet. 5. 8. findeth it not. Then he saith, I will return to my house
whence I came out; and when he is come, he findeth it
empty, swept and garnished. Then goeth he and taketh 5
Mk. 16. 9. with himself seven other spirits, more evil than himself,
and they enter in and dwell there: and the last state of
2 Pet. 2. 20. that man becometh worse than the first. Even so shall
it be also unto this evil generation.

94. *Who are blessed.*

AND it came to pass, as he said these things, a
certain woman out of the multitude lifted up her voice,

---

93. S. Matthew xii. 43—45; S. Luke xi. 24—26
94. S. Luke xi. 27, 28.

and said unto him, Blessed is the womb that bare thee,
and the breasts which thou didst suck. But he said, Mt. 12. 49..
5 Yea rather, blessed are they that hear the word of God, 53
and keep it.

95. *The Sign of Jonah. Nineveh. Queen of the South.*

BUT when the multitudes were gathering together
unto him, certain of the scribes and Pharisees, tempting 69
him, answered, saying, Master, we would see a sign from 1 Cor. 1. 22.
thee from heaven. But he answered and said unto them,
5 An evil and adulterous generation seeketh after a sign;
and there shall no sign be given to it but the sign of
Jonah the prophet: for as Jonah was three days and Jon. 1. 17.
three nights in the belly of the whale; so shall the Son
of man be three days and three nights in the heart of the
10 earth. *And* even as Jonah became a sign unto the
Ninevites, so shall also the Son of man be to this
generation. The men of Nineveh shall stand up in the
judgement with this generation, and shall condemn it:
for they repented at the preaching of Jonah, and behold Jon. 3. 10.
15 a greater than Jonah is here. The queen of the south
shall rise up in the judgement with the men of this
generation, and shall condemn them: for she came from
the ends of the earth to hear the wisdom of Solomon; 1 Ki. 10.
and behold a greater than Solomon is here.

96. *The Light in a Man.*

No man, when he hath lighted a lamp, putteth it in Mt. 5. 15.
a cellar, neither under the bushel, but on the stand, that 43*
they which enter in may see the light. The lamp of thy Mt. 6. 22.
body is thine eye: when thine eye is single, thy whole
5 body also is full of light; but when it is evil, thy body
also is full of darkness. Look therefore whether the
light that is in thee be not darkness. If therefore thy
whole body be full of light, having no part dark, it shall
be wholly full of light, as when the lamp with its bright
10 shining doth give thee light.

95. S. Luke xi. 29—32; S. Matthew xii. 38—42.
96. S. Luke xi. 33—36.

97. *The Pharisees and Lawyers.*

Now as he spake, a Pharisee asketh him to dine with
him : and he went in, and sat down to meat. And when
the Pharisee saw it, he marvelled that he had not first
washed before dinner. And the Lord said unto him,
Mt.23.25.. Now do ye Pharisees cleanse the outside of the cup and 5
135 of the platter; but your inward part is full of extortion
and wickedness. Ye foolish ones, did not he that made
the outside make the inside also? Howbeit give for alms
Lk. 12. 33. those things which are within; and behold, all things are
clean unto you.   10
Mt.23.23..   But woe unto you Pharisees! for ye tithe mint and
rue and every herb, and pass over judgement and the
love of God : but these ought ye to have done, and not
to leave the other undone. Woe unto you Pharisees!
Mt. 23. 5. for ye love the chief seats in the synagogues, and the 15
salutations in the marketplaces. Woe unto you! for ye
Mt. 23. 27. are as the tombs which appear not, and the men that
walk over them know it not.
And one of the lawyers answering saith unto him,
Master, in saying this thou reproachest us also. And he 20
said, Woe unto you lawyers also ! for ye lade men with
Mt. 23. 4. burdens grievous to be borne, and ye yourselves touch
not the burdens with one of your fingers. Woe unto
Mt.23.29.. you ! for ye build the tombs of the prophets, and your
fathers killed them. So ye are witnesses and consent 25
unto the works of your fathers : for they killed them, and
ye build their tombs. Therefore also said the wisdom of
Mt. 23. 34. God, I will send unto them prophets and apostles ; and
some of them they shall kill and persecute ; that the
blood of all the prophets, which was shed from the 30
foundation of the world, may be required of this genera-
Gen. 4. 8. tion ; from the blood of Abel unto the blood of Zachariah,
2Ch.24.22. who perished between the altar and the sanctuary : yea,
I say unto you, it shall be required of this generation.
Woe unto you lawyers ! for ye took away the key of 35
Mt. 23. 13. knowledge : ye entered not in yourselves, and them that
were entering in ye hindered.
And when he was come out from thence, the scribes
and the Pharisees began to press upon him vehemently,

40 and to provoke him to speak of many things; laying
wait for him, to catch something out of his mouth.

98. *Whom to fear. Of confessing Christ.*

IN the mean time, when the many thousands of the
multitude were gathered together, insomuch that they
trode one upon another, he began to say unto his
disciples first of all, Beware ye of the leaven of the Mt. 16. 6.
5 Pharisees, which is hypocrisy. But there is nothing Mk. 4. 22.
covered up, that shall not be revealed: and hid, that Mt. 10. 26..
shall not be known. Wherefore whatsoever ye have said **51. 59**
in the darkness shall be heard in the light; and what ye
have spoken in the ear in the inner chambers shall be
10 proclaimed upon the housetops. And I say unto you
my friends, Be not afraid of them which kill the body, Is. 51. 12..
and after that have no more that they can do. But I Jas. 4. 12.
will warn you whom ye shall fear: Fear him, which after
he hath killed hath power to cast into hell; yea, I say
15 unto you, Fear him. Are not five sparrows sold for two
farthings? and not one of them is forgotten in the sight
of God. But the very hairs of your head are all numbered.
Fear not: ye are of more value than many sparrows.
And I say unto you, Every one who shall confess me
20 before men, him shall the Son of man also confess before
the angels of God: but he that denieth me in the 2Tim.2.12.
presence of men shall be denied in the presence of the
angels of God. And every one who shall speak a word
against the Son of man, it shall be forgiven him: but Mt. 12. 31.
25 unto him that blasphemeth against the Holy Spirit it **92**
shall not be forgiven. And when they bring you before
the synagogues, and the rulers, and the authorities, be
not anxious how or what ye shall answer, or what ye shall Mt. 10. 19.
say: for the Holy Spirit shall teach you in that very hour Lk. 21. 14.
30 what ye ought to say. **59. 137**

99. *Covetousness. The Rich Fool. Be not anxious.*

AND one out of the multitude said unto him, Master,
bid my brother divide the inheritance with me. But he
said unto him, Man, who made me a judge or a divider Jn. 8. 11.

---

98. S. Luke xii. 1—12.   99. S. Luke xii. 13—34.

over you? And he said unto them, Take heed, and
1 Tim. 6. 9. keep yourselves from all covetousness: for a man's life 5
consisteth not in the abundance of the things which he
possesseth. And he spake a parable unto them, saying,
Ecclus. The ground of a certain rich man brought forth plenti-
11. 19. fully: and he reasoned within himself, saying, What shall
Ps. 49. 16.. I do, because I have not where to bestow my fruits? 10
And he said, This will I do: I will pull down my barns,
and build greater; and there will I bestow all my corn
and my goods. And I will say to my soul, Soul, thou
hast much goods laid up for many years; take thine
ease, eat, drink, be merry. But God said unto him, 15
Job 27. 8. Thou foolish one, this night is thy soul required of thee;
Jas. 4. 14. and the things which thou hast prepared, whose shall
Ps. 39. 6. they be? So is he that layeth up treasure for himself,
1Tim.6.18. and is not rich toward God.

And he said unto his disciples, Therefore I say unto 20
Mt. 6. 25... you, Be not anxious for your life, what ye shall eat; nor
43* yet for your body, what ye shall put on. For the life is
more than the food, and the body than the raiment.
Consider the ravens, that they sow not, neither reap;
Job 38. 41. which have no store-chamber nor barn; and God feedeth 25
Ps. 147. 9. them: of how much more value are ye than the birds!
And which of you by being anxious can add a cubit unto
Lk. 19. 3. his stature? If then ye are not able to do even that which
Gr. is least, why are ye anxious concerning the rest? Con-
sider the lilies, how they grow: they toil not, neither do 30
they spin; yet I say unto you, Even Solomon in all his
glory was not arrayed like one of these. But if God
Ps. 104. 14. doth so clothe the grass in the field, which to-day is, and
Jas. 1. 10. to-morrow is cast into the oven; how much more shall
he clothe you, O ye of little faith? And seek not ye 35
Ps. 55. 22. what ye shall eat, and what ye shall drink, neither be ye
1 Pet. 5. 7. of doubtful mind. For all these things do the nations of
Phil. 4. 6. the world seek after: but your Father knoweth that ye
have need of these things. Howbeit seek ye his kingdom,
1 Ki. 3. 13. and these things shall be added unto you. Fear not, 40
1 Tim. 4. 8. little flock; for it is your Father's good pleasure to give
Acts 4. 34. you the kingdom. Sell that ye have, and give alms;
Mt. 6. 20. make for yourselves purses which wax not old, a treasure
43*. 119 in the heavens that faileth not, where no thief draweth
near, neither moth destroyeth. For where your treasure 45
is, there will your heart be also.

100. *Watchfulness. Stripes. Division. Make peace betimes.*

LET your loins be girded about, and your lamps Eph. 6. 14.
burning; and be ye yourselves like unto men looking for 1 Pet. 1. 13.
their lord, when he shall return from the marriage feast; Mt. 25. 1...
that, when he cometh and knocketh, they may straight-
5 way open unto him. Blessed are those servants, whom Mt. 24. 46.
the lord when he cometh shall find watching: verily I   137
say unto you, that he shall gird himself, and make them
sit down to meat, and shall come and serve them. And Rev. 3. 20.
if he shall come in the second watch, and if in the third,
10 and find them so, blessed are those servants. But know
this, that if the master of the house had known in what Mt. 24. 43.
hour the thief was coming, he would have watched, and 1 Th. 5. 2.
not have left his house to be broken through. Be ye 2 Pet. 3. 10.
also ready: for in an hour that ye think not the Son of Rev. 3. 3.
15 man cometh.

And Peter said, Lord, speakest thou this parable
unto us, or even unto all? And the Lord said, Who Mt. 24. 44..
then is the faithful and wise steward, whom his lord 1 Cor. 4. 2.
shall set over his household, to give them their portion of
20 food in due season? Blessed is that servant, whom his
lord when he cometh shall find so doing. Of a truth I
say unto you, that he will set him over all that he hath.
But if that servant shall say in his heart, My lord
delayeth his coming; and shall begin to beat the men- 2 Pet. 3. 4.
25 servants and the maidservants, and to eat and drink, and
to be drunken; the lord of that servant shall come in a
day when he expecteth not, and in an hour when he
knoweth not, and shall cut him asunder, and appoint his
portion with the unfaithful. And that servant, which Ro. 2. 12...
30 knew his lord's will, and made not ready, nor did ac- Nu. 15. 30.
cording to his will, shall be beaten with many stripes; Jas. 4. 17.
but he that knew not, and did things worthy of stripes, Lev. 5. 17..
shall be beaten with few stripes. And to whomsoever 1 Tim. 1. 13.
much is given, of him shall much be required: and to
35 whom they commit much, of him will they ask the more.

I came to cast fire upon the earth; and what will I,
if it is already kindled? But I have a baptism to be Mt. 20. 22.
baptized with; and how am I straitened till it be accomplished! Think ye that I am come to give peace in

Mt. 10. 34.. the earth? I tell you, Nay; but rather division: for 40
59   there shall be from henceforth five in one house divided,
            three against two, and two against three. They shall be
Mic. 7. 6. divided, father against son, and son against father;
            mother against daughter, and daughter against her
            mother; mother in law against her daughter in law, and 45
            daughter in law against her mother in law.
Mt. 16. 2...   And he said to the multitudes also, When ye see a
69   cloud rising in the west, straightway ye say, There cometh
            a shower; and so it cometh to pass. And when ye see
Mt. 20. 12. a south wind blowing, ye say, There will be a scorching 50
Jas. 1. 11. heat; and it cometh to pass. Ye hypocrites, ye know
  Gr.   how to interpret the face of the earth and the heaven;
            but how is it that ye know not how to interpret this
            time? And why even of yourselves judge ye not what
Pro. 25. 8.. is right? For as thou art going with thine adversary 55
Mt. 5. 25... before the magistrate, on the way give diligence to be
  43*   quit of him; lest haply he hale thee unto the judge, and
            the judge shall deliver thee to the officer, and the officer
            shall cast thee into prison. I say unto thee, Thou shalt
            by no means come out thence, till thou have paid the 60
            very last mite.

101. *Of Sudden Judgements. The Fig-tree in the Vineyard.*

Now there were some present at that very season
which told him of the Galilæans, whose blood Pilate had
mingled with their sacrifices. And he answered and
said unto them, Think ye that these Galilæans were
sinners above all the Galilæans, because they have suf- 5
fered these things? I tell you, Nay: but, except ye
repent, ye shall all in like manner perish. Or those
eighteen, upon whom the tower in Siloam fell, and killed
them, think ye that they were offenders above all the
men that dwell in Jerusalem? I tell you, Nay: but, 10
except ye repent, ye shall all likewise perish.
            And he spake this parable; A certain man had a fig
Mt. 21. 19. tree planted in his vineyard; and he came seeking fruit
  127   thereon, and found none. And he said unto the vine-
            dresser, Behold, these three years I come seeking fruit 15
            on this fig tree, and find none: cut it down; why doth

---

101. S. Luke xiii. 1—9.

it also cumber the ground? And he answering saith
unto him, Lord, let it alone this year also, till I shall
dig about it, and dung it: and if it bear fruit thence-
20 forth, well; but if not, thou shalt cut it down.

102. *The Infirm Woman healed on the Sabbath.*

AND he was teaching in one of the synagogues on 37—40
the sabbath day. And behold, a woman which had a 77. 106
spirit of infirmity eighteen years; and she was bowed
together, and could in no wise lift herself up. And
5 when Jesus saw her, he called her, and said to her,
Woman, thou art loosed from thine infirmity. And he
laid his hands upon her: and immediately she was made Mk. 10. 16.
straight, and glorified God. And the ruler of the synagogue, being moved with indignation because Jesus had
10 healed on the sabbath, answered and said to the multitude, There are six days in which men ought to work: Ex. 20. 9.
in them therefore come and be healed, and not on the
day of the sabbath. But the Lord answered him, and
said, Ye hypocrites, doth not each one of you on the Lk. 14. 5.
15 sabbath loose his ox or his ass from the stall, and lead
him away to watering? And ought not this woman,
being a daughter of Abraham, whom Satan had bound, Lk. 19. 9.
lo, these eighteen years, to have been loosed from this
bond on the day of the sabbath? And as he said these
20 things, all his adversaries were put to shame: and all the
multitude rejoiced for all the glorious things that were
done by him.

103. *Parables of the Mustard-seed and Leaven.*

HE said therefore, Unto what is the kingdom of God
like? and whereunto shall I liken it? It is like unto a Mt. 13. 31..
grain of mustard seed, which a man took, and cast into 51
his own garden; and it grew, and became a tree; and
5 the birds of the heaven lodged in the branches thereof. Dan. 4. 12.
And again he said, Whereunto shall I liken the kingdom
of God? It is like unto leaven, which a woman took and Mt. 13. 33.
hid in three measures of meal, till it was all leavened. Ex. 16. 36.
cp.Gr.&H.

102. S. Luke xiii. 10—17.   103. S. Luke xiii. 18—21.

104. *Are there few that be saved?*

AND he went on his way through cities and villages, teaching, and journeying on unto Jerusalem. And one said unto him, Lord, are they few that be saved? And he said unto them, Strive to enter in by the narrow door: for many, I say unto you, shall seek to enter in, and 5 shall not be able. When once the master of the house is risen up, and hath shut to the door, and ye begin to stand without, and to knock at the door, saying, Lord, open to us; and he shall answer and say to you, I know you not whence ye are; then shall ye begin to say, We 10 did eat and drink in thy presence, and thou didst teach in our streets; and he shall say, I tell you, I know not whence ye are; depart from me, all ye workers of iniquity. There shall be the weeping and gnashing of teeth, when ye shall see Abraham, and Isaac, and Jacob, 15 and all the prophets, in the kingdom of God, and yourselves cast forth without. And they shall come from the east and west, and from the north and south, and shall sit down in the kingdom of God. And behold, there are last which shall be first, and there are first which shall be 20 last.

Mt. 7. 13...
43*

Mt. 25. 10..
138

Mt. 7. 21...

Ps. 6. 8.

Lk. 16. 23..
112

Mal. 1. 11.

Is. 59. 19.

Mt. 19. 30.

105. *Answer to Herod's threats.*

IN that very hour there came certain Pharisees, saying to him, Get thee out, and go hence: for Herod would fain kill thee. And he said unto them, Go and say to that fox, Behold, I cast out devils and perform cures today and to-morrow, and the third day I am perfected. 5 Howbeit I must go on my way to-day and to-morrow and the day following: for it cannot be that a prophet perish out of Jerusalem. O Jerusalem, Jerusalem, which killeth the prophets, and stoneth them that are sent unto her! how often would I have gathered thy children to- 10 gether, even as a hen gathereth her own brood under her wings, and ye would not! Behold, your house is left unto you desolate: and I say unto you, Ye shall not see me, until ye shall say, Blessed is he that cometh in the name of the Lord. 15

Heb. 2. 10.

Mt. 23. 37..
135

Jer. 22. 5;
— 12. 7.

Ps. 118. 26.

106. *Dinner on Sabbath. Dropsy healed.*

AND it came to pass, when he went into the house
of one of the rulers of the Pharisees on a sabbath to eat
bread, that they were watching him. And behold, there
was before him a certain man which had the dropsy.
5 And Jesus answering spake unto the lawyers and Pharisees, saying, Is it lawful to heal on the sabbath, or not? 37—40
But they held their peace. And he took him, and healed 77. 102
him, and let him go. And he said unto them, Which of
you shall have an ass or an ox fallen into a well, and
10 will not straightway draw him up on a sabbath day?
And they could not answer again unto these things.

107. *The Guests reproved. Of true Hospitality.*

AND he spake a parable unto those which were bidden, when he marked how they chose out the chief seats;
saying unto them, When thou art bidden of any man to
a marriage feast, sit not down in the chief seat; lest Pro. 25.6..
5 haply a more honourable man than thou be bidden of
him, and he that bade thee and him shall come and say
to thee, Give this man place; and then thou shalt begin
with shame to take the lowest place. But when thou
art bidden, go and sit down in the lowest place; that
10 when he that hath bidden thee cometh, he may say to
thee, Friend, go up higher: then shalt thou have glory
in the presence of all that sit at meat with thee. For Mt. 23. 12.
every one that exalteth himself shall be humbled; and Pro. 29. 23.
he that humbleth himself shall be exalted. Lk. 1. 52.
15 And he said to him also that had bidden him, When
thou makest a dinner or a supper, call not thy friends,
nor thy brethren, nor thy kinsmen, nor rich neighbours;
lest haply they also bid thee again, and a recompense be
made thee. But when thou makest a feast, bid the poor, Neh. 8. 10.
20 the maimed, the lame, the blind: and thou shalt be Tob. 4. 7...
blessed; because they have not wherewith to recompense thee: for thou shalt be recompensed in the resurrection of the just.

---

106. S. Luke xiv. 1—6.   107. S. Luke xiv. 7—14.

108. *The Great Supper.*

AND when one of them that sat at meat with him
Rev. 19. 9. heard these things, he said unto him, Blessed is he that
shall eat bread in the kingdom of God.   But he said
unto him, A certain man made a great supper; and he
Esth. 6. 14. bade many: and he sent forth his servant at supper time 5
Pro. 9. 2.. to say to them that were bidden, Come; for all things
Mt. 22. 1... are now ready.   And they all with one consent began to
130   make excuse.   The first said unto him, I have bought
Mt. 13. 34. a field, and I must needs go out and see it: I pray thee
have me excused.   And another said, I have bought five 10
Lk. 9. 62. yoke of oxen, and I go to prove them: I pray thee have
me excused.   And another said, I have married a wife,
1 Cor. 7. 33. and therefore I cannot come.   And the servant came,
and told his lord these things.   Then the master of the
house being angry said to his servant, Go out quickly 15
into the streets and lanes of the city, and bring in hither
the poor and maimed and blind and lame.   And the
servant said, Lord, what thou didst command is done,
and yet there is room.   And the lord said unto the
servant, Go out into the highways and hedges, and con- 20
strain them to come in, that my house may be filled.
Acts 13. 46. For I say unto you, that none of those men which were
bidden shall taste of my supper.

109. *Of bearing the Cross, and counting the cost.*

Now there went with him great multitudes: and he
Mt. 10. 37.. turned, and said unto them, If any man cometh unto
59   me, and hateth not his own father, and mother, and
Deu. 33. 9. wife, and children, and brethren, and sisters, yea, and
Rev. 12. 11. his own life also, he cannot be my disciple.   Whosoever 5
Mt. 16. 24. doth not bear his own cross, and come after me, cannot
71   be my disciple.   For which of you, desiring to build a
tower, doth not first sit down and count the cost, whether
he have wherewith to complete it?   Lest haply, when he
hath laid a foundation, and is not able to finish, all that 10
behold begin to mock him, saying, This man began to
build, and was not able to finish.   Or what king, as he
goeth to encounter another king in war, will not sit down

108. S. Luke xiv. 15—24.   109. S. Luke xiv. 25—35.

first and take counsel whether he is able with ten thou-
15 sand to meet him that cometh against him with twenty
thousand? Or else, while the other is yet a great way
off, he sendeth an ambassage, and asketh conditions of
peace. So therefore whosoever he be of you that re-
nounceth not all that he hath, he cannot be my disciple.
20 Salt therefore is good: but if even the salt have lost its Mt. 5. 13.
savour, wherewith shall it be seasoned? It is fit neither **43***
for the land nor for the dunghill: men cast it out. He Mk. 9. 50.
that hath ears to hear, let him hear. 75

110. *Joy in Heaven over Sinners that repent.*
The Lost Sheep. The Piece of Silver. The Prodigal Son.

Now all the publicans and sinners were drawing near
unto him for to hear him. And both the Pharisees and
the scribes murmured, saying, This man receiveth Lk. 19. 7.
sinners, and eateth with them. **122**
5 And he spake unto them this parable, saying, What
man of you, having a hundred sheep, and having lost one Mt. 18. 12.
of them, doth not leave the ninety and nine in the **75**
wilderness, and go after that which is lost, until he find Ps.
it? And when he hath found it, he layeth it on his 119. 176.
10 shoulders, rejoicing. And when he cometh home, he
calleth together his friends and his neighbours, saying,
Rejoice with me, for I have found my sheep
which was lost. I say unto you, that even so there shall
be joy in heaven over one sinner that repenteth, more
15 than over ninety and nine righteous persons, which need Lk. 5. 32.
no repentance.
Or what woman having ten pieces of silver, if she
lose one piece, doth not light a lamp, and sweep the
house, and seek diligently until she find it? And when
20 she hath found it, she calleth together her friends and
neighbours, saying, Rejoice with me, for I have found the
piece which I had lost. Even so, I say unto you, there
is joy in the presence of the angels of God over one
sinner that repenteth.
25 And he said, A certain man had two sons: and the
younger of them said to his father, Father, give me the
portion of thy substance that falleth to me. And he De.21.16...
divided unto them his living. And not many days after

the younger son gathered all together, and took his
journey into a far country; and there he wasted his 30
substance with riotous living. And when he had spent

Amos 8. 11. all, there arose a mighty famine in that country; and he
began to be in want. And he went and joined himself
to one of the citizens of that country; and he sent him
into his fields to feed swine. And he would fain have 35
been filled with the husks that the swine did eat: and no
man gave unto him. But when he came to himself he
said, How many hired servants of my father's have bread
enough and to spare, and I perish here with hunger! I
will arise and go to my father, and will say unto him, 40
Father, I have sinned against heaven, and in thy sight:
I am no more worthy to be called thy son: make me as
one of thy hired servants. And he arose, and came to

Acts 2. 39. his father. But while he was yet afar off, his father saw
Eph. 2. 17. him, and was moved with compassion, and ran, and 45
fell on his neck, and kissed him. And the son said unto

Ps. 51. 4. him, Father, I have sinned against heaven, and in thy
sight: I am no more worthy to be called thy son. But
the father said to his servants, Bring forth quickly the
best robe, and put it on him; and put a ring on his 50
hand, and shoes on his feet: and bring the fatted calf,
and kill it, and let us eat, and make merry: for this my

Eph. 2. 1. son was dead, and is alive again; he was lost, and is
Rev. 3. 1. found. And they began to be merry. Now his elder
son was in the field: and as he came and drew nigh to 55
the house, he heard music and dancing. And he called
to him one of the servants, and inquired what these
things might be. And he said unto him, Thy brother is
come; and thy father hath killed the fatted calf, because
he hath received him safe and sound. But he was angry, 60
and would not go in: and his father came out, and
intreated him. But he answered and said to his father,
Lo, these many years do I serve thee, and I never
transgressed a commandment of thine: and yet thou
never gavest me a kid, that I might make merry with my 65
friends: but when this thy son came, which hath devoured
thy living with harlots, thou killedst for him the fatted
calf. And he said unto him, Son, thou art ever with me,
and all that is mine is thine. But it was meet to make

Eph. 5. 14. merry and be glad: for this thy brother was dead, and is 70
alive again; and was lost, and is found.

111. *Of the right use of Riches. The unjust Steward.*

AND he said also unto the disciples, There was a
certain rich man, which had a steward; and the same
was accused unto him that he was wasting his goods.
And he called him, and said unto him, What is this that
5 I hear of thee? render the account of thy stewardship; 1 Cor. 4. 2.
for thou canst be no longer steward. And the steward
said within himself, What shall I do, seeing that my
lord taketh away the stewardship from me? I have not
strength to dig; to beg I am ashamed. I am resolved
10 what to do, that, when I am put out of the stewardship,
they may receive me into their houses. And calling to
him each one of his lord's debtors, he said to the first,
How much owest thou unto my lord? And he said, A
hundred measures of oil. And he said unto him, Take
15 thy bond, and sit down quickly and write fifty. Then
said he to another, And how much owest thou? And he
said, A hundred measures of wheat. He saith unto him,
Take thy bond, and write fourscore. And his lord
commended the unrighteous steward because he had
20 done wisely: for the sons of this world are for their own
generation wiser than the sons of the light. And I say 1 The. 5. 5.
unto you, Make to yourselves friends by means of the Dan. 4. 27.
mammon of unrighteousness; that, when it shall fail, they 1 Tim. 6. 18.
may receive you into the eternal tabernacles. He that Mt. 25. 21.
25 is faithful in a very little is faithful also in much: and he **139**
that is unrighteous in a very little is unrighteous also in Lk. 19. 17.
much. If therefore ye have not been faithful in the **123**
unrighteous mammon, who will commit to your trust the Rev. 3. 18.
true riches? And if ye have not been faithful in that
30 which is another's, who will give you that which is your
own? No servant can serve two masters: for either he Mt. 6. 24.
will hate the one, and love the other; or else he will hold **43***
to one, and despise the other. Ye cannot serve God and
mammon.
35 And the Pharisees, who were lovers of money, heard
all these things; and they scoffed at him. And he said
unto them, Ye are they that justify yourselves in the Lk. 10. 29.
sight of men; but God knoweth your hearts: for that 1 Sa. 16. 7.
which is exalted among men is an abomination in the

Mt. 11. 12. sight of God. The law and the prophets were until 40
  46   John: from that time the gospel of the kingdom of God
            is preached, and every man entereth violently into it.
Mt. 5. 18. But it is easier for heaven and earth to pass away, than
            for one tittle of the law to fall. Every one that putteth
Mt. 5. 32. away his wife, and marrieth another, committeth adultery: 45
  43*   and he that marrieth one that is put away from a husband
Mt. 19. 9. committeth adultery.
  117

112. *Of the wrong use of Riches. Dives and Lazarus.*

Now there was a certain rich man, and he was
clothed in purple and fine linen, faring sumptuously
every day: and a certain beggar named Lazarus was
laid at his gate, full of sores, and desiring to be fed with
Mt. 15. 27. the crumbs that fell from the rich man's table; yea, even 5
Ps. 22. 16. the dogs came and licked his sores. And it came to
            pass, that the beggar died, and that he was carried away
Lk. 23. 43. by the angels into Abraham's bosom: and the rich man
            also died, and was buried. And in Hades he lifted up
            his eyes, being in torments, and seeth Abraham afar off, 10
            and Lazarus in his bosom. And he cried and said,
            Father Abraham, have mercy on me, and send Lazarus,
            that he may dip the tip of his finger in water, and cool
Mk. 9. 48. my tongue; for I am in anguish in this flame. But
            Abraham said, Son, remember that thou in thy lifetime 15
Lk. 6. 24. receivedst thy good things, and Lazarus in like manner
— 6. 20. evil things: but now here he is comforted, and thou art in
            anguish. And beside all this, between us and you there
            is a great gulf fixed, that they which would pass from
            hence to you may not be able, and that none may cross 20
            over from thence to us. And he said, I pray thee there-
            fore, father, that thou wouldest send him to my father's
            house; for I have five brethren; that he may testify
            unto them, lest they also come into this place of torment.
Is. 34. 16. But Abraham saith, They have Moses and the prophets; 25
            let them hear them. And he said, Nay, father Abraham:
            but if one go to them from the dead, they will repent.
Jn. 5. 47. And he said unto him, If they hear not Moses and the
Jn. 11.46..; prophets, neither will they be persuaded, if one rise from
— 12. 10. the dead.   30

---

112. S. Luke xvi. 19—31.

113.   *Of tempting others.   Forgiveness, Faith, Service.*

AND he said unto his disciples, It is impossible but Mt. 18. 7.
that occasions of stumbling should come : but woe unto   **75**
him, through whom they come !   It were well for him if ¹ Co.11.19.
a millstone were hanged about his neck, and he were
5 thrown into the sea, rather than that he should cause one
of these little ones to stumble.   Take heed to yourselves:
if thy brother sin, rebuke him ; and if he repent, forgive Lev. 19. 17.
him.   And if he sin against thee seven times in the day, Mt. 18. 21.
and seven times turn again to thee, saying, I repent ;   **76**
10 thou shalt forgive him.

And the apostles said unto the Lord, Increase our
faith.   And the Lord said, If ye have faith as a grain of Mt. 17. 20.
mustard seed, ye would say unto this sycamine tree, Be   **127**
thou rooted up, and be thou planted in the sea ; and it ¹ Co. 13. 3.
15 would have obeyed you.   But who is there of you, having
a servant plowing or keeping sheep, that will say unto
him, when he is come in from the field, Come straightway and sit down to meat ; and will not rather say unto
him, Make ready wherewith I may sup, and gird thyself, Lk. 12. 37.
20 and serve me, till I have eaten and drunken ; and afterward thou shalt eat and drink?   Doth he thank the
servant because he did the things that were commanded?
Even so ye also, when ye shall have done all the things
that are commanded you, say, We are unprofitable Job 22. 3;
25 servants ; we have done that which it was our duty to do. — 35. 7.

114.   *Ten Lepers cleansed.   One gives thanks.*

AND it came to pass, as they were on the way to
Jerusalem, that he was passing through the midst of
Samaria and Galilee.   And as he entered into a certain   **34**
village, there met him ten men that were lepers, which
5 stood afar off : and they lifted up their voices, saying, Lev.13.46.
Jesus, Master, have mercy on us.   And when he saw
them, he said unto them, Go and shew yourselves unto Lev. 14. 2..
the priests.   And it came to pass, as they went, they
were cleansed.   And one of them, when he saw that he
10 was healed, turned back, with a loud voice glorifying
God ; and he fell upon his face at his feet, giving him
thanks : and he was a Samaritan.   And Jesus answering

---

113. S. Luke xvii. 1—10.   114. S. Luke xvii. 11—19.

said, Were not the ten cleansed? but where are the
nine? Were there none found that returned to give
glory to God, save this stranger? And he said unto 15
Lk. 8. 48. him, Arise, and go thy way: thy faith hath made thee
whole.

115. *How the Kingdom of God cometh.*

AND being asked by the Pharisees, when the kingdom
of God cometh, he answered them and said, The
kingdom of God cometh not with observation: neither
shall they say, Lo, here! or, There! for lo, the kingdom
Ro. 14. 17. of God is within you.   5
And he said unto the disciples, The days will come,
Mt. 9. 15. when ye shall desire to see one of the days of the Son of
man, and ye shall not see it. And they shall say to you,
Mt. 24. 23.. Lo, there! Lo, here! go not away, nor follow after
137   them: for as the lightning, when it lighteneth out of the 10
one part under the heaven, shineth unto the other part
under heaven; so shall the Son of man be in his day.
Lk. 9. 22. But first must he suffer many things and be rejected of
this generation. And as it came to pass in the days of
Gen. 7.   Noah, even so shall it be also in the days of the Son of 15
man. They ate, they drank, they married, they were
given in marriage, until the day that Noah entered into
the ark, and the flood came, and destroyed them all.
Gen. 19.   Likewise even as it came to pass in the days of Lot:
they ate, they drank, they bought, they sold, they planted, 20
they builded; but in the day that Lot went out from
Sodom it rained fire and brimstone from heaven, and
destroyed them all: after the same manner shall it be in
2 The. 1. 7. the day that the Son of man is revealed. In that day,
Mt. 24. 17. he which shall be on the housetop, and his goods in the 25
house, let him not go down to take them away: and let
him that is in the field likewise not return back. Re-
Gen. 19. 26. member Lot's wife. Whosoever shall seek to gain his
Mt. 16. 25. life shall lose it: but whosoever shall lose his life shall
71   preserve it. I say unto you, In that night there shall be 30
two men on one bed; the one shall be taken, and the
Mt. 24. 40. other shall be left. There shall be two women grinding
together; the one shall be taken, and the other shall be
left. And they answering say unto him, Where, Lord?

115. S. Luke xvii. 20—37.

35 And he said unto them, Where the body is, thither will Mt. 24. 28.
the eagles also be gathered together.   **137**

116. *Pray without ceasing. How to pray.*

AND he spake a parable unto them to the end that
they ought always to pray, and not to faint; saying, 1 Th. 5. 17.
There was in a city a judge, which feared not God,
and regarded not man: and there was a widow in that
5 city; and she came oft unto him, saying, Avenge me of
mine adversary.   And he would not for a while: but
afterward he said within himself, Though I fear not God,
nor regard man; yet because this widow troubleth me, I Lk. 11. 8.
will avenge her, lest she wear me out by her continual 1 Cor. 9. 17.
10 coming.   And the Lord said, Hear what the unrighteous   Gk.
judge saith.   And shall not God avenge his elect, which
cry to him day and night, and he is longsuffering over Rev. 6. 9..
them?   I say unto you, that he will avenge them Ecclus.
speedily.   Howbeit when the Son of man cometh, shall   35. 17...
15 he find faith on the earth?   2 Pe. 3. 8...
And he spake also this parable unto certain which
trusted in themselves that they were righteous, and set Is. 65. 5.
all others at nought: Two men went up into the temple
to pray; the one a Pharisee, and the other a publican.
20 The Pharisee stood and prayed thus with himself, God,
I thank thee, that I am not as the rest of men, extor- Rev. 3. 17.
tioners, unjust, adulterers, or even as this publican.   I
fast twice in the week; I give tithes of all that I get.
But the publican, standing afar off, would not lift up so
25 much as his eyes unto heaven, but smote his breast, Jn. 17. 1.
saying, God, be merciful to me a sinner.   I say unto
you, This man went down to his house justified rather
than the other: for every one that exalteth himself shall Mt. 23. 12.
be humbled; but he that humbleth himself shall be   **135**
30 exalted.

117. *Of Marriage, Adultery, and Divorce.*

AND it came to pass when Jesus had finished these
words, he departed from Galilee, and came into the
borders of Judæa and beyond Jordan: and great multitudes come together unto him again, and followed him;

---

116. S. Luke xviii. 1—14.
117. S. Matthew xix. 1—12 ; S. Mark x. 1—12.

J. H.   8

and he healed them there ; and as he was wont he taught 5
them again.

And there came unto him Pharisees, tempting him,
and asked him, saying, Is it lawful for a man to put away
his wife for every cause? And he answered and said,
Have ye not read that he which made them from the 10
beginning made them male and female, and said, For this
cause shall a man leave his father and mother and shall
cleave to his wife ; and the twain shall become one flesh?
So that they are no more twain, but one flesh. What
therefore God hath joined together, let not man put 15
asunder. They say unto him, Why then did Moses
command to give a bill of divorcement and to put her
away? He saith unto them, Moses for your hardness of
heart suffered you to put away your wives : but from the
beginning it hath not been so. And I say unto you, 20
Whosoever shall put away his wife, except for fornication,
and shall marry another, committeth adultery : and he
that marrieth her when she is put away committeth
adultery. The disciples say unto him, If the case of the
man is so with his wife, it is not expedient to marry. 25
But he said unto them, All men cannot receive this
saying, but they to whom it is given. For there are
eunuchs, which were so born from their mother's womb ;
and there are eunuchs, which were made eunuchs by
men : and there are eunuchs, which made themselves 30
eunuchs for the kingdom of heaven's sake. He that is
able to receive it, let him receive it. And in the house
the disciples asked him again of this matter. And he
said unto them, Whosoever shall put away his wife, and
marry another, committeth adultery against her : and if 35
she herself shall put away her husband, and marry
another, she committeth adultery.

Marginal references:
Gen. 1. 27.
— 2. 24.
Gr.
Mal. 2. 14..
Eph. 5. 28..
Deu. 24.
Mt. 5. 32.
43*
Lk. 16. 18.
111
1 Cor. 7. 1.
Is. 39. 7.
1 Cor. 7. 7.
1 Cor. 7. 11.
1 Cor. 7. 10,
— 39.

118. *Babes brought to Christ.*

THEN they brought unto him also their babes, that
he should lay his hands upon them and pray : but when
the disciples saw it, they rebuked them. But when
Jesus saw it, he was moved with indignation, and called
them unto him, and said unto them, Suffer the little 5

children to come unto me, and forbid them not : for of   Mt. 18. 3...
such is the kingdom of God. Verily I say unto you,   **75**
Whosoever shall not receive the kingdom of God as a   1 Co. 14. 20.
little child, he shall in no wise enter therein. And he   1 Pet. 2. 2.
10 took them up in his arms, and blessed them, laying his
hands upon them ; and departed thence.

119. *Counsel of Perfection. Riches a hindrance.*

AND as he was going forth into the way, a certain
ruler ran to him, and kneeled to him, and asked him,
saying, Good Master, what good thing shall I do that I
may inherit eternal life? And Jesus said unto him, Why
5 callest thou me good? *and* askest thou me concerning
that which is good? None is good save one, even
God. But if thou wouldest enter into life keep the commandments. He saith unto him, Which? And Jesus
said, Thou shalt not kill, Thou shalt not commit adultery,   Ex. 20. 13..
10 Thou shalt not steal, Thou shalt not bear false witness,   Deu. 5. 16.
Honour thy father and thy mother: and, Thou shalt love   Lev. 19. 18.
thy neighbour as thyself. And the young man said unto   Rom. 13. 9.
him, Master, all these things have I observed from my
youth up : what lack I yet? And Jesus looking upon
15 him loved him, and said unto him, One thing thou lackest
yet : if thou wouldest be perfect, go, sell all that thou   Lk. 12. 33.
hast and distribute to the poor, and thou shalt have   **99**
treasure in heaven: and come, follow me. But when   Acts 4. 34..
the young man heard the saying his countenance fell,
20 and he went away exceeding sorrowful : for he was one
that had great possessions.

And Jesus looked round about, and seeing him, saith
unto his disciples, How hardly shall they that have
riches enter into the kingdom of God! And the dis-
25 ciples were amazed at his words. But Jesus answereth
again, and saith unto them, Children, how hard it is for   Job 31. 24.
them that trust in riches to enter into the kingdom of   Ps. 62. 10.
God! It is easier for a camel to go through a needle's   1 Tim. 6. 17.
eye, than for a rich man to enter into the kingdom of
30 God. And when the disciples heard it, they were astonished exceedingly, saying unto him, Who then can
be saved? And Jesus looking upon them saith, With

---

119. S. Mark x. 17—27; S. Matthew xix. 16—26;
S. Luke xviii. 18—27.

Gen.18.14. men this is impossible, but not with God: for all things
Job 42. 2. are possible with God.
Zech. 8. 6.

120. *Of those who have left all. Labourers in the Vineyard.*

THEN answered Peter and began to say unto him,
Lo, we have left all, and followed thee; what then shall
we have? And Jesus said unto them, Verily I say unto
Re. 21.1,5. you, that ye which have followed me, in the regeneration
Acts 3. 21. when the Son of man shall sit upon the throne of his 5
1 Co. 6. 2. glory, ye also shall sit upon twelve thrones, judging the
Lk. 22. 30. twelve tribes of Israel. And there is no man that hath
145 left house, or wife, or brethren, or sisters, or father, or
mother, or children, or lands, for my sake and for the
2 Ch. 25. 9. gospel's sake, who shall not receive a hundredfold now 10
1 Tim. 4. 8. in this time, houses, and brethren, and sisters, and
2 Tim. 3. 12. mothers, and children, and lands, with persecutions:
and in the world to come eternal life. But many shall
be last that are first, and first that are last. For the
kingdom of heaven is like unto a man that is a house- 15
holder, which went out early in the morning to hire
labourers into his vineyard. And when he had agreed
Tob. 5. 14. with the labourers for a penny a day, he sent them into
Lk. 10. 35. his vineyard. And he went out about the third hour,
and saw others standing in the marketplace idle; and 20
to them he said, Go ye also into the vineyard, and whatsoever is right I will give you. And they went their
way. Again he went out about the sixth and the ninth
hour, and did likewise. And about the eleventh hour he
went out, and found others standing; and he saith unto 25
them, Why stand ye here all the day idle? They say
unto him, Because no man hath hired us. He saith
unto them, Go ye also into the vineyard. And when
Lev. 19. 13. even was come, the lord of the vineyard saith unto his
Deu. 24. 15. steward, Call the labourers, and pay them their hire, 30
Tob. 4. 14. beginning from the last unto the first. And when they
came that were hired about the eleventh hour, they received every man a penny. And when the first came,
they supposed that they would receive more; and they
likewise received every man a penny. And when they 35

120. S. Matthew xix. 27—xx. 16; S. Mark x. 28—31;
S. Luke xviii. 28—30.

received it, they murmured against the householder, saying, These last have spent but one hour, and thou hast
made them equal unto us, which have borne the burden
of the day and the scorching heat. But he answered Jas. 1. 11.
40 and said to one of them, Friend, I do thee no wrong: Gr.
didst not thou agree with me for a penny? Take up
that which is thine, and go thy way; it is my will to give Eze. 18. 4.
unto this last, even as unto thee. Is it not lawful for me Rom. 9. 20.
to do what I will with mine own? or is thine eye evil, Deu. 15. 9.
45 because I am good? So the last shall be first, and the Pro. 28. 22.
first last. Tob. 4. 7.

121. *Passion foretold. Request of James and John.*

AND they were in the way, going up to Jerusalem;
and Jesus was going before them: and they were amazed,
and they that followed were afraid. And he took again
the twelve disciples apart, and began to tell them the Mt. 16. 21.
5 things that were to happen unto him, saying, Behold, we **71**
go up to Jerusalem, and all things that are written by the
prophets shall be accomplished unto the Son of man.
For he shall be delivered up unto the chief priests and
the scribes; and they shall condemn him to death, and
10 shall deliver him unto the Gentiles: and they shall mock
him, and shamefully entreat him, and shall spit upon
him, and shall scourge him, and shall crucify him; and
after three days he shall rise again. And they under- Lk. 9. 45.
stood none of these things; and this saying was hid from **73**
15 them, and they perceived not the things that were said.
Then came to him the mother of the sons of Zebedee, Mt. 27. 56.
with her sons, worshipping him, and saying, Master, we Mk. 15. 40.
would that thou shouldest do for us whatsoever we shall
ask of thee. And he said unto them, What would ye
20 that I should do for you? And they said unto him,
Grant unto us that we may sit, one on thy right hand, Mt. 19. 28.
and one on thy left hand in thy glory. But Jesus an- **120**
swered and said unto them, Ye know not what ye ask.
Are ye able to drink the cup that I am about to drink? Mt. 26. 39.
25 or to be baptized with the baptism that I am baptized Lk. 12. 50.
with? And they said unto him, We are able. And
Jesus said unto them, The cup indeed that I drink ye

121. S. Mark x. 32—45; S. Matthew xx. 17—28;
S. Luke xviii. 31—34.

Acts 12. 2. shall drink; and with the baptism that I am baptized
Rev. 1. 9. withal shall ye be baptized: but to sit on my right hand
and on my left hand is not mine to give: but it is for 30
them for whom it hath been prepared of my Father.
And when the ten heard it, they began to be moved
with indignation concerning the two brethren, James
and John. But Jesus called them unto him, and saith
unto them, Ye know that they which are accounted to 35
rule over the Gentiles lord it over them; and their great

1 Pet. 5. 3. ones exercise authority over them. But it is not so
Mt. 18. 1... among you: but whosoever would become great among
75. 145 you shall be your minister: and whosoever would be
first among you, shall be servant of all. For verily the 40

Phil. 2. 7. Son of man came not to be ministered unto, but to
minister, and to give his life a ransom for many.

122. *Two Blind Men at Jericho. Zacchæus.*

AND it came to pass, as he drew nigh unto Jericho, a
certain blind man sat by the way side begging: and hearing a multitude going by, he enquired what this meant.
And they told him that Jesus of Nazareth passeth by.

And he entered and was passing through Jericho. 5
And behold, a man called by name Zacchæus; and he
was a chief publican, and he was rich. And he sought
to see Jesus who he was; and could not for the crowd,
because he was little of stature. And he ran on before,
and climbed up into a sycomore tree to see him: for he 10
was to pass that way. And when Jesus came to the
place, he looked up, and said unto him, Zacchæus, make

Lk. 4. 43; haste, and come down; for to-day I must abide at thy
— 13. 33. house. And he made haste, and came down, and received him joyfully. And when they saw it, they all 15

Lk. 5. 30; murmured, saying, He is gone in to lodge with a man
— 15. 4. that is a sinner. And Zacchæus stood, and said unto
110 the Lord, Behold, Lord, the half of my goods I give to

Lk. 3. 13. the poor; and if I have wrongfully exacted aught of any
Ex. 22. 1, 4. man, I restore fourfold. And Jesus said unto him, To- 20
day is salvation come to this house, forasmuch as he also

Lk. 13. 16; is a son of Abraham. For the Son of man came to seek
— 15. 4, 7. and to save that which was lost.

<hr>

122. S. Luke xviii. 35—xix. 10; S. Mark x. 46—52;
S. Matthew xx. 29—34.

And as he went out from Jericho with his disciples
25 and a great multitude, the son of Timæus, Bartimæus, a
blind beggar, was sitting *with another* by the way side.
And when he heard that it was Jesus of Nazareth, he
began to cry out and say, Jesus, thou son of David, have Mt. 15. 22.
mercy on me. And many of them that went before re-
30 buked him that he should hold his peace: but he cried
out the more a great deal, Thou son of David have
mercy on me. And Jesus stood still, and said, Call ye
him. And they call the blind man, saying unto him,
Be of good cheer: rise, he calleth thee. And he casting
35 away his garment, sprang up and came to Jesus. And,
when he was come near, Jesus answered him and said,
What wilt thou that I should do unto thee? And the
blind man said unto him, Rabboni, that I may receive Jn. 20. 16.
my sight. And Jesus said unto him, Go thy way, receive
40 thy sight: thy faith hath made thee whole. And being Mk. 5. 34.
moved with compassion, he touched their eyes; and im- Mk. 7. 53.
mediately they received their sight, and followed him in Lk. 22. 51.
the way, glorifying God: and all the people when they
saw it, gave praise unto God.

123. *Parable of the Pounds.*

AND as they heard these things, he added and spake
a parable, because he was nigh to Jerusalem, and because
they supposed that the kingdom of God was immedi- Acts 1. 6.
ately to appear. He said therefore, A certain nobleman
5 went into a far country, to receive for himself a kingdom,
and to return. And he called ten servants of his, and Mt. 25. 14..
gave them ten pounds, and said unto them, Trade ye   **139**
herewith till I come. But his citizens hated him, and
sent an ambassage after him, saying, We will not that Jn. 1. 11.
10 this man reign over us. And it came to pass, when he
was come back again, having received the kingdom, that
he commanded these servants, unto whom he had given
the money, to be called to him, that he might know what
they had gained by trading. And the first came before
15 him, saying, Lord, thy pound hath made ten pounds
more. And he said unto him, Well done, thou good
servant: because thou wast found faithful in a very little, Lk. 16.10..
have thou authority over ten cities. And the second

139   came, saying, Thy pound, Lord, hath made five pounds.
And he said unto him also, Be thou also over five cities. 20
And another came, saying, Lord, behold, here is thy
pound, which I kept laid up in a napkin: for I feared
thee, because thou art an austere man: thou takest up
that thou layest not down, and reapest that thou didst
Job 15. 6.   not sow.   He saith unto him, Out of thine own mouth 25
Mt. 12. 37.   will I judge thee, thou wicked servant.   Thou knewest
that I am an austere man, taking up that I laid not
down, and reaping that I did not sow; then wherefore
gavest thou not my money into the bank, and I at my
coming should have required it with interest?   And he 30
said unto them that stood by, Take away from him the
pound, and give it unto him that hath the ten pounds.
And they said unto him, Lord, he hath ten pounds.   I
Mt. 13. 12.   say unto you, that unto every one that hath shall be
49   given; but from him that hath not, even that which he 35
hath shall be taken away from him.   Howbeit these
Mt. 21. 41;   mine enemies, which would not that I should reign over
— 22. 7.   them, bring hither, and slay them before me.
129. 130   And when he had thus spoken, he went on before,
going up to Jerusalem.   40

124.   *Passover at hand.   Conspiracy to kill Jesus and Lazarus.*

Now the passover of the Jews was at hand: and
many went up to Jerusalem out of the country before
Lev. 7. 21.   the passover, to purify themselves.   They sought there-
Jn. 18. 28.   fore for Jesus, and spake one with another, as they stood
Act. 21. 24.   in the temple, What think ye?   That he will not come 5
Jn. 7. 11.   to the feast?   Now the chief priests and the Pharisees
had given commandment, that, if any man knew where
he was, he should shew it, that they might take him.
Jesus therefore six days before the passover came to
Jn. 11. 1.   Bethany, where Lazarus was, whom Jesus raised from 10
83   the dead.   So they made him a supper there, in the
Lk. 10. 38.   house of Simon the leper: and Martha served; but
90   Lazarus was one of them that sat at meat with him.
The common people therefore of the Jews learned
that he was there: and they came, not for Jesus' sake 15
only, but that they might see Lazarus also, whom he had

---

124. S. John xi. 55—xii. 2 and xii. 9—11.

raised from the dead. But the chief priests took counsel
that they might put Lazarus also to death; because that Lk. 16. 31.
by reason of him many of the Jews went away, and be-
20 lieved on Jesus.

125. *Mary anoints Jesus. Judas plans to betray Him.*

MARY therefore, having an alabaster cruse of spike- Lk. 7. 37.
nard, exceeding precious, came unto him and brake the 47
cruse, and poured it upon his head, as he sat at meat,
and she anointed the feet of Jesus, and wiped his feet
5 with her hair: and the house was filled with the odour of
the ointment. But Judas Iscariot, one of his disciples,
which should betray him, saith, To what purpose hath
this waste of the ointment been made? Why was not
this ointment sold for three hundred pence, and given to
10 the poor? Now this he said, not because he cared for Jn. 6. 70.
the poor; but because he was a thief, and having the bag, Jn. 13. 29.
took away what was put therein. And they murmured
against her. But Jesus perceiving it, said, Let her alone;
why trouble ye her? Suffer her to keep it against the
15 day of my burying. She hath wrought a good work on
me. For the poor ye have always with you, and when- Deu.15.11.
soever ye will ye can do them good: but me ye have
not always. She hath done what she could: she hath
anointed my body aforehand for the burying. And
20 verily I say unto you, Wheresoever this gospel shall be
preached throughout the whole world, that also which
this woman hath done shall be spoken of for a memorial
of her.
Then Satan entered into Judas Iscariot, him that was
25 of the number of the twelve, and he went away and communed with the chief priests and captains, and said,
What are ye willing to give me, and I will deliver him Gen.37.28.
unto you? And they were glad, and covenanted to give
him money. And he consented. And they weighed to
30 him thirty pieces of silver. And from that time he sought Zec. 11. 12.
opportunity to deliver him unto them in the absence of Ex. 21. 32.
the multitude.

125. S. John xii. 3—8; S. Mark xiv. 3 —11; S. Matthew xxvi. 6—16;
S. Luke xxii. 3—6.

126. *Jesus entereth Jerusalem as King.*

AND it came to pass on the morrow when they drew
nigh unto Jerusalem, and came unto Bethphage and
Zec. 14. 4. Bethany at the mount that is called the Mount of Olives,
then sent Jesus two of his disciples, saying unto them, Go
Mk. 14. 13. your way into the village that is over against you : and 5
144 straightway as ye enter in ye shall find an ass tied, and a
Num. 19. 2. colt with her, whereon no man ever yet sat : loose them,
Deu. 21. 3. and bring them unto me. And if any one ask you, Why
1 Sa. 6. 7. do ye loose them? thus shall ye say, The Lord hath need
of them; and straightway he will send them back hither. 10
Now this is come to pass that it might be fulfilled which
was spoken by the prophet, saying,
Is. 62. 11.   Tell ye the daughter of Zion,
Zec. 9. 9.   Behold thy king cometh unto thee,
                    Meek, and riding upon an ass,   15
                    And upon a colt the foal of an ass.
And they that were sent went away, and did even as
Jesus appointed them, and found a colt tied at the door
without in the open street; and they loose him. And
as they were loosing the colt, the owners thereof said 20
unto them, What do ye, loosing the colt? And they
said, The Lord hath need of him : and they let them go.
And they brought the ass and the colt unto Jesus, and
they threw their garments upon the colt, and set Jesus
1 Ki. 9. 13. thereon. And the most part of the multitude spread 25
their garments in the way; and others cut branches from
the trees and spread them in the way. And a great
multitude that had come to the feast, when they heard
1 Macc. that Jesus was coming to Jerusalem, took the branches
13. 51. of the palm trees, and went forth to meet him. And as 30
Lev. 23. 40. he was now drawing nigh, even at the descent of the
Rev. 7. 9. mount of Olives, the whole multitude of the disciples,
both they which went before and they that followed,
began to rejoice and praise God with a loud voice for
all the mighty works which they had seen; and they cried 35
Ps. 118. 25. saying, Hosanna to the son of David : Blessed is he that
cometh in the name of the Lord, even the King of Israel.
Blessed is the kingdom that cometh, the kingdom of our

126. S. Matthew xxi. 1—11; S. Mark xi. 1—11;
S. Luke xix. 29—44; S. John xii. 12—19.

father David : peace in heaven, and glory in the highest. Lk. 2. 14.
40 Hosanna in the highest. And some of the Pharisees
from the multitude said unto him, Master, rebuke thy
disciples. And he answered and said, I tell you that,
if these shall hold their peace, the stones will cry out. Hab. 2. 11.
And when he drew nigh, he saw the city and wept Jn. 11. 35.
45 over it, saying, If thou hadst known in this day, even
thou, the things which belong unto peace ! but now they
are hid from thine eyes. For the days shall come upon
thee, when thine enemies shall cast up a bank about Is. 29. 3.
thee, and compass thee round, and keep thee in on Deu. 28. 52.
50 every side, and shall dash thee to the ground, and thy Ps. 137. 7..
children within thee ; and they shall not leave in thee
one stone upon another ; because thou knewest not the
time of thy visitation. Lk. 1. 68.
And when he was come into Jerusalem, all the city
55 was stirred, saying, Who is this ? And the multitude
said, This is the prophet, Jesus, from Nazareth of Galilee.
These things understood not his disciples at the Jn. 2. 22;
first : but when Jesus was glorified, then remembered — 7. 39.
60 they that these things were written of him, and that they
had done these things unto him. The multitude therefore that was with him when he called Lazarus out of Jn. 11. 43.
the tomb, and raised him from the dead, bare witness. **83**
For this cause also the multitude went and met him, for
65 that they heard that he had done this sign. The Pharisees therefore said among themselves, Behold how ye
prevail nothing : lo, the world is gone after him.
And he entered into Jerusalem, into the temple; and Lk. 2. 59.
when he had looked round about upon all things, it being
70 now eventide, he went out into Bethany with the twelve.

127. *The Barren Fig-tree cursed. The Temple cleansed.*

AND on the morrow, when they were come out from
Bethany, as he returned to the city in the morning, he
hungered. And seeing a fig tree afar off by the wayside
having leaves, he came to it, if haply he might find any-
5 thing thereon ; and when he came to it he found nothing Lk. 13. 7.
thereon but leaves only ; for it was not the season of figs. **101**

---

127. S. Mark xi. 12—25 ; S. Matthew xxi. 12—22 ;
S. Luke xix. 45—48.

Lk. 3. 9.   And he answered and said unto it, No man eat fruit
from thee henceforward for ever.   And his disciples
heard it.   And immediately the fig tree withered away.

Jn. 2. 13...   And they come to Jerusalem, and Jesus entered into 10
21   the temple of God, and began to cast out all them that
De. 14.24..   sold and them that bought in the temple, and overthrew
the tables of the money changers, and the seats of them
that sold the doves; and he would not suffer that any man
should carry a vessel through the temple.   And he 15
taught, and said unto them, Is it not written, My house

Is. 56. 7.   shall be called a house of prayer for all the nations?   But

Jer. 7. 11.   ye have made it a den of robbers.   And the chief priests
and the scribes, and the principal men of the people
heard it, and sought how they might destroy him: for 20
they feared him, for all the multitude were astonished at
his teaching.   And they could not find what they might
do, for all the people hung upon him, listening.

And the blind and the lame came to him in the
temple: and he healed them.   But when the chief priests 25
and the scribes saw the wonderful things that he did,
and the children that were crying in the temple and

Ps. 118.26.   saying, Hosanna to the son of David; they were moved
with indignation, and said unto him, Hearest thou what
these are saying?   And Jesus saith unto them, Yea: 30

Ps. 8. 2.   did ye never read, Out of the mouth of babes and
Gr.   sucklings thou hast perfected praise?   And he left them.
And every evening he went forth out of the city to
Bethany and lodged there.   And he was teaching daily
in the temple.   35

And as they passed by in the morning, they saw the
fig tree withered away from the roots.   And Peter calling
to remembrance saith unto him, Rabbi, behold, the fig
tree which thou cursedst is withered away.   And Jesus
answering saith unto them, Have faith in God.   Verily I 40

1 Co. 13. 2.   say unto you, Whosoever shall say unto this mountain,
Be thou taken up and cast into the sea; and shall not
doubt in his heart, but shall believe that what he saith

1 Jn. 5. 15.   cometh to pass; he shall have it.   Therefore I say unto
you, All things whatsoever ye pray and ask for, believe 45
that ye have received them, and ye shall have them.

Mt. 6. 14..   And whensoever ye stand praying, forgive, if ye have
43*. 76   aught against any one; that your Father also which is in
heaven may forgive you your trespasses.

128. *Authority questioned. The Two Sons.*

AND they come again to Jerusalem. And it came to
pass on one of the days, as he was walking in the
temple and teaching the people and preaching the
gospel, there came upon him the chief priests and the
5 scribes with the elders; and they spake, saying unto him,
Tell us: By what authority doest thou these things? or Acts 4. 7.
who is he that gave thee this authority to do these things?
And Jesus answered and said unto them, I also will ask
you one question, which if ye tell me, I likewise will tell
10 you by what authority I do these things. The baptism
of John, whence was it? from heaven or from men?
And they reasoned with themselves, saying, If we shall
say, From heaven; he will say unto us, Why then did ye
not believe him? But if we shall say, From men;
15 all the people will stone us: for they be persuaded that Lk. 7. 29.
John was a prophet. And they answered Jesus, and Mt. 14. 5.
said, That they knew not whence it was. And Jesus said
unto them, Neither tell I you by what authority I do
these things.
20   But what think ye? A man had two sons; and he
came to the first, and said, Son, go work to-day in the
vineyard. And he answered and said, I will not: but
afterward he repented himself, and went. And he came
to the second, and said likewise. And he answered and
25 said, I go, sir: and went not. Whether of the twain did
the will of his father? They say, The first. Jesus saith
unto them, Verily I say unto you, that the publicans and Lk. 7. 29..
the harlots go into the kingdom of God before you.   46
For John came unto you in the way of righteousness,
30 and ye believed him not: but the publicans and the
harlots believed him: and ye, when ye saw it, did not
even repent yourselves afterward, that ye might believe
him.

129. *The Wicked Husbandmen.*

HEAR another parable. There was a man that was a
householder, which planted a vineyard, and set a hedge Is. 5. 1...

---

128. S. Mark xi. 27—33; S. Luke xx. 1—8; S. Matthew xxi. 23—32.
    129. S. Matthew xxi. 33—46; S. Mark xii. 1—12;
        S. Luke xx. 9—19.

Jer. 2. 21. about it, and digged a pit for the winepress in it, and
Ps. 80. 8 .. built a tower, and let it out to husbandmen, and went
Can. 8. 11· into another country.   And when the season of the fruits 5
drew near, he sent unto the husbandmen a servant, that
Lk. 16. 5... he might receive of the husbandmen of the fruits of the
vineyard.   And they took him, and beat him, and sent
him away empty.   And again he sent unto them another
servant ; and him also they beat, and handled him shame- 10
fully, wounding him in the head, and sent him away
empty.   And he sent yet a third : and him also they
wounded and cast him forth : and many others ; beating
Acts 7. 52. some, and killing some.   And the lord of the vineyard
He. 11. 37. said, What shall I do ?   I will send my beloved son : it 15
may be they will reverence him.   But when the husband-
men saw him, they reasoned one with another, saying,
Jn. 11. 48... This is the heir: come, let us kill him, and the inheritance
He. 13. 12. shall be ours.   And they took him and cast him forth
out of the vineyard, and killed him.   When therefore 20
the lord of the vineyard shall come, what will he do unto
those husbandmen ?   They say unto him, He will
miserably destroy those miserable men, and will let out
the vineyard unto other husbandmen, which shall render
him the fruits in their seasons.   And when they heard it, 25
they said, God forbid.   But he looked upon them and
said, What then is this that is written,
Ps. 118. 22.   The stone which the builders rejected,
Acts 4. 11.   The same was made the head of the corner:
                   This was from the Lord,   30
                   And it is marvellous in our eyes?
Is. 8. 14... Everyone that falleth on that stone shall be broken
Dan. 2. 35; in pieces ; but on whomsoever it shall fall, it will scatter
— 44.   him as dust.   Therefore I say unto you, the kingdom of
1 Pet. 2. 7.. heaven shall be taken from you, and shall be given to a 35
Acts 28. 28. nation bringing forth the fruits thereof.
            And when the scribes and the chief priests and the
            Pharisees heard his parables, they perceived that he
            spake of them.   And they sought to lay hands on him in
            that very hour ; and they feared the people, because they 40
            took him for a prophet.   And they left him and went
            away.

130. *The King's Marriage Feast.*

AND Jesus answered and spake again in parables Lk.14.15..
unto them, saying, The kingdom of heaven is likened **108**
unto a certain king, which made a marriage feast for his Rev. 19. 9.
son, and sent forth his servants to call them that were Est. 6. 14.
5 bidden to the marriage feast : and they would not come.
Again he sent forth other servants, saying, Tell them that
are bidden, Behold, I have made ready my dinner : my Pro. 9. 2.
oxen and my fatlings are killed, and all things are ready :
come to the marriage feast. But they made light of it,
10 and went their ways, one to his own farm, another to his
merchandise : and the rest laid hold on his servants, and
entreated them shamefully, and killed them. But the
king was wroth ; and he sent his armies, and destroyed De.28.49..
those murderers, and burned their city. Then saith he Dan. 9. 26.
15 to his servants, The wedding is ready, but they that were
bidden were not worthy. Go ye therefore unto the Acts 13.46.
partings of the highways, and as many as ye shall find,
bid to the marriage feast. And those servants went out
into the highways, and gathered together all as many as
20 they found, both bad and good : and the wedding was Mt. 13. 47.
filled with guests. But when the king came in to behold
the guests, he saw there a man which had not on a wedding- Zeph. 1. 8.
garment : and he saith unto him, Friend, how camest Gal. 3. 27.
thou in hither not having a wedding-garment? And he Rev. 19. 8.
25 was speechless. Then the king said to the servants,
Bind him hand and foot, and cast him out into the
outer darkness ; there shall be the weeping and gnashing
of teeth. For many are called, but few chosen.

131. *Question of Tribute to Cæsar.*

THEN went the Pharisees and took counsel how they
might ensnare him in his talk. And they watched him,
and sent forth spies, certain of their own disciples and of
the Herodians, which feigned themselves to be righteous, Mk. 8. 15.
5 that they might take hold of his speech, so as to deliver
him up to the rule and authority of the governor. And
when they were come, they say unto him, Master, we

---

130. S. Matthew xxii. 1—14.
131. S. Mark xii. 13—17 ; S. Luke xx. 20—26 ;
S. Matthew xxii. 15—22.

know that thou art true, and sayest and teachest rightly, and carest not for any one : for thou regardest not the
Acts 10.34. person of men, but of a truth teachest the way of God. 10 Tell us therefore, what thinkest thou ?   Is it lawful for us to give tribute unto Cæsar, or not ?   Shall we give, or shall we not give ?   But Jesus perceived their wickedness, and said, Why tempt ye me, ye hypocrites ?   Shew me the tribute-money, that I may see it.   And they brought 15 unto him a penny.   And he saith unto them, Whose is this image and superscription ?   They say unto him, Cæsar's.   And Jesus said unto them, Then render unto
Rom. 13. 7. Cæsar the things that are Cæsar's, and unto God the things that are God's.   And when they heard it, they 20 were not able to take hold of the saying before the people : and they marvelled greatly at his answer, and held their peace : and they left him and went their way.

132.   *Question of the Resurrection.*

AND on that day there came unto him certain of the
Acts 23. 8. Sadducees, they which say that there is no resurrection ; and they asked him, saying, Master, Moses wrote unto us,
Deu. 25. 5. If a man die and leave a wife behind him and leave no
Gen. 38. 8. child, that his brother should marry his wife and raise up 5 seed unto his brother.   Now there were with us seven brethren : and the first took a wife, and died childless, and the second took her, and dying, left no seed behind him ; and the third took her, and likewise the seven also left no children ; and died.   Last of all the woman also 10 died.   In the resurrection therefore whose wife shall she be of the seven ? for they all had her to wife.   Jesus said unto them, Is it not for this cause that ye err, that ye know not the scriptures, nor the power of God ?   The sons of this world marry and are given in marriage : but 15 they that are accounted worthy to attain to that world,
1 Co. 7. 29. and the resurrection from the dead, neither marry nor are given in marriage: for neither can they die any more :
1 Jn. 3. 2. for they are equal unto the angels ; and are sons of God, being sons of the resurrection.   But as touching the dead, 20 that they are raised; have ye not read in the book of Moses, in the place concerning the Bush, how God spake

---

132. S. Luke xx. 27—40 ; S. Mark xii. 18—27 ;
S. Matthew xxii. 23—33.

unto him, saying, I am the God of Abraham and the Ex. 3. 6.
God of Isaac and the God of Jacob? Now he is not the He. 11. 16.
25 God of the dead, but of the living: for all live unto him. Ro. 14. 8..
Ye do greatly err. And certain of the scribes answering
said, Master, thou hast well said. For they durst not
any more ask him any question. And when the multitudes
heard it they were astonished at his teaching.

133. *Question of the Great Commandment.*

BUT the Pharisees, when they heard that he had put
the Sadducees to silence, gathered themselves together.
And one of them, a scribe, asked him a question, tempting him, Master, what commandment is first of all in the
5 law? Jesus answered, The first is, Hear, O Israel, the Deu. 6. 4...
Lord our God, the Lord is one : and thou shalt love the Mt. 4. 10.
Lord thy God with all thy heart, and with all thy soul, Lk. 10. 26..
and with all thy mind, and with all thy strength. This **89**
is the first and great commandment. And the second
10 like unto it is this : Thou shalt love thy neighbour as Lev. 19. 18.
thyself. There is none other commandment greater than Ro. 13. 8..
these. On these two commandments hangeth the whole
law and the prophets. And the scribe said unto him,
Of a truth, Master, thou hast well said that he is one;
15 and there is none other but he : and to love him with all Deu. 4. 35.
the heart, and with all the understanding, and with all
the strength, and to love his neighbour as himself, is
much more than all whole burnt offerings and sacrifices. 1 Sa. 15. 22.
And when Jesus saw that he answered discreetly, he said
20 unto him, Thou art not far from the kingdom of God.
And no man after that durst ask him any question.

134. *Christ's question of David's Son.*

Now while the Pharisees were gathered together,
Jesus asked them a question, as he taught in the temple,
saying, What think ye of the Christ? Whose son is he?
They say unto him, The son of David. He saith unto Ps. 132. 11.
5 them, How then doth David himself in the Holy Spirit
call him Lord, saying in the book of Psalms,
The Lord said unto my Lord, Ps. 110. 1.

---

133. S. Mark xii. 28—34; S. Matthew xxii. 34—40.
134. S. Matthew xxii. 41—46; S. Mark xii. 35—37;
S. Luke xx. 41—44.

Acts 2. 34.   Sit thou on my right hand,
Heb. 1. 3.   Till I make thine enemies the footstool of thy feet.
Eph. 1. 20. If David himself then calleth him Lord, how is he 10
Ro. 1. 3... his son? And no man was able to answer him a word,
neither durst any man from that day forth ask him any
Lk. 4. 22. more questions. And the common people heard him
gladly.

135. *The Scribes and Pharisees condemned.*

THEN spake Jesus in his teaching to the multitudes
and to his disciples, in the hearing of all the people,
Mal. 2. 7.. saying, The scribes and the Pharisees sit on Moses' seat:
all things therefore whatsoever they bid you, these do
and observe: but do not ye after their works; for they 5
Lk. 11. 46. say, and do not. Yea, they bind heavy burdens and
97   grievous to be borne, and lay them on men's shoulders;
Acts 15.10. but they themselves will not move them with their finger.
Mt. 6. 1. But all their works they do for to be seen of men: for
Nu.15.38.. they make broad their phylacteries, and enlarge the 10
Deu.22.12. borders of their garments, and desire to walk in long
Lk. 11. 43. robes, and love the chief places at feasts, and the chief
seats in the synagogues, and the salutations in the market-
places, and to be called of men, Rabbi. But be not ye
Jas. 3. 1. called Rabbi: for one is your teacher, and all ye are 15
brethren. And call no man your father on the earth:
Is. 63. 16. for one is your Father, which is in heaven. Neither be
ye called masters: for one is your master, even the
Christ. But he that is greatest among you shall be your
Lk. 14. 11. servant. And whosoever shall exalt himself shall be 20
107   humbled; and whosoever shall humble himself shall be
Jas.4.6,10. exalted.
2 Ki. 4. 1. They which devour widows' houses, and for a pretence
Mt. 6. 5. make long prayers: these shall receive greater condem-
nation.   25
But woe unto you, scribes and Pharisees, hypocrites!
Lk. 11. 52. because ye shut the kingdom of heaven against men:
for ye enter not in yourselves, neither suffer ye them that
are entering in to enter.
Woe unto you, scribes and Pharisees, hypocrites! for 30
ye compass sea and land to make one proselyte; and

when he is become so, ye make him twofold more a son of hell than yourselves.

Woe unto you, ye blind guides, which say, Whosoever
35 shall swear by the temple, it is nothing; but whosoever Mt. 5. 34.
shall swear by the gold of the temple, he is a debtor.
Ye fools and blind: for whether is greater, the gold, or
the temple that hath sanctified the gold? And, Whosoever shall swear by the altar, it is nothing; but whoso-
40 ever shall swear by the gift that is upon it, he is a debtor. Mt. 5. 23.
Ye blind: for whether is greater, the gift, or the altar
that sanctifieth the gift? He therefore that sweareth Ex. 29. 37.
by the altar, sweareth by it, and by all things thereon.
And he that sweareth by the temple, sweareth by it, and
45 by him that dwelleth therein. And he that sweareth by 1 Ki. 8. 13.
the heaven, sweareth by the throne of God, and by him
that sitteth thereon.   Rev. 4. 2..

Woe unto you, scribes and Pharisees, hypocrites! for
ye tithe mint and anise and cummin, and have left undone Lk. 18. 12.
50 the weightier matters of the law, judgement, and mercy, Lk. 11. 42.
and faith: but these ye ought to have done, and not to   97
have left the other undone. Ye blind guides, which
strain out the gnat, and swallow the camel.

Woe unto you, scribes and Pharisees, hypocrites! Lk. 11. 39.
55 for ye cleanse the outside of the cup and of the platter,
but within they are full from extortion and excess. Thou
blind Pharisee, cleanse first the inside of the cup and of Is. 1. 16.
the platter, that the outside thereof may become clean Eze. 36. 25.
also.
60   Woe unto you, scribes and Pharisees, hypocrites! for
ye are like unto whited sepulchres, which outwardly Acts 23. 3.
appear beautiful, but inwardly are full of dead men's Lk. 11. 44.
bones, and of all uncleanness. Even so ye also outwardly appear righteous unto men, but inwardly ye are
65 full of hypocrisy and iniquity.

Woe unto you, scribes and Pharisees, hypocrites! for
ye build the sepulchres of the prophets, and garnish the Lk. 11. 47..
tombs of the righteous, and say, If we had been in the
days of our fathers, we should not have been partakers
70 with them in the blood of the prophets. Wherefore ye
witness to yourselves, that ye are sons of them that slew
the prophets. Fill ye up then the measure of your
fathers. Ye serpents, ye offspring of vipers, how shall Mt. 3. 7.
ye escape the judgement of hell? Therefore, behold, Gen. 3. 15.

Acts 7. 59; I send unto you prophets, and wise men, and scribes : 75
— 12. 2. some of them shall ye kill and crucify; and some of
Acts 5. 40. them shall ye scourge in your synagogues, and persecute
    from city to city : that upon you may come all the
Rev.18.24. righteous blood shed on the earth, from the blood of
    Abel the righteous unto the blood of Zachariah son of 80
2Ch.24.22. Barachiah, whom ye slew between the sanctuary and the
    altar. Verily I say unto you, All these things shall come
Lk. 21. 20. upon this generation.
Lk. 13.34.   O Jerusalem, Jerusalem, which killeth the prophets,
  105 and stoneth them that are sent unto her! how often 85
Deu.32.11. would I have gathered thy children together, even as a
    hen gathereth her chickens under her wings, and ye
Jer. 22. 5. would not! Behold, your house is left unto you desolate.
— 12. 7. For I say unto you, Ye shall not see me henceforth, till
Ps.118.26. ye shall say, Blessed is he that cometh in the name of the 90
Ro. 11. 26. Lord.

136. *The Widow's Mite.*

2 Ki. 12. 9.   AND he sat down over against the treasury. And he
    looked up, and beheld how the multitude cast money
Nu. 7. 2. into the treasury : and many that were rich cast in much.
1 Sa. 9. 8. And he saw a certain poor widow casting in thither two
    mites, which make a farthing. And he called unto him 5
    his disciples, and said unto them, Of a truth I say unto
2 Co.8.12. you, this poor widow cast in more than all they which
    are casting into the treasury : for all these did of their
    superfluity cast in unto the gifts: but she of her want did
    cast in all that she had, even all her living.   10

137. *Of Christ's Second Coming.*

    AND Jesus went out from the temple, and was going
    on his way; and his disciples came to him to shew him
Jn. 2. 20. the buildings of the temple, and how it was adorned with
    goodly stones and offerings; and one saith unto him,
    Master, behold, what manner of stones, and what manner 5
    of buildings! And Jesus answered and said unto him,
1 Ki. 9. 7.. Seest thou these great buildings? Verily I say unto you,
Mic. 3. 12. as for these things which ye behold, the days will come, in

136. S. Mark xii. 41—44 ; S. Luke xxi. 1—4.
137. S. Matthew xxiv. 1—51 ; S. Mark xiii. 1—37 ;
S. Luke xxi. 5—36.

which there shall not be left here one stone upon another, Ps. 79. 1.
10 which shall not be thrown down.   Dan. 8. 11.

And as he sat on the mount of Olives over against
the temple, Peter and James and John and Andrew
asked him privately, saying, Master, tell us when shall
these things be? and what shall be the sign when these 1 Th. 5. 1..
15 things are all about to be accomplished, and of thy
coming, and of the end of the world?   And Jesus began
to say unto them, Take heed that no man lead you
astray.   For many shall come in my name, saying, I am Acts 21. 38.
the Christ, and, The time is at hand: and shall lead Jn. 5. 43.
20 many astray; go ye not after them.   And when ye shall
hear of wars and rumours of wars, see that ye be not
troubled: for these things must needs come to pass first,
but the end is not immediately.   For nation shall rise
against nation and kingdom against kingdom: and there Is. 19. 2.
25 shall be great earthquakes in divers places: there shall be
famines and pestilences; there shall be terrors and great
signs from heaven.   But all these things are the begin- Ro. 8. 22.
ning of travail.

But take ye heed to yourselves: for before all these Mt. 10. 17..
30 things they shall lay their hands upon you, and shall   **59**
persecute you, delivering you up unto tribulation, to
councils, to the synagogues and prisons; and in synagogues shall ye be beaten, and before governors and
kings shall ye stand for my name's sake.   It shall turn
35 unto you for a testimony.   And they shall kill you: and Jn. 16. 2.
ye shall be hated of all the nations for my name's sake. Acts 28. 22.
And then shall many stumble, and shall deliver up one 1 Co. 4. 13.
another and shall hate one another.   And many false
prophets shall arise and shall lead many astray.   And 2 Pet. 2. 1.
40 because iniquity shall be multiplied, the love of the
many shall wax cold.   But he that endureth to the end Ja. 1. 12.
the same shall be saved.   And this gospel of the kingdom Rev. 2. 3.
must first be preached in the whole world for a testimony Ro. 10. 18.
unto all the nations; and then shall the end come. Col. 1. 23.
45 And when they lead you to judgement, and deliver you Mt. 10. 19.
up, settle it in your hearts not to meditate beforehand or Lk. 12. 11..
to be anxious what ye shall speak: but whatsoever shall   **59. 98**
be given you in that hour, that speak ye: for it is not ye 1 Co. 2. 13.
that speak, but the Holy Ghost.   For I will give you a
50 mouth and wisdom, which all your adversaries shall not Acts 6. 10.
be able to withstand or to gainsay.   And brother shall

Mic. 7. 6. deliver up brother to death, and the father his child, and
children shall rise up against parents and shall cause
them to be put to death.   And not a hair of your head
Is. 26. 3.. shall perish.   In your patience ye shall win your souls.   55
But when ye see Jerusalem compassed with armies,
Dan. 9. 27; and the abomination of desolation, which was spoken of
— 11. 31; by Daniel the prophet, standing in the holy place, where
— 12. 11. he ought not (let him that readeth understand), then
know that her desolation is at hand.   Then let them 60
Heb. 11. 7. that are in Judæa flee unto the mountains ; and let them
that are in the midst of her depart out ; and let not them
that are in the country enter therein : let him that is on
Lk. 17. 31. the housetop not go down, nor enter in, to take anything
115 out of his house : and let him that is in the field not 65
return back to take his cloke.   For these are days of
Hos. 9. 7. vengeance, that all things which are written may be
fulfilled.   But woe unto them that are with child, and to
them that give suck in those days ! for there shall be
great distress upon the land, and wrath unto this people. 70
And they shall fall by the edge of the sword, and shall be
Zech. 12. 3. led captive into all the nations : and Jerusalem shall be
Gr. trodden down of the Gentiles, until the times of the
Is. 63. 18. Gentiles shall be fulfilled.   And pray ye that your flight
Dan. 8. 13.. be not in the winter, neither on a sabbath : for then 75
Dan. 12. 1. shall be great tribulation, such as hath not been from the
beginning of the creation which God created until now,
no, nor ever shall be.   And except the Lord had
shortened those days, no flesh would have been saved :
Is. 65. 8.. but for the elect's sake, whom he chose, those days shall 80
Lk. 17. 23.. be shortened.   And then if any man say unto you, Lo
here is the Christ ; or, Lo there ; believe it not : for there
Deu. 13. 1.. shall arise false Christs and false prophets, and shall shew
2 Th. 2. 9... great signs and wonders ; so as to lead astray, if possible,
even the elect.   But take ye heed : behold I have told 85
2 Pet. 3. 17. you all things beforehand.   If therefore they shall say
unto you, Behold, he is in the wilderness ; go not forth :
Behold, he is in the inner chambers ; believe it not.
Lk. 17. 24. For as the lightning cometh forth from the east, and is seen
even unto the west ; so shall be the coming of the Son of 90
Job 39. 30. man.   Wheresoever the carcase is, there will the eagles
be gathered together.
Ezek. 32. 7. But immediately, after the tribulation of those days
Joel 2. 31. the sun shall be darkened, and the moon shall not give

95 her light, and the stars shall be falling from heaven ; and Is. 13. 10.
upon the earth shall be distress of nations, in perplexity — 34. 4.
for the roaring of the sea and the billows ; men fainting
for fear, and for expectation of the things which are
coming upon the world : for the powers of the heavens
100 shall be shaken.   And then shall appear the sign of the Dan. 7. 13.
Son of man in heaven : and then shall all the tribes of Zec. 12. 12.
the earth mourn, and they shall see the Son of man
coming on the clouds of heaven with power and great Rev. 1. 7.
glory.   And then shall he send forth his angels with a 1Co.15.52.
105 great sound of a trumpet, and they shall gather together 1 Th. 4. 16.
his elect from the four winds, from the uttermost part of Deu. 30. 4.
the earth to the uttermost part of heaven.   But when
these things begin to come to pass, look up, and lift up
your heads ; because your redemption draweth nigh.
110   Now from the fig tree learn her parable : when her
branch is now become tender and putteth forth its leaves,
ye see it, and know of your own selves that the summer
is now nigh.   Even so ye also, when ye see all these
things coming to pass, know ye that he is nigh, even at Jas. 5. 9.
115 the doors.   Verily I say unto you, This generation shall Mt. 16. 28.
not pass away until all these things be accomplished.
Heaven and earth shall pass away : but my words shall Is. 51. 6.
not pass away.   But of that day or that hour knoweth no Acts 1. 7.
one, not even the angels of heaven, neither the Son, but
120 the Father only.   And as were the days of Noah, so 2 Pet. 2. 5.
shall be the coming of the Son of man.   For as in those
days which were before the flood they were eating and Gen. 6. 1...
drinking, marrying and giving in marriage, until the day
that Noah entered into the ark, and they knew not until Gen. 7. 7;
125 the flood came, and took them all away ; so shall be the   21...
coming of the Son of man.   Then shall two men be in
the field ; one is taken, and one is left: two women shall Lk. 17.34..
be grinding at the mill ; one is taken, and one is left.   **115**
Watch therefore : for ye know not on what day your
130 Lord cometh.   But know this, that if the master of the Lk.12.39..
house had known in what watch the thief was coming, he   **100**
would have watched, and would not have suffered his
house to be broken through.   Therefore be ye also
ready : for in an hour that ye think not the Son of man Rev. 3. 3.
135 cometh.   But take heed to yourselves, lest haply your
hearts be overcharged with surfeiting, and drunkenness, 1 Th. 5. 2..
and cares of this life, and that day come on you suddenly

Rev.16.15. as a snare: for so shall it come upon all them that dwell
Is. 24. 17. on the face of all the earth. But watch ye at every
season, making supplication, that ye may prevail to 140
escape all these things that shall come to pass, and to
Ro. 13. 11. stand before the Son of man. Watch and pray, for ye
know not when the time is. It is as when a man, so-
Mt. 25. 14. journing in another country, having left his house, and
139 given authority to his servants, to each one his work, 145
commanded also the porter to watch. Watch therefore:
for ye know not when the Lord of the house cometh,
Lk. 12. 38. whether at even, or at midnight, or at cockcrowing, or in
100 the morning; lest coming suddenly he find you sleeping.
And what I say unto you I say unto all, Watch. Who 150
Lk.12.42.. then is the faithful and wise servant, whom his lord hath
set over his household, to give them their food in due
season? Blessed is that servant, whom his lord when he
cometh shall find so doing. Verily I say unto you, that
Lk. 19. 17. he will set him over all that he hath. But if that evil 155
2 Pet. 3.4.. servant shall say in his heart, My lord tarrieth; and shall
begin to beat his fellow-servants, and shall eat and drink
with the drunken; the lord of that servant shall come in
a day when he expecteth not, and in an hour when he
knoweth not, and shall cut him asunder, and appoint his 160
portion with the hypocrites: there shall be the weeping
Mt. 8. 12. and gnashing of teeth.

138. *The Ten Virgins.*

THEN shall the kingdom of heaven be likened unto
2 Cor.11.2. ten virgins, which took their lamps, and went forth to
Eph.5.25.. meet the bridegroom. And five of them were foolish,
Rev. 21. 2. and five were wise. For the foolish, when they took
Lk. 12. 35. their lamps, took no oil with them: but the wise took 5
oil in their vessels with their lamps. Now while the
bridegroom tarried, they all slumbered and slept. But
at midnight there is a cry, Behold, the bridegroom!
Amos4.12. Come ye forth to meet him. Then all those virgins arose,
and trimmed their lamps. And the foolish said unto the 10
wise, Give us of your oil; for our lamps are going out.
But the wise answered, saying, Peradventure there will
Ps. 49. 7. not be enough for us and you: go ye rather to them that
Is. 55. 1. sell, and buy for yourselves. And while they went away

15 to buy, the bridegroom came; and they that were ready   Ps. 45. 14..
went in with him to the marriage feast : and the door was   Lk. 13. 25.
shut.   Afterward come also the other virgins, saying,   **104**
Lord, Lord, open to us.   But he answered and said,   He. 3. 18..
Verily I say unto you, I know you not.   Watch there-   Mt. 7. 22..
20 fore, for ye know not the day nor the hour.   Jn. 10. 14.

139.   *The Talents.*

FOR it is as when a man, going into another country,
called his own servants, and delivered unto them his   Lk. 19. 12..
goods.   And unto one he gave five talents, to another two,   **123**
to another one; to each according to his several ability;   Jas. 1. 17.
5 and he went on his journey.   Straightway he that   1 Co. 12. 4.
received the five talents went and traded with them, and
made other five talents.   In like manner he also that
received the two gained other two.   But he that received
the one went away and digged in the earth, and hid his
10 lord's money.   Now after a long time the lord of those
servants cometh, and maketh a reckoning with them.
And he that received the five talents came and brought
other five talents, saying, Lord, thou deliveredst unto me
five talents : lo, I have gained other five talents.   His   1 Th. 2. 19.
15 lord said unto him, Well done, good and faithful servant:
thou hast been faithful over a few things, I will set thee   Lk. 16. 10.
over many things : enter thou into the joy of thy lord.   **111**
And he also that received the two talents came and said,   2 Tim. 2. 12.
Lord, thou deliveredst unto me two talents : lo, I have   He. 12. 2.
20 gained other two talents.   His lord said unto him, Well
done, good and faithful servant ; thou hast been faithful
over a few things, I will set thee over many things :
enter thou into the joy of thy lord.   And he also that
had received the one talent came and said, Lord, I knew
25 thee that thou art a hard man, reaping where thou didst
not sow, and gathering where thou didst not scatter :
and I was afraid, and went away and hid thy talent in   Rev. 21. 8.
the earth : lo, thou hast thine own.   But his lord answered and said unto him, Thou wicked and slothful
30 servant, thou knewest that I reap where I sowed not,
and gather where I did not scatter ; thou oughtest therefore to have put my money to the bankers, and at my
coming I should have received back mine own with

139. S. Matthew xxv. 14—30.

interest. Take ye away therefore the talent from him,
and give it unto him that hath the ten talents.   For unto 35
Mt. 13. 12. every one that hath shall be given, and he shall have
50   abundance : but from him that hath not, even that
which he hath shall be taken away.   And cast ye out the
unprofitable servant into the outer darkness : there shall
Mt. 8. 12. be the weeping and gnashing of teeth.   40

140. *The Last Judgement.*

Re. 20. 11. . . BUT when the Son of man shall come in his glory,
Dan. 9. 10. . . and all the angels with him, then shall he sit on the
2 Co. 5. 10. throne of his glory : and before him shall be gathered all
the nations : and he shall separate them one from
Mt. 13. 49. another, as the shepherd separateth the sheep from the 5
goats : and he shall set the sheep on his right hand, but
the goats on the left.   Then shall the King say unto
1 Jn. 3. 1. them on his right hand, Come, ye blessed of my Father,
1 Co. 2. 9. . inherit the kingdom prepared for you from the foundation
Is. 58. 7. of the world : for I was an hungred, and ye gave me 10
Ezek. 18. 7. meat : I was thirsty, and ye gave me drink : I was a
Lk. 10. 37; stranger, and ye took me in ; naked, and ye clothed me :
Job 31. 17;
19; 32. I was sick, and ye visited me : I was in prison, and ye
came unto me.   Then shall the righteous answer him,
saying, Lord, when saw we thee an hungred, and fed 15
thee? or athirst, and gave thee drink?   And when saw
we thee a stranger, and took thee in? or naked, and
clothed thee?   And when saw we thee sick, or in prison,
and came unto thee?   And the King shall answer and
Heb. 2. 11. say unto them, Verily I say unto you, Inasmuch as ye 20
— 6. 10. did it unto one of these my brethren, even these least, ye
Pro. 19. 27. did it unto me.   Then shall he say also unto them on
Mt. 7. 23. the left hand, Depart from me, ye cursed, into the
Jn. 5. 37. eternal fire which is prepared for the devil and his
angels : for I was an hungred, and ye gave me no meat : 25
I was thirsty, and ye gave me no drink : I was a stranger,
and ye took me not in ; naked, and ye clothed me not ;
sick, and in prison, and ye visited me not.   Then shall
they also answer, saying, Lord, when saw we thee an
hungred, or athirst, or a stranger, or naked, or sick, or in 30
prison, and did not minister unto thee?   Then shall he
Acts 9. 4. answer them, saying, Verily I say unto you, Inasmuch

as ye did it not unto one of these least, ye did it not
unto me.   And these shall go away into eternal punish-   Dan. 12. 2.
35 ment: but the righteous into eternal life.   Jn. 5. 29.

141.   *Greeks come to Christ.   Voice from Heaven.*

AND every day he was teaching in the temple; and
every night he went out, and lodged in the mount that is
called the mount of Olives.   And all the people came   Zec. 11. 4.
early in the morning to him in the temple, to hear him.
5   Now there were certain Greeks among those that   1 Ki.8.41..
went up to worship at the feast: these therefore came to   Acts 17. 4.
Philip, which was of Bethsaida of Galilee, and asked him,
saying, Sir, we would see Jesus.   Philip cometh and
telleth Andrew: Andrew cometh, and Philip, and they
10 tell Jesus.   And Jesus answereth them, saying, The
hour is come, that the Son of man should be glorified.   Jn. 13. 31.
Verily, verily, I say unto you, Except a grain of wheat
fall into the earth and die, it abideth by itself alone; but   1Co.15.36..
if it die, it beareth much fruit.   He that loveth his life
15 loseth it; and he that hateth his life in this world shall   Mt. 10. 39.
keep it unto life eternal.   If any man serve me, let him   **59**
follow me; and where I am, there shall also my servant   1 Th.4. 17.
be: if any man serve me, him will the Father honour.
Now is my soul troubled; and what shall I say?   Father,   Ps. 42. 5;
20 save me from this hour.   But for this cause came I unto   — 6. 3.
this hour.   Father, glorify thy name.   There came therefore a voice out of heaven, saying, I have both glorified   Mt. 3. 17;
it, and will glorify it again.   The multitude therefore,   — 17. 5.
that stood by, and heard it, said that it had thundered: **16. 72**
25 others said, An angel hath spoken to him.   Jesus answered and said, This voice hath not come for my sake,
but for your sakes.   Now is the judgement of this world:
now shall the prince of this world be cast out.   And I,   Jn. 16. 11.
if I be lifted up from the earth, will draw all men unto   Jn. 3. 14;
30 myself.   But this he said, signifying by what manner of   — 8. 28.
death he should die.   The multitude therefore answered   **22. 79**
him, We have heard out of the law that the Christ   Ps. 110. 4.
abideth for ever: and how sayest thou, The Son of man
must be lifted up? who is this Son of man?   Jesus there-
35 fore said unto them, Yet a little while is the light among   Jn. 9. 5.
you.   Walk while ye have the light, that darkness over-   Jer. 13. 16.

141. S. Luke xxi. 37, 38; S. John xii. 20—36.

Eph. 5. 8. take you not : and he that walketh in the darkness
1 Jn. 2. 11. knoweth not whither he goeth. While ye have the
1 Th. 5. 5. light, believe on the light, that ye may become sons of
light.   40

142. *S. John on the unbelief of the Jews.   Of true Faith.*

THESE things spake Jesus, and he departed and hid
. himself from them.   But though he had done so many
signs before them, yet they believed not on him : that
the word of Isaiah the prophet might be fulfilled, which
he spake,   5

Is. 53. 1.   Lord, who hath believed our report?
Ro. 10. 16.   And to whom hath the arm of the Lord been revealed ?

For this cause they could not believe, for that Isaiah
said again,

Is. 6. 9...   He hath blinded their eyes, and he hardened their 10
heart ;

Lest they should see with their eyes, and perceive
with their heart,

And should turn,

And I should heal them.

Is. 6. 1... These things said Isaiah, because he saw his glory ;
Jn. 8. 48. and he spake of him.   Nevertheless even of the rulers 15
many believed on him ; but because of the Pharisees
Jn. 9. 22. they did not confess it, lest they should be put out of the
80 synagogue : for they loved the glory of men more than
Jn. 5. 44. the glory of God.
40
And Jesus cried and said, He that believeth on me, 20
believeth not on me, but on him that sent me.   And he
Jn. 14. 9. that beholdeth me beholdeth him that sent me.   I am
Jn. 3. 19. come a light into the world, that whosoever believeth on
15 me may not abide in the darkness.   And if any man hear
Jn. 3. 17; my sayings, and keep them not, I judge him not : for I 25
— 8. 15. came not to judge the world, but to save the world.   He
that rejecteth me, and receiveth not my sayings, hath
De. 18. 19. one that judgeth him : the word that I spake, the same
shall judge him in the last day.   For I spake not from
Jn. 5. 19. myself ; but the Father which sent me, he hath given 30
De. 18. 18. me a commandment, what I should say, and what I should
speak.   And I know that his commandment is life eternal :

the things therefore which I speak, even as the Father hath said unto me, so I speak.

143. *Christ declares His Death at hand. The Conspiracy.*

AND it came to pass when Jesus had finished all these words, he said unto his disciples, Ye know that after two days the passover cometh and the Son of man is delivered up to be crucified. Then were gathered
5 together the chief priests, and the scribes and the elders of the people, unto the court of the high priest who was called Caiaphas; and they took counsel together that Ps. 2. 2. they might take Jesus by subtlety, and kill him. But they said, Not during the feast lest haply a tumult arise
10 among the people; for they feared the people.

144. *Preparation for the Passover.*

AND on the first day of unleavened bread, when they Ex. 12. 6. sacrificed the passover, the disciples come to Jesus, and say unto him, Where wilt thou that we go and make ready that thou mayest eat the passover? And he
5 sendeth two of his disciples, Peter and John, saying, Behold, when ye are entered into the city, there shall Mt. 21. 2. meet you a man bearing a pitcher of water; follow him **126** into the house whereinto he goeth: and ye shall say unto the goodman of the house, The Master saith unto thee,
10 my time is at hand; where is my guest-chamber where I shall eat the passover with my disciples? And he will himself shew you a large upper room furnished and Acts 1. 13. ready, and there make ready for us. And the disciples went forth, and came into the city, and found as he had
15 said unto them: and they made ready the passover.

145. *Jesus' love. Precedence. The first cup.*

NOW before the feast of the Passover, Jesus knowing that his hour was come that he should depart out of this world unto the Father, having loved his own which were Eph. 5. 2. in the world, he loved them unto the end.

143. S. Matthew xxvi. 1—5; S. Mark xiv. 1, 2; S. Luke xxii. 1, 2.
144. S. Mark xiv. 12—16; S. Luke xxii. 7—13;
S. Matthew xxvi. 17—19.
145. S. John xiii. 1; S. Luke xxii. 14; 24—30; 15—18;
S. Mark xiv. 17; S. Matt. xxvi. 20.

And when it was evening he cometh with the twelve, 5
and he sat down and the apostles with him.

Mk. 9. 34.   And there arose also a contention among them, which
75   of them is accounted to be greatest.   And he said unto
Mt. 20. 25..   them, The kings of the Gentiles have lordship over them;
121   and they that have authority over them are called Bene- 10
1 Pet. 5. 3.   factors.   But ye shall not be so: but he that is the
greater among you, let him become as the younger;
and he that is chief, as he that doth serve.   For whether
Lk. 17. 8.   is greater, he that sitteth at meat, or he that serveth? is
Lk. 12. 37.   not he that sitteth at meat? but I am in the midst of you 15
as he that serveth.   But ye are they which have con-
Heb. 4. 15.   tinued with me in my temptations; and I appoint unto
you a kingdom, even as my Father appointed unto me,
Rev. 19. 9.   that ye may eat and drink at my table in my kingdom;
Mt. 19. 28.   and ye shall sit on thrones judging the twelve tribes of 20
120   Israel.

And he said unto them, With desire I have desired to
eat this passover with you before I suffer: for I say unto
1 Co. 5. 7..   you, I will not eat it, until it be fulfilled in the kingdom
of God.   And he received a cup, and when he had given 25
thanks, he said, Take this, and divide it among yourselves: for I say unto you, I will not drink from henceforth of the fruit of the vine, until the kingdom of God
shall come.

146.   *Jesus washes His Disciples' feet.*

Mt. 26. 14..   AND during supper, the devil having already put into
125   the heart of Judas Iscariot, Simon's son, to betray him,
Heb. 2. 8.   Jesus, knowing that the Father had given all things into
his hands, and that he came forth from God, and goeth
unto God, riseth from supper, and layeth aside his gar- 5
Lk. 12. 37.   ments; and he took a towel, and girded himself.   Then
100   he poureth water into the bason, and began to wash the
disciples' feet, and to wipe them with the towel wherewith he was girded.   So he cometh to Simon Peter.   He
saith unto him, Lord, dost thou wash my feet? Jesus 10
answered and said unto him, What I do thou knowest
not now; but thou shalt understand hereafter.   Peter
saith unto him, Thou shalt never wash my feet.   Jesus
Jn. 3. 5.   answered him, If I wash thee not, thou hast no part with
1 Co. 6. 11.

146. S. John xiii. 2—20.

15 me. Simon Peter saith unto him, Lord, not my feet only, but also my hands and my head. Jesus saith to him, He that is bathed needeth not save to wash his feet, 2 Pet. 1. 9. but is clean every whit: and ye are clean, but not all. Tit. 3. 5. For he knew him that should betray him; therefore said Jn. 6. 64. 20 he, Ye are not all clean.

So when he had washed their feet, and taken his garments, and sat down again, he said unto them, Know ye what I have done to you? Ye call me, Master, and, Lord: and ye say well; for so I am. If I then, the 25 Lord and the Master, have washed your feet, ye also Gal. 6. 2. ought to wash one another's feet. For I have given you 1 Pet. 5. 5. an example, that ye also should do as I have done to you. Verily, verily, I say unto you, A servant is not Mt. 10. 24. greater than his lord; neither one that is sent greater **59** 30 than he that sent him. If ye know these things, blessed Jas. 1. 25. are ye if ye do them. I speak not of you all: I know Jn. 6. 70... whom I have chosen: but that the scripture may be ful- **64** filled, He that eateth my bread lifted up his heel against Ps. 41. 9. me. From henceforth I tell you before it come to pass, 35 that, when it is come to pass, ye may believe that I am Jn. 14. 29. he. Verily, verily, I say unto you, He that receiveth **150** whomsoever I send receiveth me; and he that receiveth Mt. 10. 40. me receiveth him that sent me. **59**

147. *The Betrayal foretold. The Traitor leaves.*

WHEN Jesus had thus said he was troubled in spirit, Jn. 12. 27. and testified, and said, Verily, verily, I say unto you, that one of you shall betray me, even he that eateth with me. Ps. 41. 9. The disciples looked one on another, doubting of whom 5 he spake. And they began to be exceeding sorrowful, and to say unto him one by one, Is it I, Lord? And he answered and said, It is one of the twelve, he that dip- peth with me in the dish. For the Son of man indeed goeth even as it is written of him: but woe unto that Jn. 17. 12. 10 man through whom the Son of man is betrayed. Good Mt. 18. 7. were it for that man if he had not been born. And they began to question among themselves which of them it was that should do this thing. And Judas which betrayed him answered and said, Is it I, Rabbi? he saith unto

147. S. John xiii. 21—35; S. Matthew xxvi. 21—25;
S. Mark xiv. 18—21; S. Luke xxii. 21—23.

him, Thou hast said. There was at the table reclining
Jn. 20. 2; in Jesus' bosom one of his disciples, whom Jesus loved.
— 21. 7; Simon Peter therefore beckoneth to him, and saith unto
20. him, Tell us who it is of whom he speaketh. He leaning back, as he was, on Jesus' breast saith unto him, Lord, who is it? Jesus therefore answereth, He it is, for whom I shall dip the sop, and give it him. So when he had dipped the sop, he taketh and giveth it to Judas, the son of Simon Iscariot. And after the sop, then
Lk. 22. 3. entered Satan into him. Jesus therefore saith unto him, That thou doest, do quickly. Now no man at the table knew for what intent he spake this unto him. For some
Jn. 12. 6. thought, because Judas had the bag, that Jesus said unto him, Buy what things we have need of for the feast; or, that he should give something to the poor. He then having received the sop went out straightway: and it
1 Th. 5. 5.. was night.

Jn. 12. 23. When therefore he was gone out, Jesus saith, Now
1 Pet. 4. 11. is the Son of man glorified, and God is glorified in him;
Jn. 17. 1... and God shall glorify him in himself, and straightway
154 shall he glorify him. Little children, yet a little while
Jn. 7. 34; I am with you. Ye shall seek me: and as I said unto
— 8. 21. the Jews, Whither I go, ye cannot come; so now I say
Jn. 15. 12.. unto you. A new commandment I give unto you, that
151 ye love one another; even as I have loved you, that ye
1 Jn. 4. 21. also love one another. By this shall all men know that ye are my disciples, if ye have love one to another.

148. *Institution of the Lord's Supper.*

AND as they were eating, he took bread, and when he had given thanks, he brake it; and he gave to the
Jn. 6. 52... disciples, saying; Take ye, eat: this is my body which
64
1 Co. 10. 16. is given for you: this do in remembrance of me. And he took the cup in like manner after supper, and when he had given thanks, he gave to them, saying, Drink ye
Ex. 24. 8. all of it; for this cup is the new covenant in my blood,
Zec. 9. 11. even that which is poured out for you and for many unto remission of sins. This do, as oft as ye drink it, in remembrance of me. Verily I say unto you, I will no
Lk. 22. 18. more drink henceforth of this fruit of the vine, until the
145

148. S. Mark xiv. 22—25; S. Matthew xxvi. 26—29; S. Luke xxii. 19, 20; S. Paul, 1 Cor. xi. 23—25.

day when I drink it new with you in my Father's Acts 10.41.
kingdom.

149. *Peter warned. Danger foretold.*

And he said, Simon, Simon, behold Satan asked to Job 1. 12.
have you that he might sift you as wheat: but I made — 2. 6.
supplication for thee that thy faith fail not: and do thou,
when once thou hast turned again, stablish thy brethren.
5 Simon Peter saith unto him, Lord, whither goest
thou? Jesus answered, Whither I go, thou canst not
follow me now; but thou shalt follow me afterwards. Jn. 21. 18.
Peter saith unto him, Lord, why cannot I follow thee **183**
even now? With thee I am ready to go both to prison 2 Pet. 1. 14.
10 and to death. I will lay down my life for thee. Jesus
answereth, Wilt thou lay down thy life for me? Verily, Mt. 26. 34.
verily I say unto thee, Peter, the cock shall not crow this **155**
day until thou shalt thrice deny that thou knowest me.
And he said unto them, When I sent you forth with- Mt. 10. 9.
15 out purse, and wallet, and shoes, lacked ye any thing? **59**
And they said, Nothing. And he said unto them, But
now, he that hath a purse, let him take it, and likewise a
wallet: and he that hath none, let him sell his cloke,
and buy a sword. For I say unto you, that this which
20 is written must be fulfilled in me, And he was reckoned Is. 53. 12.
with transgressors: for that which concerneth me hath
fulfilment. And they said, Lord, behold, here are two
swords. And he said unto them, It is enough.

150. *Of Hope, Faith, Prayer. The Comforter.*

LET not your heart be troubled: ye believe in God,
believe also in me. In my Father's house are many
mansions; if it were not so, I would have told you; for 1 Ki. 8. 13.
I go to prepare a place for you. And if I go and pre- Nu. 10. 33.
5 pare a place for you, I come again, and will receive you Heb. 6. 20.
unto myself; that where I am, there ye may be also. Jn. 12. 26.
And whither I go, ye know the way. Thomas saith 1 Th. 4. 17.
unto him, Lord, we know not whither thou goest; how
know we the way? Jesus saith unto him, I am the way, Heb. 10. 20.
10 and the truth, and the life: no one cometh unto the Jn. 1. 17.
Father, but by me. If ye had known me, ye would have — 1. 4.
— 10. 9.

---

149. S. Luke xxii. 31—38; S. John xiii. 36—38.
150. S. John xiv. 1—31; S. Matthew xxvi. 30; S. Mark xiv. 26.

Jn. 8. 19. known my Father also : from henceforth ye know him, and have seen him. Philip saith unto him, Lord, shew us the Father, and it sufficeth us. Jesus saith unto him, Have I been so long time with you, and dost thou not 15

Col. i. 15. know me, Philip? he that hath seen me hath seen the

Heb. 1. 3. Father; how sayest thou, Shew us the Father? Believest thou not that I am in the Father, and the Father in me? the words that I say unto you I speak not from myself:

Jn. 10. 37.. but the Father abiding in me doeth his works. Believe 20

    82   me that I am in the Father, and the Father in me : or else believe me for the very works' sake. Verily, verily, I say unto you, He that believeth on me, the works that

Acts 2. 41.. I do shall he do also; and greater works than these

Mt. 21. 21. shall he do ; because I go unto the Father. And what- 25

Mt. 7. 7. soever ye shall ask in my name, that will I do, that the

Jn. 16. 23.. Father may be glorified in the Son. If ye shall ask me

  153   anything in my name, that will I do. If ye love me, ye

1 Jn. 5. 3. will keep my commandments. And I will pray the Father, and he shall give you another Comforter, that he 30

1 Jn. 5. 7. may be with you for ever, even the Spirit of truth: whom

1 Cor. 2. 14. the world cannot receive; for it beholdeth him not, neither knoweth him : ye know him ; for he abideth with

Mt. 28. 20. you, and shall be in you. I will not leave you desolate : I come unto you. Yet a little while, and the world 35 beholdeth me no more; but ye behold me: because

Rom. 5. 10. I live, ye shall live also. In that day ye shall know that

Gal. 2. 20. I am in my Father, and ye in me, and I in you. He that hath my commandments, and keepeth them, he it is

1 Jn. 2. 3.. that loveth me : and he that loveth me shall be loved of 40 my Father, and I will love him, and will manifest myself unto him. Judas (not Iscariot) saith unto him, Lord, what is come to pass that thou wilt manifest thyself unto

Jn. 7. 4. us, and not unto the world? Jesus answered and said unto him, If a man love me, he will keep my word : and 45

Rev. 3. 20. my Father will love him, and we will come unto him, and

1 Jn. 2. 24. make our abode with him. He that loveth me not keepeth not my words : and the word which ye hear is

Jn. 7. 16. not mine, but the Father's who sent me.

    These things have I spoken unto you, while yet 50 abiding with you. But the Comforter, even the Holy

Jn. 15. 26. Spirit, whom the Father will send in my name, he shall

Jn. 16. 13.. teach you all things, and bring to your remembrance all

  152   that I said unto you. Peace I leave with you ; my peace

55 I give unto you: not as the world giveth, give I unto Is. 26. 3.
you. Let not your heart be troubled, neither let it be Phil. 4. 7.
fearful. Ye heard how I said to you, I go away, and I
come unto you. If ye loved me, ye would have rejoiced,
because I go unto the Father: for the Father is greater Phil. 2. 6.
60 than I. And now I have told you before it come to Jn. 13. 19.
pass, that, when it is come to pass, ye may believe. I **146**
will no more speak much with you, for the prince of the Jn. 12. 31.
world cometh: and he hath nothing in me; but that the **141**
world may know that I love the Father, and as the
65 Father gave me commandment, even so I do. Arise, let Heb. 5. 8.
us go hence.

And when they had sung an hymn they went out.

151. *The Vine. Christ's Commandment. Comfort.*

I AM the true vine, and my Father is the husband- I Cor. 3. 9.
man. Every branch in me that beareth not fruit, he Mt. 7. 21.
taketh it away: and every branch that beareth fruit, he Mal. 3. 3.
cleanseth it, that it may bear more fruit. Already ye are
5 clean because of the word which I have spoken unto you. Jn. 13. 10.
Abide in me, and I in you. As the branch cannot bear
fruit of itself, except it abide in the vine; so neither can
ye, except ye abide in me. I am the vine, ye are the
branches: He that abideth in me, and I in him, the I Jn. 2. 6.
10 same beareth much fruit: for apart from me ye can do Eph. 2. 12.
nothing. If a man abide not in me, he is cast forth as Phil. 4. 13.
a branch, and is withered; and they gather them, and
cast them into the fire, and they are burned. If ye Mt. 7. 19.
abide in me, and my words abide in you, ask whatsoever
15 ye will, and it shall be done unto you. Herein is my I Jn. 3. 22.
Father glorified, that ye bear much fruit; and so shall ye Phil. 1. 11.
be my disciples. Even as the Father hath loved me, I
also have loved you: abide ye in my love. If ye keep
my commandments, ye shall abide in my love; even as Jn. 14. 21.
20 I have kept my Father's commandments, and abide in
his love. These things have I spoken unto you, that
my joy may be in you, and that your joy may be ful- Jn. 17. 13.
filled. This is my commandment, that ye love one an- I Jn. 1. 4.
other, even as I have loved you. Greater love hath no Jn. 13. 34.
25 man than this, that a man lay down his life for his **147**
friends. Ye are my friends, if ye do the things which I I Th. 4. 9.
I Jn. 3. 16.

151. S. John xv. 1—25.

command you.   No longer do I call you servants ; for
Mt. 25. 24. the servant knoweth not what his lord doeth : but I have
Jas. 2. 23. called you friends ; for all things that I heard from my
Ge. 18.17.. Father I have made known unto you.   Ye did not 30
2Tim.1.11. choose me, but I chose you, and appointed you, that ye
should go and bear fruit, and that your fruit should
Jn. 14. 13. abide : that whatsoever ye shall ask of the Father in my
name, he may give it you.   These things I command
you, that ye may love one another.   If the world hateth 35
Jn. 7. 7. you, ye know that it hath hated me before it hated you.
1 Jn. 4. 5. If ye were of the world, the world would love its own :
Jn. 17. 14. but because ye are not of the world, but I chose you out
of the world, therefore the world hateth you.   Remember
Jn. 13. 16. the word that I said unto you, A servant is not greater 40
Mt. 10. 24. than his lord.   If they persecuted me, they will also
59 persecute you ; if they kept my word, they will keep
Eze. 3. 7. yours also.   But all these things will they do unto you
for my name's sake, because they know not him that sent
Jn. 9. 41. me.   If I had not come and spoken unto them, they had 45
Jas. 4. 17. not had sin : but now they have no excuse for their sin.
1 Jn. 2. 23. He that hateth me hateth my Father also.   If I had not
Jn. 7. 31. done among them the works which none other did, they
had not had sin: but now have they both seen and hated
both me and my Father.   But this cometh to pass, that 50
Ps. 35. 19. the word may be fulfilled that is written in their law,
— 69. 4. They hated me without a cause.

152.   *Office of the Holy Ghost.*

Jn. 14. 26.   BUT when the Comforter is come, whom I will send
150 unto you from the Father, even the Spirit of truth, which
Lk. 24. 49. proceedeth from the Father, he shall bear witness of me:
and ye also bear witness, because ye have been with me
from the beginning.   5
These things have I spoken unto you, that ye should
Jn. 9. 22. not be made to stumble.   They shall put you out of the
— 12. 42· synagogues : yea, the hour cometh, that whosoever
Acts 26.9.· killeth you shall think that he offereth service unto God.
And these things will they do, because they have not 10
1 Cor. 2. 8. known the Father, nor me.   But these things have I
1Tim.1.13· spoken unto you, that when their hour is come, ye may
Jn. 14. 29. remember them, how that I told you.   And these things

I said not unto you from the beginning, because I was
15 with you.   But now I go unto him that sent me; and Jn. 7. 33.
none of you asketh me, Whither goest thou?   But
because I have spoken these things unto you, sorrow Jn. 14. 1.
hath filled your heart.   Nevertheless I tell you the truth;
It is expedient for you that I go away: for if I go not Jn. 7. 39.
20 away, the Comforter will not come unto you; but if I
go, I will send him unto you.   And he, when he is come, Acts 2. 33.
will convict the world in respect of sin, and of righteousness, and of judgement: of sin, because they believe not Acts 2. 37..
on me; of righteousness, because I go to the Father, and Acts 2. 32.
25 ye behold me no more; of judgement, because the prince Jn. 12. 31.
of this world hath been judged.   I have yet many things Lk. 10. 18.
to say unto you, but ye cannot bear them now.   How- 1 Cor. 3. 2.
beit when he, the Spirit of truth, is come, he shall guide Jn. 14. 26.
you into all the truth : for he shall not speak from him-   **150**
30 self; but what things soever he shall hear, these shall he 1 Jn. 2. 27.
speak : and he shall declare unto you the things that are
to come.   He shall glorify me: for he shall take of
mine, and shall declare it unto you.   All things whatso- Mt. 11. 27.
ever the Father hath are mine: therefore said I, that he Jn. 13. 3.
35 taketh of mine, and shall declare it unto you.

153. *Of Christ's Resurrection.   Of Prayer in His Name.* *The Disciples declare their belief, and are warned.*

A LITTLE while, and ye behold me no more; and Jn. 7. 33;
again a little while, and ye shall see me.   Some of his   — 13. 33.
disciples therefore said one to another, What is this that
he saith unto us, A little while, and ye behold me not ;
5 and again a little while, and ye shall see me : and,
Because I go to the Father?   They said therefore, What
is this that he saith, A little while?   We know not what
he saith.   Jesus perceiveth that they were desirous to
ask him, and he said unto them, Do ye inquire among
10 yourselves concerning this, that I said, A little while,
and ye behold me not; and again a little while, and ye
shall see me?   Verily, verily, I say unto you, that ye
shall weep and lament, but the world shall rejoice: ye Mt. 9. 15.
shall be sorrowful, but your sorrow shall be turned into Jn. 20. 20.
15 joy.   A woman when she is in travail hath sorrow, Gen. 3. 16.
because her hour is come: but when she is delivered Is. 26. 17.

of the child, she remembereth no more the anguish, for
Gen. 4. 1. the joy that a man is born into the world. And ye
therefore now have sorrow: but I will see you again, and
Is. 66. 14. your heart shall rejoice, and your joy no one taketh 20
1 Pet. 1.8. away from you. And in that day ye shall ask me
Mt. 7. 7. nothing. Verily, verily, I say unto you, If ye shall ask
Jn. 14. 13. anything of the Father, he will give it you in my name.
    150   Hitherto have ye asked nothing in my name: ask, and
Mt. 21. 22. ye shall receive, that your joy may be fulfilled.   25

These things have I spoken unto you in proverbs:
the hour cometh, when I shall no more speak unto you
in proverbs, but shall tell you plainly of the Father.   In
that day ye shall ask in my name: and I say not unto
you, that I will pray the Father for you; for the Father 30
Jn. 14. 21. himself loveth you, because ye have loved me, and have
Jn. 8. 42. believed that I came forth from the Father.   I came out
from the Father, and am come into the world: again, I
Jn. 13. 3. leave the world, and go unto the Father.   His disciples
say, Lo, now speakest thou plainly, and speakest no 35
Jn. 21. 17. proverb.   Now know we that thou knowest all things,
and needest not that any man should ask thee: by this
Jn. 17. 8. we believe that thou camest forth from God.   Jesus
answered them, Do ye now believe?   Behold, the hour
Mt. 26. 56. cometh, yea, is come, that ye shall be scattered, every 40
man to his own, and shall leave me alone: and yet I am
Jn. 8. 29. not alone, because the Father is with me.   These things
Is. 26. 3. have I spoken unto you, that in me ye may have peace.
In the world ye have tribulation: but be of good cheer;
1 Jn. 5. 4.. I have overcome the world.   45

154. *Christ's Prayer for Them and for His Church.*

Lk. 18. 13.   THESE things spake Jesus; and lifting up his eyes to
heaven, he said, Father, the hour is come; glorify thy
Phil. 2. 9.. Son, that the Son may glorify thee: even as thou gavest
Mt. 28. 18. him authority over all flesh, that whatsoever thou hast
Jn. 6. 37. given him, to them he should give eternal life. And this 5
1 Jn. 5. 12. is life eternal, that they should know thee the only true
Jn. 6. 40. God, and him whom thou didst send, even Jesus Christ.
I glorified thee on the earth, having accomplished the
Jn. 5. 36. work which thou hast given me to do. And now, O
Father, glorify thou me with thine own self with the 10

glory which I had with thee before the world was. I Jn. 1. 1..
manifested thy name unto the men whom thou gavest me Jn. 1. 18.
out of the world: thine they were, and thou gavest them Jn. 10. 29;
to me; and they have kept thy word. Now they know
15 that all things whatsoever thou hast given me are from
thee: for the words which thou gavest me I have given Jn. 7. 16.
unto them; and they received them, and knew of a truth
that I came forth from thee, and they believed that thou didst Jn. 16. 27.
send me. I pray for them: I pray not for the world, but for
20 those whom thou hast given me; for they are thine: and all Jn. 10. 29.
things that are mine are thine, and thine are mine: and — 16. 15.
I am glorified in them. And I am no more in the Jn. 16. 28.
world, and these are in the world, and I come to thee.
Holy Father, keep them in thy name which thou hast Ps. 121. 5.
25 given me, that they may be one, even as we are. While Jude 1.
I was with them, I kept them in thy name which thou
hast given me: and I guarded them, and not one of Jude 24.
them perished, but the son of perdition; that the 2 Th. 2. 3.
scripture might be fulfilled. But now I come to thee; Ps. 109. 8.
30 and these things I speak in the world, that they may — 41. 9.
have my joy fulfilled in themselves. I have given them
thy word; and the world hated them, because they are Jn. 15. 18.
not of the world, even as I am not of the world. I pray 1 Jn. 3. 13.
not that thou shouldest take them from the world, but
35 that thou shouldest keep them from the evil one. They 1 Jn. 5. 18..
are not of the world, even as I am not of the world.
Sanctify them in the truth: thy word is truth. As thou Eph. 5. 26.
didst send me into the world, even so sent I them into Jn. 20. 21.
the world. And for their sakes I sanctify myself, that 1 Cor. 1. 30.
40 they themselves also may be sanctified in truth. Neither Heb. 10. 10.
for these only do I pray, but for them also that believe
on me through their word; that they may all be one; Rom. 12. 5.
even as thou, Father, art in me, and I in thee, that they Eph. 4. 4.
also may be in us: that the world may believe that thou
45 didst send me. And the glory which thou hast given me
I have given unto them; that they may be one, even as
we are one; I in them, and thou in me, that they may
be perfected into one; that the world may know that Col. 3. 14.
thou didst send me, and lovedst them, even as thou
50 lovedst me. Father, that which thou hast given me, I Jn. 12. 26.
will that, where I am, they also may be with me; that
they may behold my glory, which thou hast given me: 1 Th. 4. 17.
for thou lovedst me before the foundation of the world.

Jn. 16. 3. O righteous Father, the world knew thee not, but I knew
Jn. 16.27. thee; and these knew that thou didst send me; and I 55
made known unto them thy name, and will make it
known; that the love wherewith thou lovedst me may be
Jn. 15. 9. in them, and I in them.

155.   *The Disciples and Peter again warned.*

WHEN Jesus had spoken these words, he went forth
2 Sa.15.23. with his disciples over the brook Kidron, and went, as
Zech. 14.4. his custom was, unto the mount of Olives; and the
disciples also followed him.   And Jesus saith unto them,
Mt. 11. 6. All ye shall be offended in me this night: for it is written, 5
Zech. 13. 7. I will smite the shepherd, and the sheep of the flock
shall be scattered abroad.   Howbeit, after I am raised up,
Mt. 28. 10. I will go before you into Galilee.   But Peter said unto
Prov.16.18. him, Although all shall be offended in thee, yet will I
Jn.13.36... never be offended.   And Jesus saith unto him, Verily, 10
I say unto thee, that thou to-day, even this night, before
149   the cock crow twice, shalt deny me thrice.   But he
spake exceeding vehemently, If I must die with thee, I
will not deny thee.   And in like manner also said all
the disciples.   15

156.   *Gethsemane.*

THEN cometh Jesus with them unto a place which
was named Gethsemane, where was a garden, into the
which he entered, himself and his disciples.   And he
saith unto his disciples, Sit ye here, while I go yonder
Mk. 5. 37; and pray.   And he taketh with him Peter and James 5
Mt. 17. 1. and John, and began to be greatly amazed, and sore
Ph. 2. 26. troubled.   Then saith he unto them, My soul is ex-
Gr.   ceeding sorrowful, even unto death: abide ye here and
watch with me and pray that ye enter not into temp-
tation.   And he went forward a little about a stone's 10
Dan. 6. 10. cast, and he kneeled down, and fell on his face on
Acts 21. 5. the ground, and prayed that, if it were possible, the
hour might pass away from him.   And he said, Abba,
Mk. 10.27. Father, all things are possible unto thee: if thou be will-

155. S. Mark xiv. 26—31 ; S. Matthew xxvi. 30—35 ;
S. Luke xxii. 39; S. John xviii. 1.
156. S. Mark xiv. 32—42 ; S. Matt. xxvi. 36—46 ;
S. Luke xxii. 40—46 ; S. John xviii. 1.

15 ing, remove this cup from me : nevertheless not as I will, Mt. 20. 22.
but as thou wilt. And there appeared unto him an
angel from heaven, strengthening him. And being in Mt. 4. 11.
an agony, he prayed more earnestly : and his sweat Heb. 5. 7.
became as it were great drops of blood falling down upon
20 the ground. And when he rose up from his prayer, he
cometh unto the disciples, and findeth them sleeping for
sorrow, and saith unto Peter, Simon, sleepest thou ?
couldest thou not watch one hour ? Watch and pray,
that ye enter not into temptation : the spirit indeed is Rom. 7. 18.
25 willing, but the flesh is weak. Again the second time Gal. 5. 17.
he went away and prayed, saying, O my Father, if this
cannot pass away, except I drink it, thy will be done.
And again he came and found them sleeping, for their Mk. 9. 6.
eyes were very heavy ; and they wist not what to answer
30 him. And he left them again, and went away, and
prayed a third time, saying again the same words. Then
cometh he to the disciples the third time, and saith unto
them, Sleep on now, and take your rest : it is enough ;
the hour is come ; behold, the Son of man is betrayed Jn. 13. 1.
35 into the hands of sinners. Arise, let us be going :
behold, he that betrayeth me is at hand.

157. *The Betrayal and Arrest.*

Now Judas also one of the twelve, which betrayed
him, knew the place : for Jesus ofttimes resorted thither
with his disciples. Judas then having received the
band of soldiers, and officers from the chief priests
5 and the Pharisees and elders of the people, cometh
thither, and with him a great multitude with swords and Acts 1. 16.
staves and lanterns and torches. Now he that betrayed
him had given them a token, saying, Whomsoever I shall
kiss, that is he : take him, and lead him away safely.
10 And straightway he came to Jesus, and saith, Hail, Rabbi, 2 Sa. 20. 9.
and kissed him. But Jesus said unto him, Judas, be-
trayest thou the Son of man with a kiss ?
Jesus therefore, knowing all the things that were
coming upon him, went forth, and saith unto them,
15 Whom seek ye ? They answered him, Jesus of Nazareth.
Jesus saith unto them, I am he. And Judas also which

157. S. John xviii. 2—11; S. Mark xiv. 43—52;
S. Matt. xxvi. 47—56; S. Luke xxii. 47—53.

betrayed him, was standing with them. When therefore
Jn. 7. 45... he said unto them, I am he, they went backward, and
fell to the ground. Again therefore he asked them,
Whom seek ye? And they said, Jesus of Nazareth. 20
Jesus answered, I told you that I am he: if therefore
ye seek me, let these go their way: that the word might
Jn. 17. 12. be fulfilled which he spake, Of those whom thou hast
given me I lost not one. Then saith he unto Judas,
Mt. 22. 12. Friend, do that for which thou art come. Then they 25
came and laid hands on Jesus, and took him. And
when they that were about him saw what would follow,
Lk. 22. 35. they said, Lord, shall we smite with the sword? Simon
Peter therefore having a sword, drew it, and struck the
high priest's servant, and cut off his right ear. Now the 30
servant's name was Malchus. But Jesus answered and
said, Suffer ye thus far. And he touched his ear and
healed him. Jesus therefore saith unto Peter, Put up
Rev.13.10. the sword into the sheath: for all they that take the
156   sword shall perish with the sword. The cup which the 35
Mt. 20. 22. Father hath given me shall I not drink it? Or thinkest
thou that I cannot beseech my Father and he shall even
2 Ki. 6. 17. now send me more than twelve legions of angels? How
then should the scriptures be fulfilled, that thus it must
be? In that hour said Jesus to the multitudes, and to 40
Acts 5. 24. the chief priests and captains of the temple and elders,
which were come against him, Are ye come out as against
a robber, with swords and staves to seize me? I sat
Jn. 7. 44... daily with you in the temple teaching, and ye took me
77   not, neither stretched ye forth your hands against me : 45
but this is your hour, and the power of darkness. And
all this is come to pass, that the scriptures of the prophets
Jn. 16. 32. might be fulfilled. Then all the disciples left him and
fled.

And a certain young man followed with him, having 50
a linen cloth cast about him, over his naked body : and
they lay hold on him; but he left the linen cloth, and
fled naked.

158. *Jesus before Annas.*

So the band and the chief captain and the officers of
the Jews, seized Jesus and bound him, and led him to

---

158. S. John xviii. 12—14 ; 19—24 ; S. Luke xxii. 63—65.

Annas first; for he was father in law to Caiaphas, which Lk. 3. 2.
was high priest that year. Now Caiaphas was he which Acts 4. 6.
5 gave counsel to the Jews, that it was expedient that one Jn.11.49...
man should die for the people. 83

The high priest therefore asked Jesus of his disciples,
and of his teaching. Jesus answered him, I have spoken
openly to the world; I ever taught in synagogues, and Lk. 4. 15.
10 in the temple, where all the Jews come together; and in Jn. 7. 28.
secret spake I nothing. Why askest thou me? ask them Jn. 8. 26.
that have heard me, what I spake unto them: behold,
these know the things which I said. And when he had
said this, one of the officers standing by struck Jesus Acts 23. 2.
15 with his hand, saying, Answerest thou the high priest so?
Jesus answered him, If I have spoken evil, bear witness
of the evil: but if well, why smitest thou me? Annas
therefore sent him bound unto Caiaphas the high priest.

And the men that held Jesus mocked him and beat
20 him. And they blindfolded him, and asked him, saying,
Prophesy: who is he that struck thee? And many other Is. 53. 7.
things spake they against him, reviling him. 1 Pet.2.23.

159. *Peter thrice denies Him.*

AND Simon Peter followed Jesus afar off, and so did
another disciple. Now that disciple was known unto the Mk. 1. 20.
high priest, and entered in with Jesus into the court of
the high priest; but Peter was standing at the door with-
5 out. So the other disciple which was known unto the
high priest, went out and spake unto her that kept the Acts 12.13.
door, and brought in Peter; and he entered in and sat
with the officers to see the end. Now the servants and
the officers were standing there, having made a fire of
10 coals; for it was cold: and Peter also was with them,
standing and warming himself in the light of the fire.
The maid therefore that kept the door, seeing him as he
sat in the light of the fire, came unto him and looking
steadfastly upon him, said, Art thou also one of this man's
15 disciples? But he denied before them all, saying, Wo- Jn. 13. 38.
man, I am not. I neither know nor understand what 149
thou sayest. And he went out into the porch; and the Mt. 26. 34.
cock crew. And when he was gone out into the porch 155

the maid saw him, and began again to say to them that
stood by, This is one of them. They said therefore unto 20
him, Art thou also one of his disciples? And again he
Mt.10. 32. denied with an oath, and said, Man, I am not. I know
not the man. And after the space of about one hour
another confidently affirmed, saying to them that stood
by, Of a truth this man also was with him: for he is a 25
Jud. 12. 6. Galilæan, *and* his speech bewrayeth him. One of the
servants of the high priest, being a kinsman of him
whose ear Peter cut off, saith, Did I not see thee in the
garden with him? Peter therefore denied again, and
began to curse and to swear, *saying*, Man, I know not 30
this man of whom ye speak, nor what thou sayest. And
immediately, while he yet spake, the second time the
cock crew. And the Lord turned, and looked upon
Peter. And Peter remembered the word of the Lord,
how that he said unto him, Before the cock crow twice 35
Jn. 21. 17. this day, thou shalt deny me thrice. And when he
thought thereon he went out and wept bitterly.

160. *Jesus before the Sanhedrim.*

AND as soon as it was day, the assembly of the elders
of the people was gathered together, both the chief priests
and the elders and the scribes. And they led him away
into their council, saying, If thou art the Christ, tell us.
But he said unto them, If I tell you, ye will not believe: 5
and if I ask you, ye will not answer. Now the chief
2 Ki.21.10. priests and the whole council sought false witness against
him, that they might put him to death; and found it not,
Ps. 35. 11. though many false witnesses came. For many bare false
witness against him, and their witness agreed not together. 10
But afterward came two, which stood up and bare false
witness against him, saying, We heard this man say, I
Jn. 2. 19. will destroy this temple that is made with hands, and in
21 three days I will build another made without hands.
And not even so did their witness agree together. And 15
the high priest stood up in the midst, and asked Jesus,
saying, Answerest thou nothing? What is it which these
Ps. 39. 9. witness against thee? But Jesus held his peace, and

160. S. Mark xiv. 53—65; S. Matthew xxvi. 57—68;
S. Luke xxii. 66—71.

answered nothing. Again the high priest asked him, Is. 53. 7.
20 and said unto him, I adjure thee by the living God, that Lev. 5. 1.
thou tell us whether thou be the Christ, the Son of the
Blessed? Jesus saith unto him, I am: nevertheless I
say unto you, Henceforth ye shall see the Son of man Dan. 7. 13.
sitting at the right hand of power, and coming in the Ps. 110. 1.
25 clouds of heaven. And they said, Art thou then the 1Th. 4. 16.
Son of God? And he said unto them, Ye say that I am.
Then the high priest rent his garments, saying, He hath 2 Ki. 19. 1.
spoken blasphemy: what further need have we of wit- Acts 14. 14.
nesses? behold now we ourselves have heard the blas-
30 phemy from his own mouth: what think ye? And they
all answered and said, He is worthy of death. And
some began to spit on him, and to cover his face and to Is. 50. 6.
buffet him: and some smote him with the palms of
their hands, saying, Prophesy unto us, thou Christ: who
35 is he that struck thee?

161. *Suicide of Judas.*

THEN Judas, which betrayed him, when he saw that
he was condemned, repented himself, and brought back
the thirty pieces of silver to the chief priests and elders,
saying, I have sinned, in that I betrayed innocent blood.
5 But they said, What is that to us? see thou to it. And 2 Ki. 10. 9.
he cast down the pieces of silver into the sanctuary, and
departed; and he went away and hanged himself. And 2Sa. 17. 23.
falling headlong he burst asunder in the midst and all 1 Sa. 31. 4.
his bowels gushed out. And the chief priests took the
10 pieces of silver, and said, It is not lawful to put them
into the treasury, since it is the price of blood. And Deu. 23. 18.
they took counsel, and bought with them the potter's
field, to bury strangers in. And it became known to all
the dwellers in Jerusalem, insomuch that in their lan-
15 guage that field was called Akeldama, that is, the field
of blood. Then was fulfilled that which was spoken by
Jeremiah the prophet, saying, And they took the thirty Zec. 11. 12.
pieces of silver, the price of him that was priced, whom
certain of the children of Israel did price; and they gave
20 them for the potter's field, as the Lord appointed me.

161. S. Matthew xxvii. 3—10; Acts i. 18, 19.

162. *Jesus before Pilate.*

AND straightway in the morning, the chief priests
with the elders and the scribes, and the whole council,
held a consultation against Jesus to put him to death,
and they bound him, and the whole company of them
rose up and carried him away, and delivered him up to 5
Pilate the governor. They lead Jesus therefore from
Caiaphas into the palace: and it was early; and they
themselves entered not into the palace, that they might
not be defiled, but might eat the passover. Pilate therefore went out unto them, and saith, What accusation 10
bring ye against this man? They answered and said
unto him, If this man were not an evil-doer, we should
not have delivered him up unto thee. Pilate therefore
said unto them, Take him yourselves, and judge him
according to your law. The Jews said unto him, It is 15
not lawful for us to put any man to death: that the word
of Jesus might be fulfilled, which he spake, signifying by
what manner of death he should die.

And they began to accuse him, saying, We found this
man perverting our nation, and forbidding to give tribute 20
to Cæsar, and saying that he himself is Christ, a king.
Pilate therefore entered again into the palace, and called
Jesus, and said unto him, Art thou the King of the Jews?
Jesus answered, Sayest thou this of thyself, or did others
tell it thee concerning me? Pilate answered, Am I a 25
Jew? Thine own nation and the chief priests delivered
thee unto me: what hast thou done? Jesus answered,
My kingdom is not of this world: if my kingdom were
of this world, then would my servants fight, that I should
not be delivered to the Jews: but now is my kingdom 30
not from hence. Pilate therefore said unto him, Art
thou a king then? Jesus answered, Thou sayest that I
am a king. To this end have I been born, and to this
end am I come into the world, that I should bear witness
unto the truth. Every one that is of the truth heareth 35
my voice. Pilate saith unto him, What is truth?

And Pilate said unto the chief priests and multitudes,
I find no fault in this man. But they were the more
urgent, and accused him of many things; and when he

Marginal references:
Acts 10.28.
— 12. 4.
Acts 25.16.
Acts 24. 6.
Mt. 20. 19.
121
Mt. 22. 21.
131
Col. 1. 13.
Rev. 11. 15.
1 Ti. 6. 13.
1 Jn. 4. 6.

---

162. S. John xviii. 28—38; S. Matthew xxvii. 1, 2; 11—14;
S. Mark xv. 1—5; S. Luke xxiii. 1—4.

40 was accused by the chief priests and elders he answered
nothing. And Pilate again asked him, saying, Answerest Is. 53. 7.
thou nothing?   Hearest thou not how many things they
accuse thee of, and witness against thee?   But Jesus no
more answered anything, not even to one word, insomuch
45 that the governor marvelled greatly.

163. *Jesus before Herod.*

And they said, He stirreth up the people, teaching
throughout all Judæa, and beginning from Galilee even
unto this place.   But when Pilate heard it, he asked
whether the man were a Galilæan.   And when he knew
5 that he was of Herod's jurisdiction, he sent him unto Lk. 3. 1.
Herod, who himself also was at Jerusalem in these days.
Now when Herod saw Jesus, he was exceeding glad :
for he was of a long time desirous to see him, because Lk. 9. 9.
he had heard concerning him ; and he hoped to see Mk. 6. 20.
10 some miracle done by him.   And he questioned him in Jn. 4. 48.
many words ; but he answered him nothing.   And the
chief priests and the scribes stood, vehemently accusing
him.   And Herod with his soldiers set him at nought, Acts 4. 27.
and mocked him, and arraying him in gorgeous apparel
15 sent him back to Pilate.   And Herod and Pilate became
friends with each other that very day : for before they
were at enmity between themselves.

164. *Barabbas preferred. Jesus condemned.*

AND Pilate called together the chief priests and
the rulers and the people, and went out again unto
them, and said unto them, Ye brought unto me this
man as one that perverteth the people : and behold,
5 I, having examined him before you, found no fault in
this man touching those things whereof ye accuse him :
no, nor yet Herod, for he hath sent him back unto us ;
and behold, nothing worthy of death hath been done by
him.   I will therefore chastise him, and release him.
10   Now at the feast the governor was wont to release
unto the multitude one prisoner, whom they asked of

163. S. Luke xxiii. 5—12.
164. S. Matthew xxvii. 15—26 ; S. Luke xxiii. 13—25 ;
    S. Mark xv. 6—15 ; S. John xviii. 39, 40.

him. And they had then a notable prisoner called
Barabbas, lying bound with them that had made a
certain insurrection in the city, men who in the insurrection had committed murder.   And the multitude 15
went up and began to ask him to do as he was wont to
do unto them.   And Pilate answered them saying, Ye
have a custom that I should release unto you one at the
passover : will ye therefore that I release unto you the
King of the Jews? They cried out therefore again 20
saying, Not this man, but Barabbas.   Pilate said, Whom
Jos. 24. 15. will ye that I release unto you?   Barabbas, or Jesus
which is called Christ?   For he knew that for envy they
had delivered him up.

And while he was sitting on the judgement seat, his 25
wife sent unto him, saying, Have thou nothing to do
with that righteous man : for I have suffered many
things this day in a dream because of him.

Now the chief priests and the elders stirred up the
multitude and persuaded them that they should ask for 30
Barabbas and destroy Jesus.   But the governor answered
and said unto them, Whether of the twain will ye that I
release unto you? and they cried out altogether, saying,
Away with this man, and release unto us Barabbas.   And
Acts 3. 13. Pilate spake unto them again, desiring to release Jesus ; 35
and said, What then shall I do unto him whom ye call
the King of the Jews?   But they all shouted, saying,
Crucify, crucify him.   And he saith unto them the third
time, Why, what evil hath this man done?   I have
found no cause of death in him : I will therefore chastise 40
him and release him.   But they were instant with loud
Is. 5. 7. voices, and cried out exceedingly, saying, Let him be
crucified.   And their voices prevailed.   So when Pilate
saw that he prevailed nothing, but that rather a tumult
was arising, he took water, and washed his hands before 45
Deu. 21. 6.. the multitude, saying, I am innocent of the blood of this
righteous man : see ye to it.   And all the people
Deu. 19. 10. answered and said, His blood be on us, and on our
Acts 5. 28. children.   Then Pilate, wishing to content the multitude,
gave sentence that what they had asked for should be 50
done.   And he released him that for insurrection and
Acts 3. 14. murder had been cast into prison, whom they asked for :
but Jesus he delivered up to their will.

165. *Jesus scourged, mocked, sentenced.*

THEN Pilate therefore took Jesus, and scourged him.
And the soldiers led him away within the court, which is
the Prætorium, and gathered unto him the whole band.
And they stripped him, and arrayed him in a purple **163**
5 garment; and they plaited a crown of thorns and put it
on his head, and a reed in his right hand : and they
came unto him and began to salute him ; and they
kneeled down before him, and mocked him, worshipping
him and saying, Hail, King of the Jews! And they struck
10 him with their hands, and spat upon him, and took the Is. 50. 6.
reed and smote him on the head.   And when they had
mocked him they took off from him the purple robe, and
put on him his garments.
And Pilate went out again, and saith unto them,
15 Behold, I bring him out to you, that ye may know that I
find no crime in him.   Jesus therefore came out,
wearing the crown of thorns and the purple garment.
And Pilate saith unto them, Behold, the man ! When
therefore the chief priests and the officers saw him, they
20 cried out, saying, Crucify him, crucify him.   Pilate saith
unto them, Take him yourselves, and crucify him : for I Jn. 18. 31.
find no crime in him.   The Jews answered him, We have
a law, and by that law he ought to die, because he made Lev. 24. 16.
himself the Son of God.   When Pilate therefore heard
25 this saying, he was the more afraid ; and he entered into
the palace again, and saith unto Jesus, Whence art thou?
But Jesus gave him no answer.   Pilate therefore saith
unto him, Speakest thou not unto me ? knowest thou
not that I have power to release thee, and have power to
30 crucify thee ?   Jesus answered him, Thou wouldest have
no power against me, except it were given thee from Jn. 7. 30.
above : therefore he that delivered me unto thee hath
greater sin.   Upon this Pilate sought to release him : Acts 3. 13.
but the Jews cried out, saying, If thou release this man,
35 thou art not Cæsar's friend : every one that maketh himself a king speaketh against Cæsar.   When Pilate therefore heard these words, he brought Jesus out, and sat
down on the judgement-seat at a place called The Pave-

---

165. S. John xix. 1—16 ; S. Matthew xxvii. 27—31 ;
S. Mark xv. 16—20.

ment, but in Hebrew, Gabbatha. Now it was the Preparation of the passover : it was about the sixth hour. 40 And he saith unto the Jews, Behold, your King! They therefore cried out, Away with him, away with him, crucify him. Pilate saith unto them, Shall I crucify your King? The chief priests answered, We have no king but Cæsar. Then therefore he delivered him unto them 45 to be crucified.

166. *Jesus is led to Calvary.*

THEY took Jesus therefore : and he went out, bearing
Mt. 16. 24. the cross for himself. And as they came out, they found one passing by, Simon of Cyrene, coming from the country, the father of Alexander and Rufus; him they
Mt. 5. 41. laid hold on and compelled to go with them, and laid on 5
Gr. him the cross, to bear it after Jesus.

And there followed him a great multitude of the people, and of women who bewailed and lamented him. But Jesus turning unto them said, Daughters of Jerusalem, weep not for me, but weep for yourselves, and for your 10 children. For behold, the days are coming, in which they shall say, Blessed are the barren, and the wombs that never bare, and the breasts that never gave suck.
Hos. 10. 8. Then shall they begin to say to the mountains, Fall on
Rev. 6. 16. us ; and to the hills, Cover us. For if they do these 15
Eze. 20. 47. things in the green tree, what shall be done in the dry?
1 Pet. 4. 18. And there were also two others, malefactors, led with him to be put to death.

Nu. 15. 36. And they bring him unto the place called The place
He. 13. 12. of a skull, which is called in Hebrew, Golgotha. And 20 they offered him wine mingled with myrrh, but when he had tasted it, he would not drink.

167. *He is crucified.*

Gal. 3. 13. AND there they crucified him, and with him the two
Is. 53. 9. malefactors, one on the right hand, and the other on the
Acts 7. 60. left, and Jesus in the midst. And Jesus said, Father,
Acts 3. 17. forgive them ; for they know not what they do. And it

166. S. Luke xxiii. 26—33 ; S. Matthew xxvii. 32—34;
S. Mark xv. 21—23 ; S. John xix. 17.
167. S. John xix. 18—24 ; S. Mark xv. 24—27 ;
S. Matthew xxvii. 35—38 ; S. Luke xxiii. 33, 34, 38.

5 was the third hour, and they crucified him. And Pilate ~Ps. 22. 16.~
wrote a title also, and they set it up over his head on
the cross. And there was written, THIS IS JESUS OF
NAZARETH THE KING OF THE JEWS. This title therefore
read many of the Jews: for the place where Jesus was
10 crucified was nigh to the city: and it was written in
Hebrew, and in Latin, and in Greek. The chief priests
of the Jews therefore said to Pilate, Write not, The King
of the Jews; but, that he said, I am King of the Jews.
Pilate answered, What I have written I have written.
15   The soldiers therefore, when they had crucified Jesus,
took his garments, and made four parts, to every soldier
a part; and also the coat: now the coat was without
seam, woven from the top throughout. They said therefore one to another, Let us not rend it, but cast lots for
20 it, whose it shall be: that the scripture might be fulfilled,
which saith,

> They parted my garments among them,   ~Ps. 22. 18.~
> And upon my vesture did they cast lots.

These things therefore the soldiers did. And they sat
and watched him there.
25

168. *Conduct of priests, people, soldiers, robbers.*

AND the people stood beholding. And they that ~Ps. 22. 7.~
passed by railed on him, wagging their heads, and say- ~Ps. 109. 25.~
ing, Ha! thou that destroyest the temple, and buildest   **160**
it in three days, save thyself. If thou art the Son of
5 God, come down from the cross. In like manner also
the chief priests mocking him among themselves with
the scribes and elders scoffed at him, saying, He saved
others, himself he cannot save; let him save himself, if
this is the Christ of God, his chosen. He is the Christ,
10 the King of Israel: let him now come down from the
cross, that we may see; and we will believe on him.
He trusteth on God; let him deliver him now if he ~Ps. 22. 8.~
desireth him: for he said, I am the Son of God. And
the robbers also that were crucified with him cast upon
15 him the same reproach. And the soldiers also mocked
him, coming to him, offering him vinegar, and saying, If
thou art the King of the Jews, save thyself.

---

168. **S. Matthew xxvii. 39—44; S. Mark xv. 29—32;**
S. Luke xxiii. 35—37.

169. *Of Jesus Himself.*

AND one of the malefactors which were hanged railed on him, saying, Art not thou the Christ? save thyself and us. But the other answered, and rebuking him said, Dost thou not even fear God, seeing thou art in the same condemnation? And we indeed justly; for we receive 5 the due reward of our deeds: but this man hath done nothing amiss. And he said, Jesus, remember me when thou comest in thy kingdom. And he said unto him,
2 Co. 12. 4. Verily I say unto thee, To-day shalt thou be with me in
Lk. 16. 22. Paradise. 10

Now there were standing by the cross of Jesus his mother, and his mother's sister, Mary the wife of Clopas, and Mary Magdalene. When Jesus therefore saw his
Jn. 21. 20. mother, and the disciple standing by, whom he loved, he saith unto his mother, Woman, behold, thy son! Then 15 saith he to the disciple, Behold, thy mother! And from o that hour the disciple took her unto his own home.

170. *His Death.*

AND when the sixth hour was come, there was
Amos 8. 9. darkness over the whole land until the ninth hour, the sun's light failing. And at the ninth hour Jesus cried with a loud voice, Eloi, Eloi, lama sabachthani? which
Ps. 22. 1. is, being interpreted, My God, my God, why hast thou 5 forsaken me? And some of them that stood by, when they heard it, said, Behold, he calleth Elijah.

After this Jesus, knowing that all things are now finished, that the scripture might be accomplished, saith, I thirst. There was set there a vessel full of vinegar, and 10 one of them ran and filling a sponge full of vinegar put
Ps. 69. 21. it upon hyssop and brought it to his mouth and gave him to drink. And the rest said, Let be; let us see whether Elijah cometh to save him.

When Jesus therefore had received the vinegar he 15
Jn. 17. 4. cried again with a loud voice and said, It is finished:
Ps. 31. 5. Father, into thy hands I commend my spirit: And he bowed his head and gave up the ghost. And behold,

169. S. Luke xxiii. 39—43; S. John xix. 25—27.
170. S. Matthew xxvii. 45—56; S. Mark xv. 33—41;
S. Luke xxiii. 44—49: S. John xix. 28—30.

the veil of the temple was rent in twain from the top to Lev. 16. 2.
20 the bottom; and the earth did quake; and the rocks Heb.9.8...
were rent; and the tombs were opened; and many
bodies of the saints that had fallen asleep were raised;
and coming forth out of the tombs after his resurrection 1 Co.15.20.
they entered into the holy city and appeared unto many.
25 And when the centurion that stood by over against him,
and they that were with him watching Jesus, saw the
earthquake, and the things that were done, and that he so
gave up the ghost, they feared exceedingly, and glorified
God, saying, Truly this man was the Son of God. And
30 all the multitudes that came together to this sight, when
they beheld the things that were done, returned smiting
their breasts. And all his acquaintance, and the women
that followed with him from Galilee, stood afar off, Ps. 88. 8;
beholding these things: among whom were both Mary — 38. 11.
35 Magdalene, and Mary the mother of James the less and
of Joses, and Salome; who when he was in Galilee,
followed him, and ministered unto him; and many other Lk. 8. 3.
women which came up with him unto Jerusalem.

171. *His Death made certain.*

THE Jews therefore, because it was the Preparation,
that the bodies should not remain on the cross upon the Deu.21.23.
sabbath (for the day of that sabbath was a high day),
asked of Pilate that their legs might be broken, and that
5 they might be taken away. The soldiers therefore came,
and brake the legs of the first, and of the other which
was crucified with him: but when they came to Jesus,
and saw that he was dead already, they brake not his
legs: howbeit one of the soldiers with a spear pierced
10 his side, and straightway there came out blood and 1 Jn. 5.6...
water. And he that hath seen hath borne witness, and
his witness is true: and he knoweth that he saith true,
that ye also may believe. For these things came to Ex. 12.46.
pass, that the scripture might be fulfilled, A bone of him Num.9.12.
15 shall not be broken. And again another scripture saith, Ps. 34. 20.
They shall look on him whom they pierced. Zec. 12.10.

171. S. John xix. 31—37.

172. *His Burial.*

AND behold, after these things, when even was now come, because it was the Preparation, that is the day before the sabbath, there came a rich man from 1 Sam.1.1. Arimathæa, a city of the Jews, named Joseph, who was a councillor of honourable estate, a good man and a 5 righteous; (he had not consented to their counsel and deed), who also himself was looking for the kingdom of Jn. 12. 42. God; being a disciple of Jesus, but secretly for fear of the Jews; this man boldly went in unto Pilate, and asked that he might take away the body of Jesus. And Pilate 10 marvelled if he were already dead: and calling unto him the centurion, he asked him whether he had been any while dead. And when he learned it of the centurion, he gave him leave, and commanded it to be given up. He came therefore, having bought a linen cloth, and took 15 Jn. 3. 1; away his body. And there came also Nicodemus, he — 7. 50. who at the first came to him by night, bringing a mixture Mt. 2. 11. of myrrh and aloes, about an hundred pound weight. So they took the body of Jesus, and bound it in clean Gen.50.2.. linen cloths with the spices, as the custom of the Jews is 20 Jn. 11. 44. to bury. Now in the place where he was crucified there was a garden; and in the garden *Joseph's* own new tomb, which he had hewn out in the rock, wherein 2 Ki.13.21. was never man yet laid. There then because of the Jews' Preparation (for the tomb was nigh at hand) they 25 Jn. 11. 38. laid Jesus. And he rolled a great stone to the door of the tomb, and departed. And Mary Magdalene was there, and Mary the mother of Joses, sitting over against the sepulchre. And the women, which had come with him out of Galilee, followed after and beheld the tomb, 30 and how his body was laid. And they returned, and prepared spices and ointments. And on the sabbath they rested, according to the commandment.

173. *Precautions against removal of His Body.*

NOW on the morrow, which is the day after the Preparation, the chief priests and the Pharisees were gathered together unto Pilate, saying, Sir, we remember

172. S. John xix. 38—42; S. Mark xv. 42—47;
S. Luke xxiii. 50—56; S. Matthew xxvii. 57—61.
173. S. Matthew xxvii. 62—66.

that that deceiver said, while he was yet alive, After three Jn. 2. 19...
5 days I rise again. Command therefore that the sepulchre
be made sure until the third day, lest haply his disciples
come and steal him away, and say unto the people, He
is risen from the dead: and the last error will be worse
than the first. Pilate said unto them, Ye have a guard:
10 go your way, make it as sure as ye can. So they went,
and made the sepulchre sure, sealing the stone, the Dan. 6. 17.
guard being with them.

174. *An Angel rolls away the Stone.*

AND behold, there was a great earthquake; for an
angel of the Lord descended from heaven, and came
and rolled away the stone, and sat upon it. His appearance was as lightning, and his raiment white as snow: Dan. 10. 6.
5 and for fear of him the watchers did quake, and became
as dead men.

175. *The Tomb empty. Angels declare that He is risen.*

AND when the sabbath was past, Mary Magdalene,
and Mary the mother of James, and Salome, and Joanna,
and other women with them, bought spices that they
might come and anoint him. And very early on the Gen. 50. 2.
5 first day of the week, they came to the tomb when the
sun was risen, bringing the spices which they had prepared. And they were saying among themselves, Who
shall roll us away the stone from the door of the tomb?
And looking up they see that the stone is rolled back:
10 for it was exceeding great.
Mary runneth therefore, and cometh to Simon Peter,
and to the other disciple, whom Jesus loved, and saith Jn. 21. 20.
unto them, They have taken away the Lord out of the
tomb, and we know not where they have laid him. Peter
15 therefore arose and went forth, and the other disciple,
and they went toward the tomb. And they ran both
together: and the other disciple outran Peter, and came
first to the tomb; and stooping and looking in, he seeth
the linen cloths lying; yet entered he not in. Simon Jn. 19. 40.

---

174. S. Matthew xxviii. 2—4.
175. S. John xx. 1—10; S. Mark xvi. 1—8; S. Luke xxiv. 1—12;
S. Matthew xxviii. 1; 5—8.

Peter therefore also cometh, following him, and entered 20
into the tomb; and he beholdeth the linen cloths lying,
Jn. 11. 44. and the napkin, that was upon his head, not lying with
the linen cloths, but rolled up in a place by itself. Then
entered in therefore the other disciple also, which came
first to the tomb, and he saw, and believed. For as yet 25
Ps. 16. 10. they knew not the scripture, that he must rise again from
Acts 2. 31. the dead. So the disciples went away again unto their
own home, wondering at that which was come to pass.

And the women entered in, and found not the body
of the Lord Jesus. And it came to pass, while they were 30
perplexed thereabout, behold, two men stood by them in
dazzling apparel; and they saw a young man sitting on
the right side, arrayed in a white robe; and they were
amazed. And as they were affrighted and bowed down
their faces to the earth, the angel answered and said 35
unto the women, Be not amazed: for I know that ye
seek Jesus, the Nazarene, which hath been crucified:
Is. 8. 19. Why seek ye the living among the dead? He is not
here; for he is risen, even as he said. Remember how
Mk. 9. 31. he spake unto you while he was yet in Galilee, saying 40
73 that the Son of man must be delivered up into the hands
of sinful men, and be crucified, and the third day rise
again. Come, behold the place where the Lord lay.
But go quickly; tell his disciples and Peter, He is risen
Mt. 26. 32. from the dead, and lo, he goeth before you into Galilee; 45
Mt. 28. 16. there shall ye see him, as he said unto you: Lo, I have
184 told you. And they went out and fled from the tomb;
for trembling and astonishment had come upon them.
And they said nothing to any one, for they were afraid.

176. *Jesus appears to Mary Magdalene.*

BUT Mary was standing without at the tomb weeping:
so, as she wept, she stooped and looked into the tomb;
and she beholdeth two angels in white sitting, one at the
head, and one at the feet, where the body of Jesus had
lain. And they say unto her, Woman, why weepest thou? 5
She saith unto them, Because they have taken away my
Lord, and I know not where they have laid him. When
she had thus said, she turned herself back, and beholdeth
Lk. 24. 16. Jesus standing, and knew not that it was Jesus. Jesus
Jn. 21. 4.

176. S. John xx. 11—18; S. Mark xvi. 9—11.

10 saith unto her, Woman, why weepest thou? whom seekest
thou? She, supposing him to be the gardener, saith unto
him, Sir, if thou hast borne him hence, tell me where
thou hast laid him, and I will take him away. Jesus
saith unto her, Mary. She turneth herself, and saith
15 unto him in Hebrew, Rabboni; which is to say, Master. Mk. 10. 51.
Jesus saith to her, Touch me not; for I am not yet
ascended unto the Father: but go unto my brethren, Rom. 8. 29.
and say to them, I ascend unto my Father and your Heb. 2. 11.
Father, and my God and your God. Mary Magdalene Eph. 1. 17.
20 cometh and telleth the disciples, I have seen the Lord; 1 Pet. 1. 3.
and how that he had said these things unto her. And
they, when they heard that he was alive, and had been
seen of her, disbelieved.

177. *Jesus appears to the other Women.*

AND *the other women* remembered his words, and
departed quickly from the tomb with fear and great joy,
and ran to bring the disciples word. And behold Jesus
met them, saying, All hail. And they came and took hold
5 of his feet and worshipped him. Then saith Jesus unto
them, Fear not: go, tell my brethren that they depart Mt. 26. 32.
into Galilee, and there shall they see me. Mt. 28. 16.
And they returned from the tomb, and told all these **184**
things unto the eleven, and to all the rest. And their
10 words appeared in their sight as idle talk; and they disbelieved them.

178. *Report and bribery of the Guards.*

Now while they were going, behold, some of the Mt. 27. 65.
guard came into the city, and told unto the chief priests **173**
all the things that were come to pass. And when they
were assembled with the elders, and had taken counsel,
5 they gave large money unto the soldiers, saying, Say ye,
His disciples came by night, and stole him away while
we slept. And if this come to the governor's ears, we Acts 12. 19.
will persuade him, and rid you of care. So they took 1 Sam. 8. 3.
the money, and did as they were taught: and this saying
10 was spread abroad among the Jews, and continueth until
this day.

---

177. S. Luke xxiv. 9—11; S. Matthew xxviii. 9, 10.
178. S. Matthew xxviii. 11—15.

179. *Jesus appears to Cleopas and another.*

AND after these things he was manifested in another
form unto two of them, as they walked on their way into
the country. *For* behold, two of them were going that
very day to a village named Emmaus, which was three-
score furlongs from Jerusalem.   And they communed 5
with each other of all these things which had happened.
And it came to pass, while they communed and questioned together, that Jesus himself drew near, and went
with them.   But their eyes were holden that they should
not know him.   And he said unto them, What communi- 10
cations are these that ye have one with another, as ye
walk?   And they stood still, looking sad.   And one of
them, named Cleopas, answering said unto him, Dost
thou alone sojourn in Jerusalem and not know the things
which are come to pass there in these days?   And he 15
said unto them, What things?   And they said unto him,
The things concerning Jesus of Nazareth, which was a
prophet mighty in deed and word before God and all
the people: and how the chief priests and our rulers
delivered him up to be condemned to death, and cruci- 20
fied him.   But we hoped that it was he which should
redeem Israel.   Yea and beside all this, it is now the
third day since these things came to pass.   Moreover
certain women of our company amazed us, having been
early at the tomb; and when they found not his body, 25
they came, saying, that they had also seen a vision of
angels, which said that he was alive.   And certain of
them that were with us went to the tomb, and found it
even so as the women had said: but him they saw not.
And he said unto them, O foolish men, and slow of heart 30
to believe in all that the prophets have spoken!   Be-
hoved it not the Christ to suffer these things, and to
enter into his glory?   And beginning from Moses and
from all the prophets, he interpreted to them in all the
scriptures the things concerning himself.   And they drew 35
nigh unto the village, whither they were going: and he
made as though he would go further.   And they constrained him, saying, Abide with us: for it is toward
evening, and the day is now far spent.   And he went

Jn. 20. 14;
— 21. 4.

Jn. 19. 25.

Lk. 1. 68.
Acts 1. 6.

Acts 17. 3.

Acts 3. 22..

Gen.32.46.
Jn. 1. 39.

---

179. S. Luke xxiv. 13—35; S. Mark xvi. 12, 13.

40 in to abide with them. And it came to pass, when he
had sat down with them to meat, he took the bread, and Lk. 9. 16.
blessed it, and brake, and gave to them. And their Lk. 22. 19.
eyes were opened, and they knew him ; and he vanished Lk. 4. 30.
out of their sight. And they said one to another, Was Jn. 8. 59.
45 not our heart burning within us, while he spake to us in
the way, while he opened to us the scriptures? And
they rose up that very hour, and returned to Jerusalem,
and found the eleven gathered together, and them that
were with them, saying, The Lord is risen indeed, and
50 hath appeared to Simon. And they rehearsed the things 1 Cor.15. 5.
that happened in the way, and how he was known of
them in the breaking of the bread.

180. *Jesus appears to His Disciples the same evening.*

WHEN therefore it was evening on that day, the first
day of the week, and when the doors were shut where Jn. 20. 26.
the disciples were for fear of the Jews, as they sat at
meat and spake these things, Jesus himself came and
5 stood in the midst of them and saith unto them, Peace Jn. 14. 27.
be unto you. But they were terrified and affrighted, and Mt. 14. 26.
supposed that they beheld a spirit. And he upbraided **63**
them with their unbelief and hardness of heart, because
they believed not them which had seen him after he was
10 risen. And he said unto them, Why are ye troubled?
and wherefore do reasonings arise in your heart? See
my hands and my feet, that it is I myself: handle me Jn. 20. 27.
and see, for a spirit hath not flesh and bones as ye see **181**
me having. And when he had said this he shewed them 1 Jn. 1. 1.
15 his hands and his feet and his side. And while they still
disbelieved for joy, and wondered, he said unto them, Gen.45.26.
Have ye here anything to eat? And they gave him a Jn. 21. 5.
piece of a broiled fish. And he took it, and did eat Acts 10.41.
before them. The disciples therefore were glad, when
20 they saw the Lord. Jesus therefore said to them again,
Peace be unto you : as the Father hath sent me, even so Jn. 17. 18.
send I you. And when he had said this, he breathed on 2 Tim. 2. 2.
them, and saith unto them, Receive ye the Holy Ghost :
whose soever sins ye forgive, they are forgiven unto them; Mt. 16. 19.
25 whose soever sins ye retain, they are retained. Mt. 18. 18.

71. 76

180. S. Luke xxiv. 36—49 ; S. John xx. 19—23 ;
S. Mark xvi. 14—18.

Mt. 28. 19.   And he said unto them, Go ye into all the world,
184   and preach the gospel to the whole creation.   He that
believeth and is baptized shall be saved ; but he that
disbelieveth shall be condemned.   And these signs shall
follow them that believe: in my name shall they cast out 30
devils; they shall speak with new tongues; they shall
Acts 28. 5. take up serpents, and if they drink any deadly thing, it
shall in no wise hurt them ; they shall lay hands on the
sick, and they shall recover.

And he said unto them, These are my words which 35
I spake unto you, while I was yet with you, how that all
things must needs be fulfilled, which are written in the
law of Moses, and the prophets, and the psalms, concern-
Acts 16. 14. ing me.   Then opened he their mind, that they might
understand the scriptures ; and he said unto them, Thus 40
Acts 26. 23. it is written, that the Christ should suffer, and rise again
from the dead the third day; and that repentance and
remission of sins should be preached in his name unto
Acts 1. 8. all the nations, beginning from Jerusalem.   Ye are wit-
Acts 3. 15. nesses of these things.   And behold, I send forth the 45
Jn. 14. 16. promise of my Father upon you : but tarry ye in the
— 15. 26. city, until ye be clothed with power from on high.

181. *Again, a week later.   Thomas.*

Jn. 11. 16.   BUT Thomas, one of the twelve, called Didymus, was
not with them when Jesus came.   The other disciples
therefore said unto him, We have seen the Lord.   But
he said unto them, Except I shall see in his hands the
print of the nails, and put my finger into the print of the 5
nails, and put my hand into his side, I will not believe.

And after eight days again his disciples were within,
Jn. 20. 19. and Thomas with them.   Jesus cometh, the doors being
Jn. 14. 27. shut, and stood in the midst, and said, Peace be unto
you.   Then saith he to Thomas, Reach hither thy finger, 10
Lk. 24. 39. and see my hands ; and reach hither thy hand, and put
180   it into my side : and be not faithless, but believing.
Thomas answered and said unto him, My Lord and my
God.   Jesus saith unto him, Because thou hast seen me,
1 Pet. 1. 8. thou hast believed : blessed are they that have not seen, 15
and yet have believed.

---

181. S. John xx. 24—31.

Many other signs therefore did Jesus in the presence Jn. 21. 25.
of the disciples, which are not written in this book : but **183**
these are written, that ye may believe that Jesus is the
20 Christ, the Son of God ; and that believing ye may have 1 Jn. 5. 13.
life in his name.

182. *Again at the Sea of Tiberias.   Draught of Fishes.*

AFTER these things Jesus manifested himself again to
the disciples at the sea of Tiberias ; and he manifested
himself on this wise.   There were together Simon Peter,
and Thomas called Didymus, and Nathanael of Cana in Jn. 1. 45...
5 Galilee, and the sons of Zebedee, and two other of his Mt. 4. 21.
disciples.   Simon Peter saith unto them, I go a fishing.
They say unto him, We also come with thee.   They
went forth, and entered into the boat ; and that night
they took nothing.   But when day was now breaking, Lk. 9. 5.
10 Jesus stood on the beach : howbeit the disciples knew **33**
not that it was Jesus.   Jesus therefore saith unto them,
Children, have ye aught to eat ?   They answered him, Lk. 24. 41.
No.   And he said unto them, Cast the net on the right
side of the boat, and ye shall find.   They cast therefore,
15 and now they were not able to draw it for the multitude
of fishes.   That disciple therefore whom Jesus loved Jn. 13. 28.
saith unto Peter, It is the Lord.   So when Simon Peter
heard that it was the Lord, he girt his coat about him
(for he was naked), and cast himself into the sea.   But
20 the other disciples came in the little boat (for they were
not far from the land, but about two hundred cubits off),
dragging the net full of fishes.   So when they got out
upon the land, they see a fire of coals there, and fish laid
thereon, and bread.   Jesus saith unto them, Bring of the
25 fish which ye have now taken.   Simon Peter therefore
went up, and drew the net to land, full of great fishes, a
hundred and fifty and three : and for all there were so
many, the net was not rent.   Jesus saith unto them,
Come and break your fast.   And none of the disciples Acts 10. 41.
30 durst inquire of him, Who art thou ? knowing that it was
the Lord.   Jesus cometh, and taketh the bread, and Lk. 24. 30.
giveth them, and the fish likewise.   This is now the **179**
third time that Jesus was manifested to the disciples,
after that he was risen from the dead.

182. S. John xxi. 1—14.

183. *Special Charge to S. Peter and S. John.*

So when they had broken their fast, Jesus saith to
Mt. 26. 33. Simon Peter, Simon, son of John, lovest thou me more
155   than these? He saith unto him, Yea, Lord; thou
knowest that I love thee. He saith unto him, Feed
Eze. 34. 2... my lambs. He saith to him again a second time, Simon, 5
son of John, lovest thou me? He saith unto him, Yea,
Lord; thou knowest that I love thee. He saith unto
1 Pet. 5. 2. him, Tend my sheep. He saith unto him the third time,
Simon, son of John, lovest thou me? Peter was grieved
Mt. 26. 75. because he said unto him the third time, Lovest thou 10
159   me? And he said unto him, Lord, thou knowest all
things; thou knowest that I love thee. Jesus saith unto
Acts 20. 28. him, Feed my sheep. Verily, verily, I say unto thee,
When thou wast young, thou girdedst thyself, and
walkedst whither thou wouldest: but when thou shalt 15
Jn. 13. 36. be old, thou shalt stretch forth thy hands, and another
shall gird thee, and carry thee whither thou wouldest
2 Pet. 1. 14. not. Now this he spake, signifying by what manner of
death he should glorify God. And when he had spoken
this, he saith unto him, Follow me. Peter, turning 20
about, seeth the disciple whom Jesus loved following;
Jn. 13. 23... which also leaned back on his breast at the supper, and
147   said, Lord, who is he that betrayeth thee? Peter therefore seeing him saith to Jesus, Lord, and what shall this
man do? Jesus saith unto him, If I will that he tarry 25
Mt. 16. 28; till I come, what is that to thee? follow thou me. This
— 24. 30. saying therefore went forth among the brethren, that that
disciple should not die: yet Jesus said not unto him,
that he should not die; but, If I will that he tarry till I
come, what is that to thee?   30
This is the disciple which beareth witness of these
things, and wrote these things: and we know that his
3 Jn. 12. witness is true.
Jn. 20. 30.   And there are also many other things which Jesus
181   did, the which if they should be written every one, I 35
suppose that even the world itself would not contain the
books that should be written.

183. S. John xxi. 15—25.

184. *Again in Galilee.*

BUT the eleven disciples went into Galilee, unto the Mt. 26. 32;
mountain where Jesus had appointed them. And when — 28. 7.
they saw him, they worshipped him : but some doubted. **175**
And Jesus came to them and spake unto them, saying,
5 All authority hath been given unto me in heaven and on Heb. 2. 8.
earth. Go ye therefore, and make disciples of all the Mk. 16.15.
nations, baptizing them into the name of the Father and **180**
of the Son and of the Holy Ghost : teaching them to
observe all things whatsoever I commanded you : and
10 lo, I am with you alway, even unto the end of the world. Ro. 8. 35,..
Then he appeared to above five hundred brethren at
once, of whom the greater part remain until now, but
some are fallen asleep ; then he appeared to James ;
then to all the apostles.

185. *And in Jerusalem, during Forty Days.*

HE shewed himself to his apostles alive after his pas- Acts 10.41.
sion by many proofs, appearing unto them by the space Lk. 24. 39.
of forty days, and speaking the things concerning the
kingdom of God : and, being assembled together with
5 them, he charged them not to depart from Jerusalem,
but to wait for the promise of the Father, which, said he, Lk. 24. 49.
ye heard from me : for John indeed baptized with water ; **180**
but ye shall be baptized with the Holy Ghost not many Mt. 3. 11.
days hence. **15**
10 They therefore, when they were come together, asked
him, saying, Lord, dost thou at this time restore the Dan. 7. 27.
kingdom to Israel ? And he said unto them, It is not Mt. 24. 36.
for you to know times or seasons, which the Father hath **137**
set within his own authority. But ye shall receive power, Acts 2. 2.
15 when the Holy Ghost is come upon you : and ye shall
be my witnesses both in Jerusalem, and in all Judæa and Acts 2. 14;
Samaria, and unto the uttermost part of the earth. — 8. 1;
— 8. 4;
— 13. 4.

---

184. S. Matthew xxviii. 16—20; St Paul, 1 Cor. xv. 6, 7.
185. Acts i. 3—8.

186. *His Ascension.*

AND when he had said these things, he led them out till they were over against Bethany ; and he lifted up his hands and blessed them. And it came to pass, while he
2 Ki. 2. 11. blessed them, while they were looking, he was parted from them, and was carried up into heaven, and a cloud 5
Eph. 1. 20. received him out of their sight, and he sat down at the
Ps. 110. 1. right hand of God. And while they were looking stead-
Mt. 28. 3. fastly into heaven as he went, behold two men stood by
Acts 13.31. them in white apparel, which also said, Ye men of Gali-lee, why stand ye looking into heaven? This Jesus 10 which was received up from you into heaven shall so
Mt. 25. 31. come in like manner as ye beheld him going into heaven.
And they worshipped him, and returned unto Jeru-salem from the mount called Olivet with great joy, and
Acts 2. 46. were continually in the temple blessing God. And they 15 went forth and preached everywhere, the Lord working
Acts 5. 12. with them, and confirming the word by the signs that followed. Amen.

187. *Of Giving and Receiving.*

REMEMBER the words of the Lord Jesus, how he himself said, It is more blessed to give than to receive.

AND EVERY CREATED THING WHICH IS IN THE HEAVEN, AND ON THE EARTH, AND UNDER THE EARTH, AND ON THE SEA, AND ALL THINGS THAT ARE IN THEM, HEARD I SAYING, UNTO HIM THAT SITTETH ON THE THRONE, AND UNTO THE LAMB, BE THE BLESSING, AND THE HONOUR, AND THE GLORY, AND THE DOMINION, FOR EVER AND EVER. AND THE FOUR LIVING CREATURES SAID, AMEN. AND THE ELDERS FELL DOWN AND WOR-SHIPPED. REV. V. 13, 14.

---

186. S. Luke xxiv. 50—53 ; Acts i. 9—11 ; S. Mark xvi. 19, 20.
187. Acts xx. 35.

VARIATIONS.

N.B.   Omissions are not noted here.

Sect. line
15. 13. that is spoken of *Mt.*
  36. think not *Mt.*
  55. baptized *Mk.*
  56. he that cometh after me is... *Mt.*
  57. whose shoes I am not worthy to bear *Mt.*
  59. and he will throughly cleanse his... ⎫ *Mt.*
  60. and he will gather... ⎭
16. 11. he saw the heavens rent asunder *Mk.*
  —. and the Holy Ghost descended *Lk.*
  14. Thou art my beloved Son, in thee... *Mk. Lk.*
17. 2. he was led up of the Spirit into the wilderness *Mt.*   led by the
    Spirit in the wilderness *Lk.*
  6. when he had fasted forty days and forty nights, he afterward hun-
    gered *Mt.*
  7. the devil said *Lk.*
  8. that these stones become bread *Mt.* (Gr. loaves)
  12 & 22. Par. 3 before 2 *Mt.*
  13. led him up and shewed *Lk.*
  18. worship me *Mt.*
27. 2. withdrew *Mt.*   came *Mk.*
28. 14. Repent ye, for the kingdom *Mt.*
29. 12. went after *Mk.*
30. 4. his word was with authority *Lk.*
  17. this word *Lk.*
  19. a rumour concerning him *Lk.*
31. 2. Peter's house *Mt.*
  6. touched her hand *Mt.*
  8. unto him *Mt.*
32. 1. when it was day *Lk.*
  10. therefore was I sent *Lk.*
34. 2. a leper *Mt. Mk.*
  8. his leprosy was cleansed *Mt.*
  13. the gift that... *Mt.*   according as... *Lk.*
  14. But so much the more went abroad the report concerning him *Lk.*
35. 3. on one of those days *Lk.*
  11. a man that was palsied *Lk.*
  17 & 30. couch *Lk.*

J. H.   12

35. 20. Man *Lk*.
  23. This man blasphemeth *Mt*. he blasphemeth *Mk*.
  25. God alone? *Lk*.
  26. perceiving their reasonings *Lk*. knowing their thoughts *Mt*.
  27. what *Lk*.
  39. were afraid *Mt*.
36. 4. a man called Matthew *Mt*.
  12. Why eateth your Master *Mt*. Why do ye eat and drink... *Lk*.
  17. I am not come *Lk*.
  20. we and the Pharisees *Mt*.
  22. eat and drink *Lk*.
  26. but the days will come: and when... *Lk*.
  28. in those days *Lk*.
  30. rendeth a piece from a new garment, and putteth it upon an old garment; else he will rend the new, and also the piece from the new will not agree with the old *Lk*.
  35. they put new wine... *Mt*. and *Mk*.
39. 7. why do ye... *Lk*.
  8. did ye never read... *Mk*.
40. 4. asked him, saying, Is it lawful to heal... *Mt*.
  11. or to kill? *Mk*.
42. 1. goeth up *Mk*.
  5. appointed *Mk*.
  9. named *Lk*. who is called *Mt*.
  14. Cananæan *Mk*. and *Mt*.
  —. Thaddæus *Mk*.
  15. which also betrayed him *Mk*. and *Mt*.
43 and **43*.** See Note p. xi. after Preface.
44. 3. παῖς *Mt*. δοῦλος *Lk*.
  6. came *Mt*.
46. 11. do hear and see *Mt*.
  22. wear soft raiment are in kings' houses *Mt*.
  23. But wherefore went ye out? to see a prophet? *Mt*.
  30. kingdom of heaven *Mt*.
  41. liken this generation? It is like *Mt*.
  43. call to their fellows and say... *Mt*.
  45. mourn... *Mt*.
  —. came neither eating nor drinking, and they say *Mt*.
  50. by her works *Mt*.
49. 1. and again he began *Lk*.
  5. on the beach *Mt*.
  5. spake to them *Mt*.
  8, 10, 14, 16. Plural throughout *Mt*.; singular throughout *Lk*.
  11. rocky places *Mt*. rock *Lk*.
  12. as soon as it grew *Lk*.
  14. no moisture *Lk*.
  15. amidst *Lk*.
  18. some a hundredfold, some sixty, some thirty *Mt*. thirtyfold, and sixtyfold, and a hundredfold *Mk*. hundredfold *Lk*.
50. 2. asked of him the parables *Mk*. asked him what this parable might be *Lk*.
  5. kingdom of heaven *Mt*.
  10. that seeing they may see and not perceive, and hearing they may

hear and not understand *Mk.* that seeing they may not see, and hearing they may not understand *Lk.*

50. 22. it should be forgiven them *Mk.*
33. the evil one *Mt.* the devil *Lk.*
—. taketh *Mk.* and *Lk.*
35, 36 &c. these are they... *Mk.*; those...are they *Lk.*; both plural throughout.
36. rock *Lk.*
39. which for a while believe, but in time of temptation fall away *Lk.*
41. others are they that are sown *Mk.*
46. becometh unfruitful *Mk.*
48. accept it *Mk.*
49. thirtyfold and sixtyfold and a hundredfold *Mk.*

51. 1. No man when he hath lighted ..covereth...putteth *Lk.*
14. kingdom of heaven *Mt.*

53. 6. they say... & 8, them *Mk.*
7. desiring to see thee *Lk.*
14. of God *Mk.*

54. 5. they *Mt.*
6. this wisdom and these mighty works *Mt.*
9. carpenter's son *Mt.*
15. did not many mighty works there... *Mt.*

55. 1. on that day *Mk.*
12. Master, carest thou not that we perish? *Mk.* Master, Master, we perish *Lk.*
19. what manner of man *Mt.*
20. water *Lk.*

56. 2. Gadarenes *Mt.*
4. two possessed with devils; and plural throughout *Mt.* a...man... who had devils *Lk.*
20. beseech *Lk.*
26. And the devils besought him, saying, If thou cast us out, send us away into the herd of swine. And he said unto them, Go *Mt.* send us into the swine *Mk.*
34. lake *Lk.*
35. were choked *Lk.*

57. 1. while he spake these things unto them, behold... *Mt.*
7. for he had an only daughter about twelve years of age, and she lay a dying *Lk.*
8. is even now dead *Mt.*
9. and she shall live *Mt.*
13. having *Lk.*
14. had spent all her living upon physicians *Lk.*
20. the issue of her blood stanched *Lk.*
24. who is it that touched me? *Lk.*
22—36. But Jesus turning and seeing her, said... *Mt.*
42. trouble not *Lk.*
43. hearing it *Lk.*
51. And all were weeping, and bewailing her; but.. *Lk.*
52. weep not *Lk.*
—. the damsel *Mt.*
59. Maiden, arise *Lk.*

59. 12. over all devils, and to cure diseases *Lk.*

59. 28. money (brass) *Mk.* money (silver) *Lk.*
　　30. save a staff only,...but to go shod with sandals, and put not on two coats *Mk.* neither have two coats *Lk.*
　　33. and thence depart *Lk.*
　　36. whatsoever place *Mk.*
　　38. depart *Lk.*
　　39. unto *Mk.*
60. 1. king Herod *Mt.*
　　6. And others said, It is a prophet, even as one of the prophets *Mt.*
　　8. John I beheaded, but who is this, about whom I hear such things? *Lk.*
　　35. was grieved *Mt.*
61. 4. Now when Jesus heard of it (death of John B.) he withdrew *Mt.*
　　8. went away *Mk.*
　　12. followed him *Mt.* and *Lk.*
　　22. even was come *Mt.* the day began to wear away *Lk.*
　　23. the time is already past *Mt.*
62. 5--10. they say unto him, We have here but five.. *Mt.* they say, Shall we go and buy two hundred ... and give them to eat? And he saith unto them, How many loaves have ye? go and see. And when they knew, they said... *Mk.* they say, We have no more than five...except we should go and buy food for all this people *Lk.*
63. 6. withdrew again into the mountain himself alone *Jn.*
65. 17. Moses *Mk.*
　　35. not that which entereth into the mouth defileth the man, but that which proceedeth out of the mouth, this defileth the man *Mt.*
　　48. into the mouth *Mt.*
66. 19. the dogs eat of the crumbs which fall from their masters' table *Mt.*
68. 8. Whence should we have so many loaves in a desert place, as to fill... *Mt.*
　　11. Seven, and a few small fishes *Mt.*
　　14. and the fishes *Mt.*
　　23. into the borders of Magadan *Mt.*
69. 18. and Sadducees *Mt.*
　　19. We took *Mt.*
71. 3. Who do the multitudes say... *Lk.*
　　20. tell no man of him *Mk.* to tell this to no man *Lk.*
　　22. that the Son of man must suffer *Mk.*
　　24. after three days rise again *Mk.*
　　37. shall save it *Mk.* & *Lk.*
　　38. forfeit his life *Mt.* & *Mk.*
　　39. for what should *Mk.*
　　47. the kingdom of God come with power *Mk.* the k. of God *Lk.*
72. 1. after six days *Mt.* & *Mk.*
　　7. glistering *Mk.* white as the light *Mt.*
　　17. let us make *Mk.*
　　19. not knowing what he said *Lk.*
　　27. lifting up their eyes *Mt.*
　　31. commanded them, saying, Tell the vision to no man, until *Mt.*
　　38. The scribes say *Mk.*
73. 3. a great multitude met him *Lk.*
　　8. Master *Mk.* & *Lk.*
　　10. is epileptic *Mt.* and behold, a spirit taketh him *Lk.*

73. 17. could not *Mt. Lk.*
22. devil *Lk.*
27. he falleth *Mt.*
41. and healed the boy *Lk.*
56. is *Mk.*
38. the third day he shall be raised up *Mt.*

75. 1. In that hour came the disciples to Jesus, saying, Who then is greatest in the kingdom of heaven? *Mt.* and there arose a reasoning among them, which of them should be greater *Lk.*
17. one such little child *Mt.* this little child *Lk.*
26. against you is for you *Lk.*
30. it were profitable...that...should be *Mt.*
38. eternal *Mt.*
43. into life *Mt.*
45. the hell of fire *Mt.*

84 parag. 2. S. Matthew records these incidents immediately after the Sermon on the Mount. " Now when Jesus saw great multitudes about him he gave commandment to depart unto the other side. And behold there came a scribe...head. And another of his disciples said unto him, Lord, suffer &c." He does not record the third.

86, 88. S. Matthew apparently records these speeches after the mission of the twelve.

86. 10. go down *Mt.*
88. 1. At that season Jesus answered and said *Mt.*
3. knoweth the Son...know the Father... *Mt.*

92. J. J. Halcombe thinks that Lk. xi. 14 to xiii. 21 has been displaced from its original position after viii. 21.
5. And he was casting out a devil which was dumb *Lk.*
7. insomuch that *Mt.*
9. marvelled *Lk.*
10. But some of them said, by Beelzebub... *Lk.*
16. If a kingdom be... that kingdom cannot stand ; and if a house... that house... *Mk.*
18. falleth *Lk.*
19. he is divided *Mt.*
24. Spirit *Mt.*
26. Or how can one [no one can *Mk.*] enter into the house of the strong man and spoil his goods, except he first bind the strong man ? and then will he spoil his house *Mt. & Mk.*
32. Verily *Mk.*
37. speak against *Mt.*
38. hath never forgiveness, but... *Mk.*

93. 3. finding none, he saith, I will turn back *Lk.*
95. 3. And others, tempting him, sought of him... *Lk.* (xi. 16)
5. he began to say, This generation is an evil generation : it seeketh... *Lk.*
13. ' the queen of the south ' before ' men of Nineveh ' *Lk.*

117. 10. What did Moses command you ? and they said, Moses suffered... *Mk*, and the words about the original institution of marriage after those about divorce.

118. 1. little children *Mt. & Mk.*
2. touch them *Mk. & Lk.*

118. 5. kingdom of heaven *Mt.*
119. 2. one *Mt.* & *Mk.* came *Mt.*
    6. One there is who is good : but if... *Mt.*
    7. Thou knowest the commandments *Mk.* & *Lk.*
   14. when Jesus heard it, he said *Lk.*
   17. give *Mt.* & *Mk.*
   20. became *Lk.*
   21. very rich *Lk.*
   23. It is hard for a rich man *Mt.*
120. 2. our own *Lk.*
    9. for the kingdom of God's sake *Lk.* for my name's sake *Mt.*
   10. manifold more *Lk.*
121. 12. kill *Mk.* & *Lk.*
   13. the third day he shall be raised up *Mt.* the third day *Lk.*
   16. James and John the sons... *Mk.*
   19. unto her *Mt.*
   21. Command that these my two sons... *Mt.*
   22. kingdom *Mt.*
   37. Not so shall it be *Mt.*
   40. your servant: even as the Son... *Mt.*
122. 4. S. Luke continues the history of his cure at once.
   26. and behold two blind men sitting... *Mt.*
   27, 29. they—us, &c. *Mt.*
   32. commanded him to be brought near *Lk.*
   38. Lord, that our eyes may be opened *Mt.*
125. 1. there came a woman having... *Mt.* & *Mk.*
    6. when the disciples saw it, they had indignation, saying.. *Mt.*
      there were some that had indignation among themselves, saying... *Mk.*
    8. for this ointment might have been sold... *Mt.* & *Mk.*
   18. for in that she poured this ointment upon my body, she did it to prepare me for burial *Mt.*
   31. how he might conveniently... *Mk.*
126. 7. him *Lk.* Jesus having found a young ass, sat thereon *Jn.*
   13. as it is written, Fear not... *Jn.*
   20. certain of them that stood there *Mk.*
   22. even as Jesus had said *Mk.*
   24. cast *Mk.*
   26. from the fields *Mk.*
   36. the king that cometh... *Lk.*
127. S. Matt. records the cleansing of the temple before the cursing of the barren fig tree.
    7. let there be no fruit on thee *Mt.*
   36. And when the disciples saw it, they marvelled, saying, How did the fig tree immediately wither away? *Mt.*
   41. if ye have faith and doubt not, ye shall not only do what is done to the fig tree, but even if ye... *Mt.*
   44. it shall be done *Mt.*
128. 9. and answer me *Mk.* and tell me *Lk.*
   15. we fear the multitude *Mt.* they feared the people *Mk.*
   —. for all verily held John to be... *Mk.*
129. 6. he sent his servants unto the husbandmen to receive his fruits. And the husbandmen took his servants, and beat one, and

killed another, and stoned another. Again he sent other servants more than the first, and they did unto them in like manner. But afterward he sent unto them his son, saying... *Mt.*

129. 13. killed *Mk.*
   15. He had yet one, a beloved son : he sent him last unto him, saying... *Mk.*
   18. that the inheritance may *Lk.*
   19. killed him, and cast him forth *Mk.*
   27. Did ye never read in the scriptures... *Mt.*
       Have ye not read even this scripture *Mk.*
   38. against them *Mt.* & *Lk.*
   40. multitude *Mk.*
131. 9. acceptest *Lk.*
   13. craftiness *Lk.*
132. 3. Moses said *Mt.*
   9. unto the seventh *Mt.*
   13. Ye do err, not knowing... *Mt.*
   19. but are as angels in heaven *Mt.*
   21. even Moses shewed *Lk.*
   22. when he calleth the Lord the God of Abraham *Lk.*
       that which was spoken to you by God, saying... *Mt.*
133. 3. And one of the scribes came, and knowing that he had answered them well, asked him, What commandment *Mk.* lawyer *Mt.*
   4. which is the great commandment *Mt.*
134. 2. And Jesus answered and said *Mk.*
   3. How say the scribes that the Christ is David's son *Mk.*
       How say they that... *Lk.*
135. 3. Beware of the scribes *Mk.* & *Lk.*
136. 4. And there came a poor widow, and she cast in *Mk.*
   6. Verily. *Mk.*
137. 2. and as some spake of the temple... *Lk.*
   7. them, See ye not all these things ? *Mt.*
   12. the disciples *Mt.* they *Lk.*
   15. when these things are about to come to pass *Lk.*
   16. answered and said *Mt.* and he said *L.*
   21. terrified *Lk.*
   23. is not yet *Mt.*
   —. then said he unto them, Nation... *Lk.*
   47. how to answer *Lk.*
   51. But ye shall be delivered up even by parents and brethren and by kinsfolk and friends, and some of you shall they cause... *Lk.*
   74. that it be not *Mk.*
   76. For those days shall be tribulation *Mk.*
   80. he shortened the days *Mk.*
   84. that they may lead *Mk.*
   93. there shall be signs in the sun and moon and stars *Lk.*
   110. And he spake to them a parable : Behold the fig tree and all the trees : when they now shoot forth... *Lk.*
   114. that the kingdom of God is nigh *Lk.*
143. 1. Now after two days was the feast of the passover and the unleavened bread *Mk.*
   —. Now the feast of unleavened bread drew near, which is called the Passover *Lk.*

143. 7. sought how *Mk.* & *Lk.*

8. for they said... *Mk.*

144. 1. on which the passover must be sacrificed *Lk.*

6. Go into the city to such a man, and say unto him *Mt.*

10. the guest-chamber *Lk.*

14. did as Jesus had appointed them *Mt.*

145. 5. the hour was come *Lk.*

147. 3. but behold, the hand of him that betrayeth me is with me on the table *Lk.*

6. every one *Mt.*

7. he that dipped his hand with me in the dish, the same shall betray me *Mt.*

9. it hath been determined *Lk.*

148. 2. blessed *Mt.* & *Mk.*

4. which is for you *P.* (v.l. broken).

5. a cup *Mt.* & *Mk.*

7. this is my blood of the covenant *Mt.* & *Mk.*

16. the kingdom of God *Mk.*

149. 13. hast denied *Jn.*

150. 67. unto the mount of Olives *Mt.* & *Mk.*

155. 9. will not I *Mk.*

13. Peter saith unto him *Mt.*

156. 2. called *Mt.*

5. the two sons of Zebedee *Mt.*

6. sorrowful *Mt.*

10. was parted from them *Lk.*

15. not my will, but thine be done *Lk.*

23. what, could not ye watch with me one hour? *Mt.*

why sleep ye? rise and pray *Lk.*

26. the same words *Mk.*

157. 1. And while he yet spake, lo, Judas...came *Mt.* and straightway, while he...cometh Judas *Mk.* while he..., behold a multitude, and he that was called Judas...went before them. *Lk.*

8. a sign *Mt.*

10. drew near *Lk.*

28. one of them that were with Jesus *Mt.* a certain one of them that stood by *Mk.* a certain one of them *Lk.*

34. its place *Mt.*

40. Jesus answered them *Mk.*

43. I was daily *Mk.*

158. 1. And they that had taken Jesus led him away to the house of Caiaphas the high priest *Mt.* And they led Jesus away to the high priest *Mk.* And they seized him, and led him away, and brought him into the high priest's house *Lk.*

159. 12. a maid *Mt.* one of the maids of the high priest *Mk.* a certain maid *Lk.*

13. In *Jn.* Peter is standing throughout; in *Lk.* and *Mt.* he is sitting at first. *Mk.* does not notice attitude.

14. Thou also wast with Jesus the Galilæan *Mt.* Thou also wast with the Nazarene, even Jesus *Mk.* Thou also wast with him *Lk.*

16. I know him not *Lk.*

19. another (maid) *Mt.* another (man) *Lk.*

159. 20. this man also was with Jesus the Nazarene *Mt.* thou also art one of them *Lk.*

24. they that stood by came and said, Of a truth thou also art one of them *Mt.*

160. 13. I am able to destroy the temple of God, and to build it in three days *Mt.*

21. Son of God *Mt.*

22. thou hast said *Mt.*

—. But from henceforth shall the Son of Man be seated at the right hand of the power of God *Lk.*

29. ye *Mt.* & *Mk.*

33. the officers received him with blows of... *Mk.*

161. 12. Now this man obtained a field with the reward of his iniquity *Lk.* (or Peter ?) in Acts i. 18.

162. 5. led him *Mt.* brought him before *Lk.*

40. And he gave him no answer *Mt.*

164. 1. And when he had said this *Jn.*

5. find no crime in him *Jn.*

11. whom they would *Mt.*

13. Barabbas was a robber *Jn.*

23. perceived *Mk.*

30. that he should rather release Barabbas *Mk.*

33. said *Mt.*

36. Jesus which is called Christ ? *Mt.*

165. 3. call together *Mk.*

4. clothe him with purple *Mk.* put on him a scarlet robe *Mt.*

11. a reed *Mk.*

166. 20. the skull *Lk.*

—. gave him to drink *Mt.*

21. with gall *Mt.*

22. received it not *Mk.*

167. 2. robbers *Mt. Mk.* others *Jn.*

6. (Pilate) put it on *Jn.*

—. accusation *Mt.* superscription *Lk.* superscription of his accusation *Mk.*

7. The King of the Jews *Mk.* This is the King of the Jews *Lk.* This is Jesus the King of the Jews *Mt.* Jesus of Nazareth the King of the Jews *Jn.*

168. 6. the rulers *Lk.*

11. and believe *Mk.*

14. reproached him *Mk.*

170. 4. Eli *Mt.*

12. a reed *Mt.*, *Mk.*

14. take him down *Mk.*

18. yielded up *Mt.* his spirit *Mt.* & *Jn.*

29. a righteous man *Lk.*

36. the mother of the sons of Zebedee *Mt.*

172. 14. granted the corpse to Joseph *Mk.*

15. taking him down *Mk.* took it down *Lk.*

19. wrapped it *Mt.* & *Lk.* wound him *Mk.*

28. the other Mary *Mt.*

175. 4. late on the sabbath day, as it began to dawn toward the first day of the week *Mt.* at early dawn *Lk.* while it was yet dark *Jn.*

175.   5.   to see (Gr. behold) the sepulchre *Mt.*
      9.   found the stone rolled away from the tomb *Lk.*   see the stone taken away from the tomb *Jn.*
    18.   stooping and looking in, he seeth the linen cloths by themselves *Lk.*
    27.   departed *Lk.*
    35.   they said unto them *Lk.*   he *Mk.*
    36.   fear not ye *Mt.*
    43.   see the place *Mt.*
    —.   where they laid him *Mk.*

176.   8—21.   Now when he was risen early on the first day of the week, he appeared first to Mary Magdalene, from whom he had cast out seven devils. She went and told them that had been with him, as they mourned and wept *Mk.*

179.   50.   And that he appeared to Cephas. S. Paul, 1 *Cor.* xv. 5.
    51.   And they went away and told it unto the rest, neither believed they them *Mk.*

180.   5.   And afterward he was manifested unto the eleven themselves *Mk.*   then [he appeared] to the twelve. S. Paul, 1 *Cor.* xv. 5.

186.   1—6.   So then the Lord Jesus, after he had spoken with them, was received up into heaven *Mk.*

Until the Harmony corresponding to this Gospel History and forming the second part of this work is published, readers are recommended to use Mr Waddy's "Harmony of the Four Gospels in the Revised Version" (T. Woolmer, 2, Castle Street, City Road, E.C.). The Sections of this do not quite correspond with my own, but may easily be found by using the following table.

J.	W.	J.	W.	J.	W.
1	2	34	34	67	78
2	3	35	35	68	79
3	3	36	36	69	80, 81
4	1	37	39	70	82
5	4	38	40	71	83, 84
6	5, 6	39	37		
7	7	40	38		
8	8	41	41	72	85
9	9	42	42	73	86, 87
10	10	43	43	74	88
11	11	43*	43	75	89
12	12	44	44	76	89
13	13	45	45	77	91, 92
14	14	46	46	78	93
		47	47	79	94
		48	48	80	95
15	15	49	52	81	96
16	16	50	52	82	97
17	17	51	53, 54, 63	83	98, 107, 108
18	18	52	63	84	110
19	19	53	5	85	111
20	20	54	68	86	111
21	21	55	64	87	112
22	22	56	65	88	112
23	23	57	66	89	113
24	25	58	67	90	114
25	25	59	69	91	115
26	26	60	24, 72, 71	92	49
27	27	61	73	93	50
28	28	62	73	94	55
29	29	63	74	95	50
30	30	64	75	96	55
31	31	65	76	97	56
32	32	66	77	98	57
33	33			99	58

Made in the USA
San Bernardino, CA
09 July 2018